Imagining Success

Imagining Success

by

Kurt A. Schneider

First Printing, July 1977
Second Printing, January 1978
Third Printing, March 1979

Library of Congress Catalog Card No. A-875582

Published by
KURT A. SCHNEIDER
P.O. Box 9358
Salt Lake City, Utah 84109
Telephone (801) 278-4015

Lithographed in the United States of America by
Publishers Press, Salt Lake City

Table of Contents

May 19, 1977

TO WHOM IT MAY CONCERN:

"Standard Relaxation," as taught by my dear friend, Kurt Schneider, is a wonderful assistance not only in managing clinically-sick patients, but also as an important link in the holistic chain essential in providing a comprehensive prevention program, maintaining buoyant abundant health through nourishing optimum adaptation to disease-formenting stress. We all are subjected to the negative buffeting by stress in our lives but when we adequately compensate, stress in a sense, rather than being destructive, helps achieve the goal we seek in daily exercise in that the challenges merely flex our defensive muscles and successful adaptative patterns are established. "There *must* needs be opposition in *all* things."

It is impossible to isolate psychological reactions from physiologic function. Learning to harness our fantastic inherent powers through programmed training, provides us with unlimited potential to cope positively with internal, as well as external, ecological demands.

Kurt Schneider, because of years of diligent study and dedicated work, is now able to condense many disciplines for you into a concise and workable program—Standard Relaxation. I am confident that S.R. will prove invaluable to you.

Robert Bliss Vance, D. O.

May 19, 1976

TO WHOM IT MAY CONCERN:

This book is the product of a lifetime of study and instruction on the new Frontiers—The "World of The Mind." The Author has finally "multiplied himself" and the good he does through this book. It most certainly contains the Golden Key to health, wealth, success, and the "Life-Positive."

Norman S. Johnson
Attorney at Law

"This book is an excellent treatment of a powerful success skill, a book that is bound to help any reader. It has helped me."

Dr. Norman Vincent Peale

"I can certainly say without reservation that it's a book everyone should read. Regardless of what endeavor in life he will find much help from the great ideas contained in *Imagining Success*."

Cavett Robert

"This book is practical and doesn't conflict with any basic Christian beliefs. It's one of the best of its kind I've read. I like it. It makes sense."

Olive D. Osmond,
Mother of the "Osmonds"

"The book is excellent! I especially benefited from your chapter regarding the subconscious mind."

Don Hutson
Pres. National Speakers' Assoc.

Acknowledgments

It would be impossible for me to adequately express my gratitude to my many friends and students of the "Golden Keys Success Seminar," associates and staff members, for their help and inspiration during the creation of this book. A special debt of gratitude is owed to my patient, understanding, sustaining wife Charlotte, Norman S. Johnson, my attorney, Jolene Dickey, and Ann Simmons.

There is no way to give credit to such mind teachers as Napoleon Hill, W. Clement Stone, Dr. Joseph Murphy, Melvin Powers, Maxwell Maltz, Harold Sherman, Jim Jones, Howard E. Hill, Emmett Fox, Alex Osborn, John K. Williams, John A. Schindler, David J. Schwarz, Claude Bristol, Norman Vincent Peale, Albert Ellis, Robert A. Harper, Catherine Ponder, William Edwards, A. H. Z. Carr, Charles M. Simmons, O. G. Mandino, M. S. Andersen, Paul Harvey, Earl Nightingale, Dorothy Jongeward, Dottie Walters, Zig Ziglar, Ben Feldman, Cavett Robert, Don Hutson, Paul J. Meyer and many others, for all of their enormous contributions to the storehouse of information regarding the world of the Subconscious.

Certainly, the Author owes a great debt to them.

Primary credit, however, must be given to the Supreme Benefactor, the Subconscious Mind, "The Wisdom In Us," that precious gift from the Almighty.

(Illustrations by Mr. Reed McGregor, Ms. Shirley Wight, Barbara Becker and Debbie Oyler, Grand Hulet.)

THIS BOOK IS DEDICATED TO MY WIFE AND CHILDREN, MY POSTERITY AND TO THE MULTITUDE OF PEOPLE IN NEED—IN NEED OF A HAPPIER, HEALTHIER, MORE SATISFYING, MORE PROSPEROUS, AND SUCCESSFUL LIFE. WITH ALL SINCERITY AND LOVE.

Introduction

The personal, family, spiritual, and business problems we face nowadays can be frightening.

After teaching numerous Seminars, giving hundreds of lectures and talking with thousands of people, I felt the need for a book to help all those who are searching for happiness, health, success, spirituality, and a new, better way of life. A student of mine at the end of a seminar said:

"Everyone of you signed up for this Seminar for reasons personal and important to yourself, and only you know those reasons. This is one field that shows no partiality or preference for any one profession. Success means different things to different people. Because of the terrific feeling I have received from these classes, I want to share my reasons with you. Success to me means feeling good within yourself, about yourself—and a bunch of money, of course!

"Five years ago I felt as if I was on top of the world, and if any one had told me what was to happen, I would never have believed it. I was one of the beautiful people—living the ideal American life. I had one husband, one son, one daughter and a family dog. This constitutes the ideal American family according to statistics. I still have all of those things, but for a while, I forgot what I had.

"I was busy with many activities, teaching a few youth classes, working a part-time job, enjoying my family and my friends. I rushed around with my head up, keeping to the paved paths, not looking to the right or to the left, not seeing the mud and the gutters on either side, and I guess this is how it happened. Very unexpectedly a very influential person gave me a good, hard shove. He didn't just trip me a little; he kicked me hard, right in the shins and I landed in the mud and the quicksand down below. There is nothing more destructive than 100% anger and that is what I was left with!

"I fought and I floundered and tried to get out of the mud, but by the time I realized the seriousness of the situation I seemed to be in too deep. My friends came by and tried to help me—assuring me there would be a way out; that the man would correct the error, that it wouldn't be long. A few special people tried to take my hand and pull, but they were surprised to find that if they did this they too might slide in with me. They soon became afraid to reach out for fear I would pull them in. We could all get very muddy.

"They still all spoke as they hurried by. 'What a shame! This should never have happened to you.' 'You're strong, you'll be O.K.' 'Keep your chin up!' They said, 'It isn't fair,' and they added, 'hang in there,' as I tried to keep from sinking completely into the quicksand. It was a desolate place in which to be alone.

"About six weeks ago someone who knew me well came and sat down by the mud pool upon the paved walk above, and said, 'I know someone who can help you.' 'Well, don't waste time, get them over here while I can still speak, for heaven's sake!' She replied, 'I can't, you'll have to go to him.' 'I can't get out of here—you know that.' But being very stubborn, she coaxed and encouraged until she had me to the side of the mud pool. 'Now,' she said, 'grab that twig and pull yourself up.'

"I looked up and saw only a spindly, bent twig hanging over me. 'That's impossible,' I said, 'that could not hold me.' The twig spoke in a booming voice, 'Nothing is impossible,' it said. And surprisingly the 'twig' spoke with a 'German' accent! It was then I noticed that the twig grew into a long, sturdy branch which fastened to a much sturdier tree which gave out so much 'positive energy' it was positively contagious!

"I grabbed at the twig and was surprised at the strength of it. It took effort and a lot of concentration on my part, but I found myself climbing up to dry ground where I heard someone say, 'Uh-huh, uh-huh—I see it coming, and I hear it humming!' Of course, you all recognize this tree as a 'Kurt Schneider' tree. There is no other species quite like it.

"I am still brushing a little of that mud off, but I know now that I am going to be in that top 5 percent. I know I can do it because I believe in the power of my mind and I believe in the power of believing. Mr. Schneider, I salute you and your positive thinking."

May Glenn

During visits to the State Mental Hospital, I have observed mentally disturbed patients who were completely dependent on the love and devotion of others.

"We are born with a sound mind," wrote Paul, but sometimes because of environmental conditions, sickness, accident, family background and false ideas about reality, emotional disturbances develop. What was once a sound mind becomes chained and handicapped by psychosis.

We have an adult son who is schizophrenic, caused by an injury at birth. This sorrow led me to study mind dynamics, to write this book, and to try to give others strength to carry their burdens and solve their problems and live, in spite of circumstances, a more meaningful and rewarding life.

If your mind and emotions function together, synchronized and well adjusted, be thankful. If you see someone acting abnormally, don't make fun. Treat everyone you meet kindly and with compassion, as you would wish to be treated. Use this affirmation: "I will always respect the minds of others. I expect to have the patience and understanding to treat and respect everyone the way I would like to be treated and respected."

Preface

I report case histories of many E.S.P. experiences concerning myself and my family. These phenomena have permeated my entire life. I relate these experiences to prove that my teachings bring results if practiced. You too can have such experiences, if you follow the simple mental exercises I give you. But you must be willing to devote time and attention to the techniques and principles, so that higher powers can work through you.

THE ROCK SPLITTER

As a boy, I did not have the right attitude toward learning. I seemed unable to concentrate. Does that sound familiar?

I could not understand why I needed to study. No one could help me realize that I needed this preparation for my later life. My grades were so poor that I had to repeat some years at school. One day my father exclaimed, "Kurt, you are of no value to anyone! All you can possibly become in your life is a 'rock-cutter,' working on the highway." At that time in Germany, rock-splitter work was the lowest form of labor one could perform. Men sat beside the highway splitting rocks to repair the road surface. My father was angry, but I knew he meant what he said. Unfortunately his words had no great effect on me. I just wouldn't wake up. It took more than his comments to bring me out of my apathy.

Father found me an apprenticeship with a steel and hardware company. About that time "Mr. Positive of Germany," Oscar Schellbach, came to the city and I was persuaded to attend one of his lectures. He gave me a blast of psychic dynamite! He changed my life. Under his leadership and motivation I started to live an exciting, positive life. There was only one way for me to go, and that was UP. I eventually became President and Director of Thyssen Rheinstahl, one of the leading steel distributing companies in Germany, Strassbourg Branch.

One day when I was traveling with my chauffeur, we saw an old ragged man sitting on the highway splitting granite rocks to make small stones for repairing the road. We stopped, and I borrowed the man's torn jacket, and I sat down in his place. My chauffeur took a photograph of me splitting rocks. I sent this picture to my father and wrote: *"Yes, Dad, you were right after all."* By that time, he knew I had had some success and he was extremely proud of me. But he still enjoyed the picture.

One lecture turned me from failure to success. It is never too late for you. You can start a new, positive life-style today.

This is a Workshop Book. Please set aside enough time to study it chapter by chapter.

My accomplishments flow from the love of my Heavenly Father, my parents and my devoted wife and family. I owe so much to wise teachers, great spiritual leaders, numerous books, and my faithful companion, My Subconscious. I wish you a more meaningful, positive, successful, and spiritual life, the best in every situation.

The Author

Introducing the Author

KURT A. SCHNEIDER

An instructor, business executive, writer, and radio personality of the program: "The Fundamental Laws of Right Thinking," Mr. Schneider established in 1960, a school and mental workshop for Subconscious Mind Training, the Golden Keys Success Seminar. It features new methods and techniques for working with the subconscious mind. The development and realization of a positive mental attitude. The self motivation, and building of success through "The Fundamental Laws of Right Thinking."

Mr. Schneider is an experienced teacher. Enthusiasm, transformation of the inner man, and positive thinking are his watchwords. He emanates those qualities and attitudes.

At 15 years of age he was rebellious, atheistic, negative, and a potential school dropout, obsessed with athletics. But one day he attended a lecture by Oscar Schellbach, a well known teacher and the "Mr. Positive" of Germany. That lecture became the turning point in his life. He learned to use time effectively, to set meaningful goals, and to strive for higher life values.

MENTAL KEYS UNLOCKED HIS MIND

He developed a drive and zest for living, completed his higher education and graduated from Business College in Bayreuth, Germany. He did not abandon athletics, he was a swimming champion. He discovered that the qualities, endurance and burning desire, that helped him to become a champion swimmer in Bavaria, caused him to succeed in business.

After a rugged three-year apprenticeship in the hardware and steel industry, he became a very successful steel executive and later president of one of the leading steel corporations of Germany.

FROM FAILURE TO SUCCESS

Mr. Schneider experienced the pre-Hitler era during which there was a 25 percent unemployment rate. He suffered persecution and imprisonment during the Hitler regime. He endured World War II with its heavy bombing and ensuing occupation, and after the defeat of Germany, industrial starvation and runaway inflation. He survived the 90 percent devaluation of the Germany currency through times impossible to adequately describe. Many thousands of people suffered mental and physical breakdowns, but he came through.

Training in Mental Transformation Meant Survival

Triggered by extraordinary stresses, he built a life filled with many spiritual and psychic experiences.

The Human Mind Is Infinitely Great and Powerful

Early in his life he turned from dead-end-living. The result was preparation and readiness for promotions and business opportunities. He developed the ability to act and to plan, according to the promptings and intuitions of the subconscious mind.

He emigrated with his family to the United States in 1951 and became a naturalized U.S. Citizen in 1957. He started a wholesale clock and figurine importing business which in a very short time developed into a thriving success in the eleven Western States. In 1955 he sold his importing business and entered the field of Life Insurance sales.

Mr. Schneider has used these laws of mind control to obtain success. He has gained many honors in the insurance field. He earned and held membership in the President's Club, the highest distinction in his company, for many years. Three times he led all 2600 men in the sales of Health and Accident and Group/Hospital Insurance. In 1970 he was "Man of the Year" for his company, and received a special award from the Governor of the State of Utah.

Mr. Schneider is active in church, social, community and philanthropic groups. He is a member of his local Chamber of Commerce.

The Schneiders have two sons and one daughter. His dynamic program has made his marriage a joy and a success. He has never been satisfied with second best. He programmed his subconscious mind for desirable opportunities and has made his way to the top.

Mr. Schneider has attended Psychology classes at the University of Utah, graduated as a Certified Hypno-Technician from the Association to Advance Ethical Hypnosis (A.A.E.H.) headed by Harry Arons, and in 1961 became a member of the Professional Association Division of the American Institute of Hypnosis headed by William J. Bryan, M.D., J.D., Ph.D.

THE WORLD OF THE MIND

These methods brought him physical fitness, health, enthusiasm, and a love of mankind. His faith-promoting lectures and sermons, packed with miraculous experiences, have stimulated many to "Walk Tall" and live upright, successful lives.

MR. SCHNEIDER IS WELL QUALIFIED IN THE FIELD OF SUB- CONSCIOUS MIND STUDIES, (RELAXOLOGY—SUGGEST- OLOGY), PROGRAMMING OF THE SUBCONSCIOUS, SELF-MOTIVATION AND SELF-IMPROVEMENT. HE IS EDUCATED IN THE EUROPEAN, AMERICAN AND ASIATIC METHODS OF MIND DEVELOPMENT

He invites you to now explore the universe of your own subconscious mind, and to break the barrier of monotonous daily chores and self-imposed limitations. His teachings can bring strength, excitement and illumination into your life. Your accumulated knowledge and wisdom will motivate you to right action with integrity. *You can achieve a rich, rewarding life by employing the powers of your Subconscious Mind.*

This book is based on the Golden Keys Success Seminar, and divided into four separate parts. The reader is taken from a state of negative self-image, outlook, and mental attitude to a positive mental attitude, a healthy self-image and a positive life style. In a workshop type atmosphere, specific, simple self-help techniques and exercises are given for daily use. These teachings and mind improving exercises will develop positive character traits.

However successful you may feel yourself to be—you are still operating well below your potential. Are you certain that you need *no* help? Dr. William James, the father of Psychology in America wrote, "Human beings can alter their lives by altering their attitudes of mind." Remember, "Today starts the rest of your life."

"The Book In A Nutshell"

PART I
THE CANDLE AND THE SUN
(Chapter 1 to 4)

Consider the power, heat and light the sun generates compared to that generated by a small candle. This is the power your subconscious mind has compared to your conscious mind. Why let such power go unused? Most of the world does. I will teach you working methods of mind control and show you how to unleash the power of your subconscious mind.

You will experience through mental picturing exercises, the compelling force and power of your subconscious mind, and you will come to understand that "what you consciously decide, plan, and expect, your subconscious mind will achieve and provide for you."

After you have practiced and experienced these exercises, utilizing your subconscious mind, you will learn to apply the same principle to materialize in your life anything that you want to have, become, or accomplish. You will learn how to change from a negative to a positive mental attitude (PMA).

Once you are taught the mental laws of right thinking you will forget your negative self-image and find a positive and harmonious life style. A simple formula used at night will re-arrange all of your thought patterns for your benefit.

You will learn a simple mental picturing exercise which will bring heightened concentration into your life.

PART II
SOCRATES AND A YOUNG MAN
(Chapter 1 to 5)

Socrates was asked by a young man for the secret of wisdom and success. Socrates took him to the beach. He then led him into the ocean, pushed his head under the water and let him struggle. The young man almost was drowned. Socrates brought him to the beach and returned to the market place to finish his lecture. After some time the young man regained his strength and came to him. He demanded, "Why did you do that? I could have drowned." Socrates asked, "What was your greatest desire after I had forced your head under the water?" The young man answered, "I wanted air more than anything else in the world." Said Socrates, "When your desire for wisdom and success becomes as great as your desire for air, you will obtain them."

Your desire for success and happiness must be as strong in you. You will learn mental laws and exercises to give you this strong desire.

A unique exercise, done for three to five minutes a few times daily, will condition your mind, program your subconscious mind and free the innate abilities within you. This exercise gives you many amazing benefits: with increased energy, you will accomplish many more times your normal work. Your nerves will relax and your emotions will be calmed. You will find new vibrant health through the healing power of the subconscious mind.

You will multiply your free time through the repetition of this exercise. You will learn how to connect yourself with God and great minds and to influence others by mental telepathy.

You will gain the ability to find lost articles and to remember names. You will have an increased awareness of the promptings, intuitions and guidance from the subconscious mind.

You will achieve harmony with the world around you.

You will enjoy many other amazing benefits through the consistent use of this marvelous relaxation and meditation exercise.

You will learn the universal laws of the mind and become the successful, happy person you were meant to be. You will know the power of the subconscious mind and its compelling feedback into your life.

You will learn to eliminate a negative vocabulary; and edit what you think and say. Thoughts are like seeds and you are the master of what you plant in your own mind, and in the minds of others. Your thoughts, speech, and actions affect not only yourself but others.

Negative and positive emotions are real "things" which can be measured and analyzed scientifically by the Kirlian equipment (Coronagraph) now available from Russia. The Coronagraph photographs the human aura. It is being studied by leading universities and psychic centers throughout the world. The aura, they have found, is a glow which radiates from each of us and is depleted through the outburst of negative emotions like anger, fear, doubt and anxiety.

You will be taught how to recharge the psychic energy of your aura so that you can be more effective. This is in preparation for the development of ESP (Extra Sensory Perception), mental telepathy and precognition, which are innate gifts in every person.

PART III
HOW TO PROGRAM YOUR SUBCONSCIOUS
MIND FOR SUCCESS
(Chapters 1 to 7)

A professional in difficulties, programmed his subconscious mind, and now is extremely successful in all phases of his life.

A salesman raised his production many-fold.

A housewife, on the verge of a nervous breakdown, now lives a happy, positive life.

You, too, can become successful.

You must be goal-directed and organized in life to be a winner. You must learn how to utilize the marvelous power of your subconscious mind through programming and the directing of your life toward specific goals in business, finance, education, family life, recreation, religion, spirituality, and health.

You will be taught two goal achievement methods, short-term and long-term. The short-term method, using positive affirmations, can be implemented and will result in achievement in only a week. The long-term method is designed to bring results over a period of months or longer. The latter method involves the reduction of goals to written form and the conscious programming of goals into the subconscious mind. Both methods involve direct programming of the subconscious mind through special relaxation exercises. You will thrill as you see the materialization of your goals in your life!

"There Is A Better Way, and You, Too, Will Find It"

You will become acquainted with universal mental laws, such as the law of service through mental telepathy or "mind-to-mind" contact.

You will learn the way to bridge the communication gap through "silent speaking" with loved ones and others. Sales people, executives and professional people will learn how to establish mental rapport.

The Law of Abundance (financial independence) is explained in detail. You will become familiar with the technique of using "money in action" to your advantage.

You will learn a dynamic method for planning time.

Through the law of "Things To Do," you will learn how to plan a day's itinerary and how to prepare mentally for it with a nightly programming. The power of the subconscious mind will take over and will carry out your itinerary for you.

"Believe That You Have Received and You Will Receive"

You will formulate a new self-image and become the person you desire to be.

So Simple—So Effective!

Get a tape printer, or label maker. Get stimulating messages such as "Today I Expect the Best in Every Situation" and put them where your eye will find them, in the office, in the home, and in the car. They will reinforce the programming of your subconscious mind.

PART IV
HAPPINESS AND SUCCESS IS AWAITING YOU
(Chapters 1 to 6)

You will learn with the help of your Subconscious Mind. Imagine having all of your problems solved through the greatest power in the world today, your Subconscious Mind! You see, the Subconscious Mind has no problems—only solutions: no questions, only answers.

Are you burdened with mental blocks, mental limitations or guilt complexes? Has someone hurt you deeply? Almost all of us are subject to or have experienced such problems or situations.

You will learn how to "Forgive and Forget" yourself and others with the help of your Subconscious Mind. You do not have to love or even like the one who has hurt you, but you must forgive in order to be free. Otherwise, you are in danger of contracting psychosomatic illnesses, living an unhappy life, and experiencing lacks and limitations of all kinds.

A program more marvelous than you can imagine will provide you with the relief from burdens and hurts. You may have tried to do this in the past without success. Why? Because you have not employed the power of your Subconscious Mind.

Sometimes people become depressed and upset for no apparent reason. The "Psycho-bio-rhythmic-cycle" explains why depressions exist and I show you how to avoid and overcome them.

Marriage is the basic institution in our lives and having a marriage full of love, excitement and harmony is the goal of most of us. The keys to a happy marriage can be acquired through the compelling force of the Subconscious Mind. You will be taught to program the correct attitudes directly into the Subconscious Mind. You can then expect the compelling feedback to create this ideal relationship.

There is yet another extraordinary concept which you will learn. I will teach you how to psychically protect yourself, your spouse, children, animals, and your property from any possible harm that could occur.

I will show you that there is a way out of any given situation at any given time, and how this complete psychic protection can benefit everyone.

You will be taught mental laws and how to use them in your life. Anger, fear, worry, resistance, lack of harmony, mental depression, criticism, and excess materialism are some of the results of mental law breaking. There are others. Breaking mental laws invariably brings destruction to mind and body. Live the mental laws and get the best. Deserve the best, and you will receive the best.

EXPERIENCE A NEW LIFE OF JOY, HAPPINESS, AND SUCCESS

WARNING: Do *not* depend *alone* on your own genius and natural strength, knowledge and wisdom; don't *ever* think they are sufficient to guarantee your success. Above and beyond all of this is Almighty God, your Heavenly Father from whom you can receive—through your Subconscious Mind—spiritual insight and help beyond all that your conscious effort can provide. Your Subconscious Mind is in direct communication with God, Infinite Intelligence.

"For without Me, ye can do nothing." (John 15:1-8)

I hope you have a glimpse of what the power of your Subconscious Mind is, and will be able to do for you.

PART I

How To Use This Book for Self Improvement

THE MONOTONOUS LIFE

Was this your life in the past—drifting with the crowd, conforming to others, monotonously performing your dull, boring, routine, life without goals? The mental exercises in this book will change YOU! *Today starts the rest of YOUR WONDERFUL, EXCITING LIFE.*

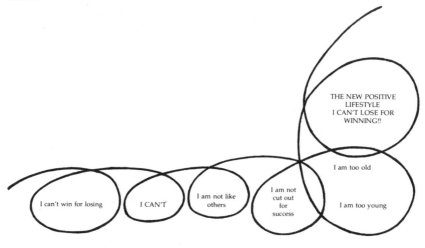

THE NEW POSITIVE LIFESTYLE I CAN'T LOSE FOR WINNING!!

I am too old

I am not cut out for success

I am too young

I can't win for losing

I CAN'T

I am not like others

SUCCESS DEPENDS ON YOUR POSITIVE MENTAL ATTITUDE

THE STEPS LEADING TO SUCCESS

Scores of people of all walks of life and all ages stand around the "STAIRWAY LEADING TO SUCCESS," looking up, saying: "I wish I could—but: It is TOO hard!" These negative, doubting, indifferent, and gloomy people are always found at the bottom of the ladder of success. There is plenty of room on the way up and on top.

I will teach you how to eliminate your doubts, fears, negative thinking and self-limitations. I will motivate you to obtain self-confidence, a new image and a positive lifestyle. All that YOU have to do is to make up your mind; set your goals and then move to the STEPS leading to Success.

I expect YOU to climb with me. With the help of the super power of your Subconscious Mind, you will be able to get on your way. You will find that it takes only one step at a time to climb the stairway leading to fulfillment, prosperity, achievement, fame, happiness, vigorous health, and SUCCESS.

REMEMBER, CLIMBING IS NOT WALKING OR
STANDING AROUND IDLY

WHAT ARE YOU WAITING FOR? START CLIMBING!!
ANYBODY CAN!!
TODAY STARTS THE REST OF YOUR LIFE!!

CONGRATULATIONS ON YOUR DECISION TO VENTURE INTO THE DEPTHS OF YOUR SUBCONSCIOUS MIND

Let me show you the way to your Subconscious Mind, which from today on will be your invaluable companion on the road to: HAPPINESS, SUCCESS, FINANCIAL INDEPENDENCE, FAITH, SPIRITUALITY, WISDOM, HEALTH, AND PEACE OF MIND.

If you are willing to learn the working methods, rules, laws, and principles of your Subconscious Mind and apply them in your daily life, you can expect to be a well-adjusted, integrated, organized, and successful personality tomorrow.

Please sign the pledge to faithfully do the exercises for the next *four weeks* and put this first and foremost in your life.

When you sign your name, you express with your signature: "I will do it; I promise." By branding this workshop book with your name, you are making a conscious decision to turn to your Subconscious Mind for help in your daily life. This is a contract between your conscious and your Subconscious Mind. Nothing in your life before has been more important in terms of your self-improvement than this promise with your signature

NAME *Dick Blungl*

DATE *Aug 21, 80*

THOUGHTS THAT WILL HELP YOU TO STICK TO YOUR GOALS:

"Human beings can alter their lives by altering their attitudes of mind."—*Dr. William James*

"Our wishes are the motivators of our talents, capabilities and qualifications."—*Wolfgang von Goethe*

"A wise man turns chances into good fortune."—*Thomas Fuller*

"To a brave man, good and bad luck are like his right and left hand. He uses both."—*St. Catherine of Siona*

Yes, you too have all the gifts and abilities. Believe it and feel it and you shall receive them. They will be yours for the asking.—*Kurt A. Schneider*

Thoughts are energy and create change. What you imagine you become. What you feel, you attract.—*Kurt A. Schneider*

You need nothing from outside: All this power is in you waiting to be freed. A spark is enough to kindle a bonfire in you.—*Kurt A. Schneider*

BE READY FOR A GREAT SURPRISE

As soon as you *start to practice these exercises*, you will automatically tune in with me through Mental Telepathy on the psycho-electro-magnetic energy thought field and obtain a clear understanding of the "Fundamental Laws of Right Thinking."

Every one of us has the ability to receive and send thoughts through Mental Telepathy. It is necessary to study and develop these gifts. Anyone can *learn* to have psychic experiences.

I have used in every chapter, psychic experiences of my own and stories from my broadcasting program: "The Fundamental Laws of Right Thinking."

CIRCUS ELEPHANTS AND LIMITATIONS

An elephant can pick up a one ton load with his trunk. Have you ever visited a circus and seen these huge creatures standing quietly while tied to a small wooden stake? In the country of Thailand I witnessed the training of elephants.

While young and weak, an elephant is tied by a heavy chain to an immovable iron stake. No matter how hard he tries, he cannot break the chain or move the stake. Later, no matter how large and strong the elephant becomes, he continues to believe he cannot move while he is fastened to the stake in the ground beside him. Many intelligent people are like circus elephants. They are limited in thoughts, actions, and results. They never question their own self-imposed limitations.

If this is true of your life . . . resolve now to uproot the stakes that hold you . . . break the chains of hindering habits . . . become the person you want to be and can become by programming your Subconscious Mind.

BREAK WITH THE NEGATIVE PAST

After a speaking assignment in a prison, I tried to find out the attitudes of the inmates toward the past. Many were very remorseful and wished they could turn back the clock and undo the things they had done.

Whether we are aware of it or not, there have been times in our lives when we could have fallen if our attitudes hadn't been positively influenced by some person or circumstance. Daily, I hear adults and teenagers say, "I wish I had: . . . married more wisely; . . . finished my education . . . gone to church . . . taken care of my health . . . listened to my parents . . . followed my inner voice . . . read more good books, etc." The trouble is that we do not learn from our experiences, so we say over and over again: "I wish I had." If we really want to have a better future with fewer regrets, we can have it with Subconscious Mind Training by applying the positive formula: "I will surely take advantage of the next opportunity."

The following technique has helped many. Use sample page with double lines across the middle of the page, dividing it into two parts. Write on the lower half: "PAST." Now fill in the double line solidly with red or any other color. At the same time impress on your mind that you have learned from negative, devastating and disappointing experiences and are now willing not to dwell on them any more. You cannot turn back the clock. Make up your mind that you will never do them again, and then free your mind from them. Great harm results from constantly dwelling on past errors.

"A man can fail many times, but he isn't a failure until he begins to blame somebody else." Buffalo News

Write on the top half of the page: TODAY IS THE BEGINNING OF THE REST OF MY LIFE. Think and plan positively and constructively for the future. Let the past fade away. Think like Charles F. Kettering, the wizard head engineer of GM, "My interest is in the future because I am going to spend the rest of my life there."

No one is too old or too young to change his attitude of mind and his self-image; to start a new positive lifestyle TODAY.

Fill in this space with color, signifying that you are willing to quit complaining and fretting about the negative past.

"There is no crying over spilt milk—that which is past cannot be recalled."—*Andrew Yarraton*
If necessary, work in connection with Part 4, Chapter IV, "Forgive and Forget." Forget and overcome your past failures and inadequacies.

WEAKNESSES WHICH I WANT TO OVERCOME

By applying the mental laws and exercises in this book:

_____

_____

_____

_____

_____

_____

_____

_____

_____

_____

_____

WHAT I WANT TO ACCOMPLISH

By applying the mental laws and exercises in this book:

CONTINUING EDUCATION

Studying the lives of many executives, vice-presidents and presidents of leading companies, I found that almost without exception they all believed in continuing education. Many didn't have much early formal education, but they later learned all they could, which led to their promotions. They were chosen because they had prepared themselves. Their advancement was no coincidence. They constantly sought for new ideas, new methods and better ways to manage, sell, produce and serve the public.

One of these executives, who rose from delivery boy to vice-president of a large corporation, said in an interview: "I think every individual has tremendous potentials. People are even 'over-built' for this world physically, mentally and spiritually. But considering what we do, the world is in a mediocre state today." If you were a dropout, failed in school, or couldn't keep up with the curriculum in high school or college, it does not matter! The important question is: Do you really want to succeed now? There are countless opportunities to succeed without a formal education, through continuing education.

"There is always a better way—FIND IT!"

I don't promise you that it will be easy, but it isn't so difficult, either. To succeed, people must change their self-images and change their attitudes. New inner self-confidence, self-mastery and self-discipline can be developed. Through Subconscious Mind Training, all this and more can be achieved, by erasing old negative character patterns from the mind and programming in new ideas of hope, happiness, joy and success. Use the following affirmation with a burning desire:

"I want to succeed. I can; I will; I do. My Subconscious Mind will bring forth my special gifts and talents with which I can serve mankind. I will help others to succeed, and compound my own successes."

THE MOTIVATION

When I was 15 years of age I decided to go into the steel business. My father was not very pleased with my decision at the time, but he helped me to obtain an apprenticeship. This was a small town where the farmers came with horses and wagons to pick up their supplies.

It was hard work. Most of the lifting was done by hand and a strong back. Being the youngest, I had to clean the yard and street, which wasn't exactly what I had envisioned when I chose this profession. I wanted to be an expert in steel, hardware and houseware. With a positive mental attitude, *I made up my mind and went to the boss.* I told him what I wanted to be and what I could do for him if he would give me a chance as a sales representative of his company. He looked at me and said, "I have watched you, Kurt, and have waited for this hour. As long as you were complacent I couldn't help you. Now I know you will go places. The world is waiting for men like you and there is plenty of room at the top."

And so it was. In a short time I set sales records for his company. With a positive mental attitude I motivated myself by programming my Subconscious Mind for a leading position in the steel industry. I had not had much schooling, but I made up my mind that I would catch up through continuous education. It is never *too* late. Wake up and live. Today starts the rest of your life!

THE SWIMMING INSTRUCTOR

One day as I waited for my little girl, Susi, to have her swimming lesson I watched the other boys and girls. They were first instructed on dry land, and then they had to go into the water. A few were reluctant and stood on the deck afraid. The instructor was very understanding. I was impressed by what she said, "You must get your feet wet first if you want to learn to swim."

The following chapters are all designed to expand your thinking and develop your foresight, ambition and determination. It really is a Subconscious Mind Training Course. If you would like to get more out of life and gain wisdom and spirituality, you must "get your feet wet" first. You have to start at the beginning. The children in the swimming school had to go from exercises on dry land to practicing in shallow water and then to swimming in deep water. So we have to study and get used to Subconscious Mind Training. I will guide you step by step, and with every exercise you learn, you will be able to open a new way of thinking. I can promise you that it will be a rewarding and exciting experience for you.

PART I
CHAPTER 1
SUMMARY

1. S.I.H.—K.I.S.—SEE IT HUGE—KEEP IT SIMPLE
2. Brand Your Book
3. How to Break With the Negative Past
4. What You Want to Accomplish
5. Stories from the Broadcasting Program, ''The Fundamental Laws of Right Thinking''

YOU DESERVE
A SECOND
CHANCE

PART I
CHAPTER 2

The Subconscious Mind Explanations

THERE IS A BETTER WAY: FIND IT

"When someone starts and continues a self-improvement program, his future is unlimited."—*Benjamin Franklin*

With conventional methods:

85% will not remember much after a few days;
10% will forget after a few months;
5% will succeed in retaining the material.

With the "NEW PROGRAMMING OF YOUR SUBCONSCIOUS MIND"

100% can succeed. It will not take many months. You will experience a marvelous change in one week. You are about to start an adventure that will reward you richly for the rest of your life.

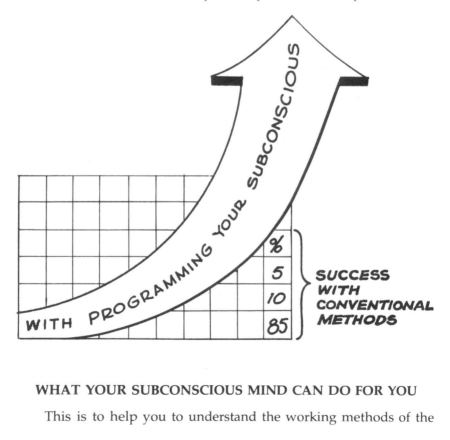

WHAT YOUR SUBCONSCIOUS MIND CAN DO FOR YOU

This is to help you to understand the working methods of the

Subconscious Mind, so that you can program any goal you choose into your Subconscious without outside help.

Are You A Winner, or a Loser?

Do you feel that life has cheated you out of happiness? Are you lonely, unhappy, living in the past, or confused? Do you feel you have failed? Are you doubtful and fearful? Do you lose your temper easily? Are you living under stress? Are you anxious, nervous, unable to sleep or relax? Do you need a self-starter? Do you need more energy and zest for work? Do you want to know how to solve your problems? Do you need more self-confidence, self-mastery, creativity, wisdom, joy, vigorous health and total success? Do you want to find the right partner?

How is Your Spiritual Life?

Have you lost faith in God, and in people?

What is Your Financial Situation?

Are you in the comfort zone? Do you need a better job, more money? Do you want to get out of debt? Do you want to be financially independent?

How to Quit Undesirable Habits:

Do you want to free your inner strength to overcome obesity, drug problems, smoking or alcoholism?

Are You Willing to Improve?

Are you willing to learn "How to Program Your Subconscious Mind" so life may bring you what you need and want? If you are, please read on.

You Can't Lose!

See yourself change through carefully managed "thought control." There is a better way, and I shall help you to find it. "As a man thinketh in his heart, so is he."

Do not scoff and say, "I have tried it all; but it doesn't work for me." Please give this new method of *HOW TO PROGRAM YOUR SUBCONSCIOUS MIND* a chance. Right at this moment, your Subconscious Mind is waiting to prove to you its limitless power.

The Four Week Trial

Reserve judgment—give the method a four-week trial. This mind energy of yours, your aura, the psycho-electro-magnetic-energy field, is a natural, universal, God-given force. You alone must determine how it will be used—negatively and destructively—or positively and creatively. You must train yourself to become an expert in using your Subconscious Mind energy and free your innate gifts of "extra" sensory perception.

100% Workable

In the past successful self-motivation and self-improvement may have been difficult for you. But these "New Techniques for Programming the Subconscious Mind" have made such processes easy, simple and 100% sure!

What is the Greatest Power?

What do you think is the greatest power available to us? Is it atomic energy, thermonuclear power, interplanetary space travel? It is none of these! The greatest power is the miraculous, incredible power of your own Subconscious Mind. Many are concerned only with the physical. But it is the mind that rules. So let us talk about the MIND.

Each of us has only one mind. The mind manifests itself however, in two kinds of mental activity, the conscious and the Subconscious. Just as your voluntary and involuntary nervous systems, both parts of your mind are capable of independent action as well as synchronized interaction. It is in your greatest interest to explore the working method of your Subconscious Mind. *The Subconscious Mind doesn't require the time-consuming process of reasoning the conscious mind does.* You simply program the Subconscious Mind with intense feelings and mental pictures of your desires. You mentally "see" and feel the accomplishment of your goals. They will be brought to pass by your Subconscious Mind precisely as you have programmed.

THE SPIRAL

In my lectures and seminars, I use a spiral made out of poster paper, about 20 inches in diameter, to illustrate our potentials. I recommend that you too make yourself a spiral according to the graph. It will be a teaching tool not only for you, but also for those you tell about it.

The Spiral

Each new level of enlightened thinking enlarges your spiritual horizon, leading you to new dimensions of understanding. On the lower level you may wake up in the morning saying sleepily: "Oh, another day." On the higher levels you wake up full of ambition and vigor and can hardly wait to accomplish something positive. You face the world with zest.

You expand to meet the higher standards of life. You climb upward in your visions. Your mind will grow and your spirit unfold in the application of knowledge and wisdom. Your life will move upwards to new dimensions of learning. Your personality will develop from level to level to the utmost reaches of your imagination and potentials.

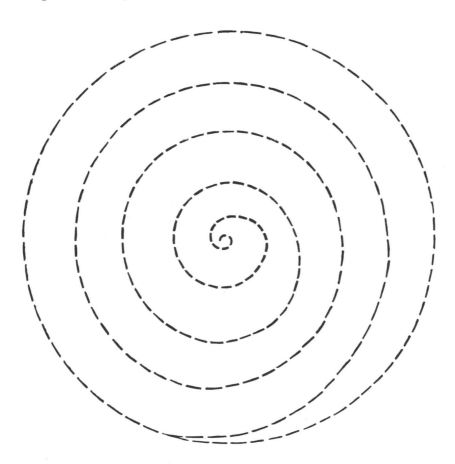

"Man's mind stretched by a new idea never goes back to its original dimensions."—Oliver Wendell Holmes

Don't constantly "re-invent the wheel." More is expected of you than to go back into the past. Take advantage of the experiences of yesterday and expect better things today. Bounteous new encounters and new growth experiences are awaiting you.

Someone said, "He who reaches for things beyond his grasp may find more happiness than one who strives only for things within reach."

THE SPIRAL

"Another day! I have to work! I can't win for losing."
Negative mental attitude. Endless want
—Sickness—Mediocrity

Nervous Breakdown, All Mixed up, No Goals, on the verge of suicide—On Drugs—Alcoholic—Psycho-Somatic Sickness

POSITIVE MENTAL ATTITUDE
Glad To Be Alive. Full of Vigor and Zest. Striving Constantly to do Good for Someone. Goal Directed. Total Success. Full Potentials.

SPIRITUALITY—BEST HEALTH
I CAN'T LOSE FOR WINNING!!

WHAT DOES E.S.P. STAND FOR

The process by which something is seen, experienced or perceived beyond the normal five senses of the conscious mind is E.S.P., or Extra-Sensory Perception. Para-psychology and Meta-physics are other collective expressions for psychic potentials. P.S.I., or psychic ability cannot be proved or disproved by reasoning or scientific observations.

The best known E.S.P. phenomenon is Mental Telepathy. For instance, someone calls on the telephone at the same instant you were thinking of or dialing this person's number. A question in someone's mind is answered by another before it is spoken.

Clairvoyance is seeing things or events happening in the present and, at a distant place.

Clairaudience is hearing a message. This frequently happens as a forewarning to prevent accidents, dangers or troubles of any kind.

Precognition is a revelation, a prophetic dream, or a view of an event happening in the future. For instance, quite a few people are known to have foreseen the assassination of President John F. Kennedy, and to have seen wars and catastrophies this way.

Postcognition occurs when past events are shown on a mental screen like a motion picture. Some have had this phenomenon occur in their lives.

Clair Sentience is a hunch or inspiration. Your telephone rings and you have a hunch who is calling you. This is an example of clair sentience.

Psychometry is the ability of a person to get strong feelings and impressions concerning another after having touched an object which had been in contact with the person in question. Missing persons have been located through psychometry.

Psycho Kinesis, or P.K., is a psychic phenomenon in which objects can be influenced by focused thoughts. Mind over matter!

THE CAVE IN YUCATAN

My wife and I visited the Yucatan Peninsula in Mexico and saw the temples and ruins of the ancient Mayas. Our guide made it possible for us to enter a newly-discovered cave, and he told us that a young boy had discovered this cave years ago. The boy had entered the cave many times, always finding his way to the place it ended, approximately one-half mile away, where the ceiling became very low. He had the feeling that there was more that he had not seen.

Years later the boy returned as a Doctor of Archaeology to satisfy his burning desire. He searched the cave, and finally discovered an unusual formation which looked man-made. He removed part of it and found a tunnel leading to a magnificent dome-like cave filled with vases, sculptures, precious stones and gold. He left us a lesson in persistence: "Just so far and progress seemed impeded—I searched a little farther and then proceeded." Emerson said: "Do the things and you will have the power."

You may ask, "What is so strange about that?" It teaches us that we shouldn't be content until we have obtained our goal, arrived at our final destination. There is no virtue in mediocrity (remember the spiral).

As a boy, he was not ready for the discovery of the entire cave. He had to mature first. Perhaps you have tried positive thinking before, or worked on developing your extra-sensory perception but failed. That is no reason to quit! You too have matured, have expanded your thinking, and are now ready to find new dimensions through understanding the Laws of Right Thinking. Why not try once more and this time discover a new life of joy, happiness, health and success?

Prepare yourself with the following affirmation: "I give thanks in advance for guidance in all situations, in thoughts and words and actions. All good things will now be realized in my life."

DISABLED

A friend of mine became totally disabled as the result of a car accident. It was a sobering experience. The man had loved to work, and was very energetic. His wife told me that she feels impatient with other people because in her opinion they are lazy. What her husband would give to be able to wake up in the morning, and start a day of hard work!

Let's be honest with ourselves. Do we not wake up many mornings saying, "Another day?" But you can change that attitude. It doesn't have to be like that. All people have the potential for joy. They can find it by obeying the Fundamental Laws of Right Thinking. We can condition ourselves to experience that joy. But nothing comes from nothing. If we program our minds with joyful thinking, we will act accordingly.

Here is the secret. Even if you don't feel like it right now, pretend you are happy. Speak and act "as if" you were happy. Say aloud: I am happy. I am happy! Then as sure as day follows night, your subconscious mind will accept this as a command and move heaven and earth to bring it into your life. You can depend on it.

We All Fall Short of Our Potential

Everyone has an enormous mind power potential. Some may use a larger part of their powers than others, but all men are falling far short of their total intellectual potential. We use only about 1/10th of one percent of our mind energy. We must find the way to release the psychic energy within us by learning to throw off inhibiting factors and complexes. No matter how long we may have used our mind in a negative manner, from the day we change our attitude and begin to think positively, positive results will follow.

I read recently in the news the story of a lady who lifted a heavy tree to free her boy who was pinned underneath.

Another woman freed her husband by lifting the front end of a truck. Both ladies acted under the stress of the moment and did what they felt had to be done, without consciously considering the fact that the performance was "impossible."

THE BUMBLEBEE

Physicists and Zoologists tell us that the bumblebee is designed in such a way that it should not be able to fly. But the bumblebee doesn't know this—so, it flies!

In shrines all over the world the "impossible" occurs daily. I saw a sick woman in Tokyo approaching a temple. She touched the "holy smoke from the offering altar," swished it all over her, and her body and mind was healed. She believed and expected that when she touched the smoke she would be healed. And so she was healed.

It is the conscious mind that limits our potentials; when the conscious mind is by-passed, miracles can be performed by the Subconscious Mind.

HEALTH STUDIO

I work out often in a fine health studio. It is interesting to see the different muscular bodies there. Some men develop their arms and chests, while others develop their legs. Others seek to bring the whole muscle system into harmonious-looking bodies. I wondered how many were concerned about mental fitness. The people I most enjoy seeing are not the "Mister America Types," but the all-around, healthy, well-developed and fit-looking people.

Just as we are generally far from healthy and fit, so have we fallen short in the development of our intellectual powers. Very few have found the secret of how to use their psychic energies. The times in which we live demand that we achieve our potentials in order to meet our complex problems and to develop a psychic shield against the emotional blows we receive daily.

A study of the Fundamental Laws of Right Thinking and their application in daily life makes it possible to maintain a positive mental attitude; to think better, and clearer, and make right decisions. Through Subconscious Mind Training we will be able to cast off mental blocks and limitations, and guilt complexes and every self-programmed negative trait, which hold us back from finding fulfillment in life. Someone said, "Procrastination is the thief of time." Start today to do something about mental fitness.

OTHER DIMENSIONS

We are so wrapped up in our daily work responsibilities, that we forget about other dimensions. There are countless things about us too small for the naked eye to see. There are sounds beyond our hearing, and colors which our eyes are not equipped to see. Radio waves, solar rays, T.V. signals continually pass by us, and through us. All of these things influence our lives, yet we cannot even recognize such influences with our five physical senses.

Our Inner Space

Probably the greatest and most powerful world of all is the world of Our Inner Space, containing the many dimensions of our minds. This is the world we should really be most concerned about. This is the world of the Subconscious Mind which we should explore.

You can learn to use the vast resources of your Subconscious

Mind, resources of knowledge, strength and inspiration which are beyond the reach of our five physical senses. The power is within you. You may have tapped this power before on rare occasions, when you experienced brief flashes called hunches, insights or inspirations. But there is a way to bring this incredible mental power under full conscious control.

Your Subconscious, Your Genie, receives your emotionalized wishes, goals, and thoughts and brings them to pass. It is on the job 24-hours a day. It never sleeps. It is your "Genie," your willing servant. Remember, the Subconscious Mind Computer is unable to determine whether your wishes, goals and thoughts are good or bad, right or wrong. It accepts them, mulls them over and moves heaven and earth to bring them to pass for you. You cannot overwork your Subconscious Mind. In fact, the more you assign to it, the better it will serve you. It is YOUR Willing Partner!!

Here are a few statements from some of my students, after only a short time of practice in programming the Subconscious Mind:

"Mr. Schneider, look at my new office and the new plant which I have established. I owe it all to you and your method of 'Programming the Subconscious Mind.' " J.C.

"I now have more business than I can handle." S.T.

"My husband and I are no longer separated. We have a happy marriage again." M.C.

"My greatest dream is fulfilled; I found my husband. We love one another deeply." L.W.

"No one believed that I could quit smoking. I had tried to quit so often before. This time it is permanent. I have re-programmed my subconscious. If I can do it, anyone can." F.B.

Four Drawings of the Workings of the Mind Follow:

Study them carefully. Before you begin the exercises, I want you to have a clear understanding of the working methods of your Subconscious Mind.

NEGATIVE VICIOUS CYCLE

If you live by the "law of averages," you are in danger of slipping farther down to failure.

The big circle represents your total mind. The two halves represent the CONSCIOUS MIND FACULTY, (CM) and the SUBCONSCIOUS MIND FACULTY, (SM). Remember, this is only figurative. The capabilities and power of the Subconscious can be compared to the light and heat of the sun and the Conscious Mind with the light and heat of one candle. The comparison could also be made with an iceberg; the small part above the water represents the

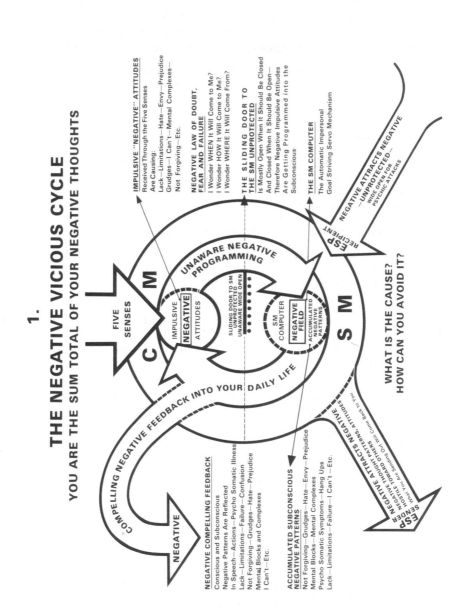

1.
THE NEGATIVE VICIOUS CYCLE
YOU ARE THE SUM TOTAL OF YOUR NEGATIVE THOUGHTS

IMPULSIVE "NEGATIVE" ATTITUDES
Received Through the Five Senses
Are Causing:
Lack—Limitations—Hate—Envy—Prejudice
Grudges—I Can't—Mental Complexes—
Not Forgiving—Etc.

NEGATIVE LAW OF DOUBT,
FEAR AND FAILURE
I Wonder WHEN It Will Come to Me?
I Wonder HOW It Will Come to Me?
I Wonder WHERE It Will Come From?

THE SLIDING DOOR TO
THE SM UNPROTECTED
Is Mostly Open When It Should Be Closed
And Closed When It Should Be Open—
Therefore Negative Impulsive Attitudes
Are Getting Programmed into the
Subconscious

THE SM COMPUTER
The Automatic Impersonal
Goal Striving Servo Mechanism

NEGATIVE ATTRACTS NEGATIVE
—UNPROTECTED—
WIDE OPEN FOR
PSYCHIC ATTACKS

FIVE
SENSES

C M

UNAWARE NEGATIVE
PROGRAMMING

IMPULSIVE
NEGATIVE
ATTITUDES

SLIDING DOOR TO SM
UNPROTECTED
UNAWARE WIDE OPEN

SM
COMPUTER

NEGATIVE
FIELD

ACCUMULATED
NEGATIVE
PATTERNS

S M

ESP
RECIPIENT

COMPELLING NEGATIVE FEEDBACK INTO YOUR DAILY LIFE

NEGATIVE

NEGATIVE COMPELLING FEEDBACK
Conscious and Subconscious
Negative Patterns Are Reflected
In Speech—Actions—Psycho Somatic Illness
Lack—Limitations—Failure—Confusion
Not Forgiving—Grudges—Hate—Prejudice
Mental Blocks and Complexes
I Can't—Etc.

ACCUMULATED SUBCONSCIOUS
NEGATIVE PATTERNS
Not Forgiving—Grudges—Hate—Envy—Prejudice
Mental Blocks—Mental Complexes
Psycho Somatic Symptoms—Hang Ups
Lack—Limitations—Failure—I Can't—Etc.

NEGATIVE ATTRACTS NEGATIVE
NEGATIVE THOUGHT PATTERNS-ATTITUDES
NEGATIVE TOWARD OTHERS Will Come Back to You
When You Are Sending Out
Hostile Vibes

ESP
SENDER

WHAT IS THE CAUSE?
HOW CAN YOU AVOID IT?

conscious and the huge mass of ice under the water represents the subconscious. The conscious mind is only a small part of our total mind power. We receive by way of conversations, movies, radio, television, books, magazines, and newspapers, compelling "negative" thoughts and ideas of which we are sometimes unaware. These in turn create a negative "thought field" in the conscious. (Circle impulsive negative attitudes, Chart 1).

Negative Field

Negative thoughts, ideas and beliefs which we accept are automatically programmed into the subconscious creating therein a forceful NEGATIVE FIELD. The subconscious not knowing what is good for you, accepts such ideas as wanted "ideal things;" or "goals." It attaches enormous power to them like an electric transformer and feeds them back again into your conscious.

Subconscious Feedback

This immense power reacts in your daily life, creating all kinds of havoc; forcing you into a negative state. It is too late to fight then with "will power" through the conscious. (Remember the comparison of the Candle, and the Sun.)

THE DEVIL MADE ME DO IT

You have probably heard the expression, "the devil made me do it." It is not the devil who makes you do it; it is your negatively programmed subconscious. You have not considered the consequences. Repeatedly you have let your mind dwell on negative ideas.

Remember, there is no life without pressure, trial, temptation and occasional failure, but these need not damage you!

BIRDS NEST

My Yoga Mind Teacher in Bangkok, Thailand, told me this story from Buddha. He said, "You can't avoid birds flying over you, but you must prevent them from building nests on top of your head."

We are the sum total of all our negative and positive thoughts of the past. Unfortunately, we are constantly bombarded by negative thoughts, feelings and attitudes, without being aware that the protective "sliding door" to the subconscious is wide open.

You have not yet learned how to deliberately open and close the door to your subconscious. The sliding door represents your heightened, focused, controlled, and selective thinking.

No wonder so many negative patterns have accumulated in your subconscious computer and have been fed back into your daily life to create trouble for you. (You permitted the birds to build their nests on your head.) Now you can see, you and you alone are to blame. (Not that I don't believe in an Adversary. But we are usually at fault, not Lucifer.) You can be the recipient of negative vibrations, mental telepathy from others. You are also open for negative psychic attacks.

Blind worries and negative thinking add to your problems because they draw to you the very things you fear, and do not want.

Even Job suffered from this and wrote about it. "For the thing which I greatly feared is come upon me, and that which I was afraid of is come unto me." (Job 3:25)

You broadcast negative thought patterns and attitudes, and even hostility toward others. Negative attracts negative. What you have been sending out forcefully has been restored in your own life again—making you more miserable.

REMEMBER: "Hell is paved with good intentions."—Samuel Johnson

"The dictionary is the only place where success comes before work."—Arthur Boisbanc

TELEPHONE PLUG

The telephone in my private lecture room can be disconnected. Sometimes I rush to the telephone and dial without being aware that the telephone is still disconnected. I dialed and dialed and couldn't understand why the telephone did not work. The telephone was in good order; the dial was working, but the cord was not plugged in.

We have to be plugged in and connected before we can enjoy real communication. We are created that way. If we are not plugged in to the Infinite, we are worthless for the purpose for which we are created, just like the disconnected telephone. After I put the four prongs into the connection piece, I dialed and reached the party I wanted.

Many of us are in the habit of blaming our environment,

circumstances, tradition, parents, school, state and government, God, or the Devil for our misfortune. It would have been foolish for me to blame the telephone for not working properly. I was the one at fault. I had disconnected it. The Fundamental Laws of Right Thinking will connect us, just as the Fundamental Laws of Negative Thinking will cut us off. The act of plugging in and dialing could be compared with focused thoughts, prayer, meditation and relaxation for programming and directing our minds.

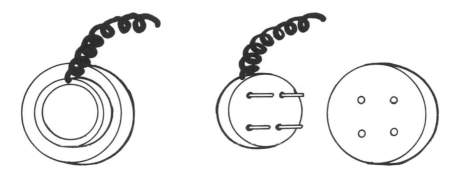

OBESITY, THE RESULT OF NEGATIVE PROGRAMMING—SANDY

A lady, whom I know very well, call her Sandy, was depressed, lonely, disappointed, overworked, fatigued, tense, worried and torn between hopes and despair. She was close to suicide. Sandy followed a common and well-accepted pattern. When troubled, she ate, and this gave her satisfaction. The relieved feelings and satisfactions from eating were programmed into her subconscious and there accepted as the solution for her problems.

The subconscious computer, not knowing what is good or bad, healthy or unhealthy for Sandy, registered this process for further use. The next time Sandy suffered from similar negative emotions and stress, the subconscious compelled her to eat again. This cycle was repeated again, and again, until she was on her way to obesity.

The Negative Feedback From the Subconscious Can Be Re-programmed

Sandy said: "I was frightfully ignorant. It was just like another person in me saying, 'Sandy, can you remember last time when you felt miserable just as you do now? You ate and felt so much better afterwards; so why don't you eat again? Make yourself a good sandwich; get a dish of ice cream; eat some cookies and candies.' "

The vicious cycle was established; the habit was formed. The compelling force of the subconscious was now so strong that Sandy could not consciously withstand this feedback with willpower any more. After she had experienced such cause-and-effect many times, the negative habit was established. Sandy has learned to re-program her subconscious in relaxation and is well-adjusted and slim.

Success in overcoming smoking, drinking, drug-use or any other undesirable habit, can be yours, by this process. The answer is overcoming the negative by re-programming. A habit has to be changed where it is deeply lodged, in the subconscious. The principle is very simple.

DRIVE-IN

A student of mine told me this story. A man had a thriving Drive-In business. He was hard of hearing and had poor eyesight; therefore, he had no radio and read no newspapers. The people liked him, felt sorry for him and patronized him. Soon he had to expand. His business was great!

One day, his son whom he was helping through college, came home saying, "Father, haven't you heard how many businesses have gone bankrupt? We are in a depression and disaster is on our doorsteps. Cut down the operation." The father took this to heart because he respected his son's knowledge. He started to cut down. He dropped his advertising. His negative, worried attitude was easy to spot. In the past, the Drive-In had been an island of optimism but almost overnight, it changed to the same negative ways of the other businesses. Day by day, business went down and he had to release nearly all of his employees. He said to his son, "I am glad you came home and warned me. We certainly are in the middle of a depression."

Every day we are bombarded by negative statements. But they can only hurt us if we accept them, dwell on them, and let fear and doubt grow in us. In and of themselves, the words you hear are powerless. The mental pictures and the colors you give them with your own thoughts are powerful and creative. They can be positive or negative, good or bad.

Let us learn from this story and train ourselves to discern and reject negative remarks. Condition yourself for the future with the following affirmation: "Negative statements will roll off me like water from a duck's back. I will be highly aware of all that is good for me."

SAILBOAT

Have you ever watched a sailboat regatta? With the breeze blowing in one direction, the boats can turn around at a given point and go in the opposite direction. The captain turns the sails in such a way that the wind power is always used, and maneuvers the boat in the desired direction.

Watching a sailboat regatta at Lake Tahoe, I compared this to our lives. We use the great potentials of our mind power in a negative or in a positive way, depending on our focused thinking, just as we can work the rudder of a ship. The boat doesn't care where you sail it. We have the mental ability and power to change our attitudes and course of life.

The mind doesn't care where you let your thoughts wander or on what you let them dwell. The sail and the rudder are like our conscious mind programming the direction of the Subconscious Mind. The wind is the influence of environment. Failure to give a ship direction; to properly maneuver it with the sails and rudder, can lead to destruction. In the same way, our thoughts, if not focused, directed, dedicated by a burning desire for accomplishment, can lead us to destruction and failure.

Watching the regatta, we were told that although the way the boat is built has great influence on its speed; the most significant influence is the skill of the captain. He has to know how to set the sails and to handle the rudders. Sometimes we lull ourselves into believing that we are left behind in life because of misfortune and bad luck. Not so. It is the skill and knowledge of how to apply the Fundamental Laws of Right Thinking in our daily lives that determine our "fortune" and "luck."

How have you set your mental sails?

THE SWEAT SHIRT

A student told me this story. A sweat shirt manufacturer sold thousands of shirts with the words printed on them, "MONEY ISN'T EVERYTHING." He went bankrupt! Many of the young people wearing the shirts suffered financial setbacks, too.

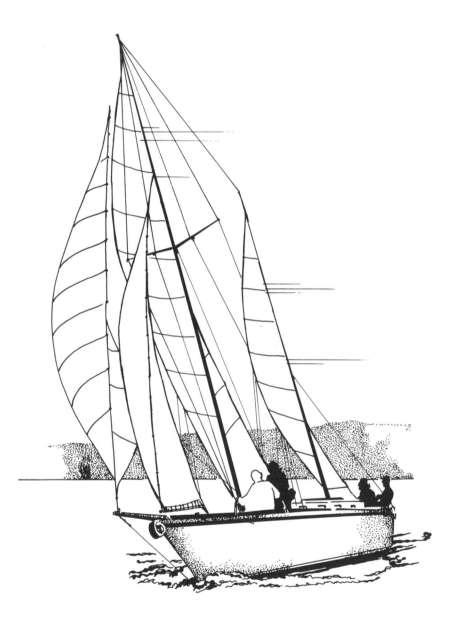

You see, *you can't fool the subconscious!* It can't take a joke! It takes everything literally, and brings what is programmed into it to pass!

TODAY STARTS THE REST OF YOUR LIFE

Your negative mental attitudes are already a part of the past because you will learn how to transform negative patterns into positive patterns on the psycho-electro-magnetic energy thought field. TODAY IS THE BEGINNING OF THE REST OF YOUR LIFE.

The great German poet Friedrich von Schiller said: "If we could free our people from FEAR—DOUBT- and NEGATIVE THINKING we could make them God-like."

During the desperate time of 1933, Franklin D. Roosevelt said: "The only thing we have to fear is fear itself."

The Elevator

What do you think would happen if you entered an elevator and pressed the UP and DOWN button at the same time? You go

nowhere! Make up your mind today and act accordingly. Press only the "POSITIVE BUTTON."

THE OCEAN LINER "FRANCE"

We saw the huge ocean liner "France" in the harbor at Hong Kong. We asked the Captain: "How can a great ship like that stay afloat?" He said, "The water of all the oceans we plow through on our world tour cannot sink that ship unless water is allowed to get inside the hull."

My wife said, "Isn't that what you teach? The negative thoughts around us have no influence unless we dwell on them—fear them, and let them become a part of our lives."

THE FROG IN THE STOMACH

Let me tell you about a lady who was obsessed with the belief that she had a frog in her stomach. In desperation, she went to see a doctor. After the examination, the physician tried to convince her that it was not possible for a frog to live in her stomach. She said, "Are you calling me a liar? I feel the frog. I feel him jumping up and down."

She went from one doctor to another, always with the same result. Finally she met a very understanding doctor. He said, "I believe you, madam. Why don't you come to the hospital tomorrow morning? We shall remove that darned frog!"

The doctor used practical psychology. He gave her anesthesia, but he didn't operate. He went downtown and bought a frog, put it in a jar, and came back to the bedside of the lady. "Here is your frog" he said. "How do you feel now?" She jumped right out of her bed, hugged the doctor and testified that she felt wonderful and was healed, instantly.

At home, she placed the jar with her frog on the mantle and invited all her friends to see it, as proof to them that she had been right after all. She felt wonderful until one of her friends remarked, "Gee, I hope the frog hasn't laid any eggs!"

You can imagine what happened to our lady. Think about this story. There is a lot of truth and wisdom in it. Daily we suffer from negative suggestions or are helped through positive compliments. Say as many positive affirmations as you can. They will help others, as well as yourself.

NEGATIVE PHRASES ARE DANGEROUS

Do NOT Lie Awake at Night with a Negative Mental Attitude

When you are in a dark room with your eyes closed, your conscious can concentrate with great power. Your imagination and mental picturing ability are not distracted and can work with full force. You can hold negative thoughts for a long time, concentrated in your conscious. From there, they will be automatically programmed into the subconscious computer. The subconscious will then take this as your command, attaching its own immense power. It will go to work and bring about what you have commanded after you fall asleep, whether it is good or bad or right or wrong for you. So if you cannot sleep, never imagine negative things or worry about a bad outcome. Think positively. Use Positive Affirmations.

DO NOT USE NEGATIVE PHRASES IN THE PRESENCE OF INJURED, SICK, UNCONSCIOUS, OR PERSONS ASLEEP, ESPECIALLY CHILDREN

Let me illustrate this with a story reported from a convention:

Cancer was detected in a woman at an early stage, and the operation was a total success. Cleaning up after the surgery, one doctor talked about a boat accident, saying, "we didn't get everything out."

The three doctors were very happy about the well-performed operation, and the patient was wheeled into the recovery room. Then something strange happened. As time went by, she didn't recover as expected. The doctors became concerned. A doctor was called in to hypnotize this lady to find out the cause. In a trance state, a regression to the time of the operation, the lady said, "I hear the doctor saying, 'we didn't get everything out.' " This was the reason her condition didn't improve. Subconsciously she had connected this statement with her cancer operation. She thought herself doomed to die, because all the cancer was not removed. When she was reassured and re-programmed by the doctor, she recovered quickly and completely.

This story shows that the Subconscious never sleeps even when a person is unconscious!

Now Turn to Chart Number 2. A Mental Guard Stop is Necessary to Protect You Against Impulsive Negative Programming

In the drawing, Mind Chart Number 2, you will notice a SLIDING DOOR which protects the subconscious. (Naturally this is figurative.) Be aware that the "SLIDING DOOR" opens easily. It glides as if on ball bearings. Many times in our lives it is open when it should really be closed, and closed when it should be open.

MAKE UP YOUR MIND

Do not contaminate your mind. It is hard to houseclean.

 What your conscious concentrates on will be programmed into the subconscious.

What your conscious does not want to concentrate on will be rejected.

What your conscious repeatedly concentrates on will be believed, expected and brought to pass by the subconscious.

This is the way habits are formed, good or bad, right or wrong.

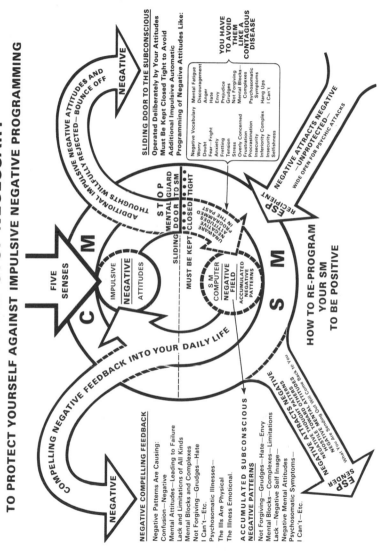

Sometimes We Become Blinded by Our Habits

Habits can be positive or negative. We can be aware or fully unaware of them; but all of them are consciously or unconsciously programmed into our subconscious and govern our lives.

Everyone has the ability to use these habit forces, for good, to control his thoughts, eliminate unwanted habits and develop new and positive traits by programming the subconscious.

No one is ever too old or too young to change negative attitudes of mind and poor self-images and start to build a new positive lifestyle.

Watchman or Guard

The word "Guard" reminds you that you have to be the watchman or guard. You have to learn to control the opening or closing of the door to your subconscious by focused, concentrated, and selective thinking. You have to guard against being influenced and brainwashed against your will and accumulating unwanted negative patterns.

Let me illustrate the point with an experience I had in Japan.

BUDDHA TEMPLE

My wife and I toured many temples in Kyoto, Japan, with a fine group of people. One lady in our group was very positive and outgoing. Everyone enjoyed her company.

In one of the temples we picked our "fortunes" from a wooden box filled with numbered sticks. We shook the box and one stick would drop out for each of us. We would then hand the stick to the Priest who gave us the fortunes written on small pieces of white rice paper which corresponded with the numbers on the sticks.

We could not read a word because our fortunes were printed in Japanese. Our guide interpreted each one for us, except the fortune picked by our nice, positive lady. He said, "No, I will not read it to you! You do not want to know it!" She begged, "Please, I paid for it, I want to know what it says." He exclaimed, "No, no, no!" After a long heated conversation, he surrendered and began to translate it for her.

He announced: "You know, I did not wish to tell you. You proceed at your own risk. It is up to you. Remember you wanted to hear this." He was serious. He believed in the fortunes. You could see how emotionally involved he was. He said, "Here it is, since you insist. You will have bad luck; bad luck in traveling; bad luck in marriage; bad luck in health, bad luck with your family; bad luck in everything." The lady started to grow paler and paler; her face turned white, and she started to cry. "Bad luck in your business," he went on. She almost passed out, but her husband caught her in his arms. He exclaimed, "Honey, can you read this?" She shook her head. "Well," he said, "this is for the Buddhists, not for the Christians." She recovered with a loud sigh and was instantly well, and happy again.

We might be tempted to laugh about the story, but doesn't something like this happen to us every day? Aren't our children and ourselves in constant danger of being negatively programmed from the environment?

IT IS SO EASY TO BE NEGATIVELY PROGRAMMED HOW CAN WE AVOID IT?

THE STEAM CLEANED MOTOR

I found exhaust fumes caused by a malfunction of the engine and carburetor infiltrating my car, so I consulted a mechanic. He lifted the hood and pointed out that the motor was soiled, gummed-up, and covered with greasy matter. There was also a leak in the gas line. To solve the problem, he said the motor had to be steam-cleaned and the gas line repaired.

It was amazing how this affected the looks, performance, and probably the life of the car. I was lucky to have discovered the problem before more damage was done.

Things like this go on in our minds. Daily we receive negative and harmful suggestions. Devastating stories about war, robberies, riots, accidents, murders bombard us! Off color jokes are sometimes told in our presence, whether we want to hear them or not. The subconscious can be programmed negatively by these things. Later it will feed these impressions back to consciousness at the wrong time, at the wrong place, and in the wrong way, doing us great harm.

I was negligent to let my engine get into that condition. I wasn't aware of it, but am I the cause? Yes, I should have been more concerned. Is this true of many of us? A little dirt here and there we feel will do no harm, but builds up to finally overwhelm us in time.

Association with negative thinkers, unbelievers unethical, immoral, dishonest, lawless people, over a period of time, can influence and shape in our subconscious a negative self-image, and undesirable habits. Let us all be on guard against these things and refresh our minds daily through the Fundamental Laws of Right Thinking. Let us stop ourselves right now before any more damage is done.

WHEELCHAIR

A friend of mine had a major operation a few weeks before her daughter and husband and their eight-month old baby were due back from Germany. She told her husband, with great conviction, "I will be at the airport to meet them, even if I have to be in a wheelchair." She emphasized this several times.

The operation was a success, and she recovered very quickly.

When the time came, she was able and ready to be at the airport for the happy event.

At the appointed hour, they were waiting for the arrival of the plane. Suddenly her husband said, "Look, the airplane with our daughter is coming." My friend turned around quickly, and strained a ligament in her leg so severely that she could neither stand nor walk. She was in terrible pain. Her husband had to support her until a wheelchair could be found. *She welcomed her family back home in a wheelchair.*

Perhaps this was coincidence. But it is a perfect example of programming the subconscious negatively: "I will be at the airport even if I have to be in a wheelchair," she said, not once, but several times.

I hope this story will show you how easy it is to be negatively programmed. Statements uttered with strong emotions, like those made by our friend, are programmed and accepted by the subconscious as commands; it brings them all to pass.

The subconscious computer is not able to decide between good or bad, right or wrong, It takes our affirmed statements to be what

we really want. It then follows through to make them come true. The idea is to program the subconscious to work for you and not against you.

IT NEVER FAILS

I know a lady who, whenever something goes wrong, exclaims: "It never fails!" She is expressing a kind of resentment against some unknown force or power in her life. She is really saying, "It is not my fault; I haven't done anything; but I always get beaten and receive the dirty deals of life. I don't know why I am always picked on!"

I urged her: "Quit saying, 'It never fails' when you are troubled. You are negatively programming your future. You expect that matters will go wrong for you. You accept the negative idea 'I will always lose!' "

The subconscious computer cannot decide between good and bad, or right and wrong. It takes the idea as a command and brings it forth with superhuman power. If your subconscious could talk back it would say—"You always want to fail. You want to feel bad, to be a loser; to have a miserable time. I will see that this happens to you. I will move heaven and earth so that you will always have a cold, so that someone will pick on you, so that everything will go wrong in your life."

My friend used this phrase only for negative things, when something went wrong. She never used it for positive things or when something good had happened to her. She would never say, "It never fails," when she had good luck or when something went right. Perhaps you make similar statements and are completely unaware that this has caused your suffering. Examine your life. Nobody is too old or too young to change his life. Today is the beginning of the rest of your life. Make it a habit to say, and think: "I can't lose for winning!"

Good Luck to you.

AIR POLLUTION

Air pollution is a grave problem, especially for big cities which have industries located in valleys. Many times I have to drive through such territories, and I am always glad when I have passed through them. Sometimes the pollution is so heavy, hanging low over the freeway, that it becomes necessary to drive with the lights on. The citizens living there urge that something be done about it, since all kinds of respiratory and eye diseases have been traced to air pollution.

There is another kind of pollution which is even more harmful; it is the pollution of the mind. Just as we cannot avoid breathing polluted air, we cannot avoid hearing negative statements all day long from people around us. Mind pollution is much more dangerous to us than the air pollution. Fortunately we don't need outside help or legislative decision to shield ourselves from this destructive condition. Everyone must be more concerned about what he says all day long. We should be more aware, filtering our thoughts before we speak, learning the positive approach and having a positive mental attitude.

Meanwhile, until more people have been educated to the Fundamental Laws of Right Thinking, we must draw a psychic shield of protection around ourselves. Whenever you are bombarded with negative statements, reword and neutralize the statements quickly in your own mind, with positive feelings. Try it out. You will see that everything will change for the better.

We Are Still Talking About Chart Number 2

Intrusive negative attitudes and thoughts from the conscious can now be stopped at will by selective thinking. They are rejected because of the changes in your thinking. You haven't learned yet how to replace accumulated negative patterns lodged in your subconscious. But at least new ones cannot easily penetrate it any more. You may be negatively influenced from your improperly programmed subconscious whenever you forget to be watchful. But you need not be controlled by it. You may receive negative mental telepathy from others if you are sensitive to what is going on around you. But you need not emit negative mental telepathy to others. What you send out will forcefully come back to you, be it good or bad.

Negative E.S.P. vs Positive E.S.P.

Now you understand why you have suffered negative feelings so often in the past, seemingly from out of nowhere. You do not have to suffer that way. A new life awaits you. Believe it; feel it; and you shall receive it. It is yours for the asking. Read and re-read every word of this explanation and study the Chart Number 2 carefully.

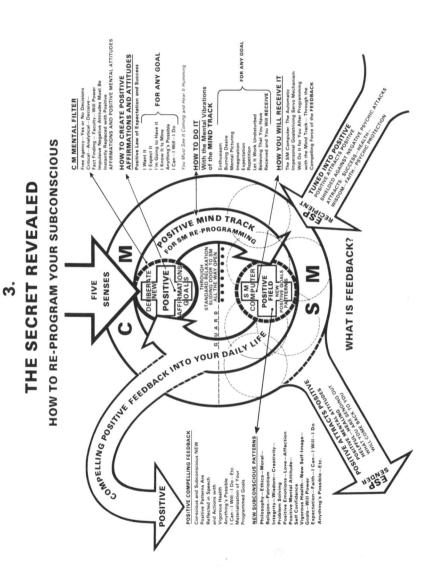

3.
THE SECRET REVEALED
HOW TO RE-PROGRAM YOUR SUBCONSCIOUS

C M MENTAL FILTER

Free Agency—Yes or No Decisions
Critical—Analytical—Decisive—
Fact Finding—Faculty—Will Power
Impulsive Negative Attitudes Must Be
Instantly Replaced with Positive
AFFIRMATIONS AND POSITIVE MENTAL ATTITUDES

FOR ANY GOAL

HOW TO CREATE POSITIVE
AFFIRMATIONS AND ATTITUDES
Positive Law of Expectation and Success

I Want It
I Expect It
I'm Going to Have It
I Know It Is Mine
Anything's Possible
I Can—I Will—I Do

You Must See It Coming and Hear It Humming

HOW TO DO IT
With the Mental Vibrations
of the MIND TRACK

Enthusiasm
Burning Desire
Mental Picturing
Imagination
Expectation
Repetition
Let It Work Undisturbed
Believing That You Have
Received and You Will RECEIVE

HOW YOU WILL RECEIVE IT

The SM Computer: The Automatic
Impersonal Goalstriving Servo Mechanism
Will Do It for You After Programming
with the Mind Track—Through the
Compelling Force of the FEEDBACK

FOR ANY GOAL

TUNED INTO POSITIVE
SHIELDED AGAINST NEGATIVE PSYCHIC ATTACKS
POSITIVE ATTRACTS POSITIVE
WISDOM - FAITH - PSYCHIC PROTECTION
ATTRACTS: SUCCESS, HEALTH,

SM
RECIPIENT

POSITIVE MIND TRACK
FOR SM RE-PROGRAMMING

FIVE
SENSES

C   M

DELIBERATE
NEW
POSITIVE
AFFIRMATIONS
GOALS

THROUGH
STANDARD RELAXATION
SLIDING DOOR TO SM
ALL THE WAY OPEN

G   U   A   R   D

SM
COMPUTER
POSITIVE
FIELD
NEW
POSITIVE GOALS
PATTERNS

S   M

WHAT IS FEEDBACK?

COMPELLING POSITIVE FEEDBACK INTO YOUR DAILY LIFE

POSITIVE ATTRACTS POSITIVE

POSITIVE MENTAL—SENDING OUT
POSITIVE—ARE YOU TO YOU
WHAT YOU SEND TO YOU
WILL COME BACK TO YOU

ESP
SENDER

POSITIVE

POSITIVE COMPELLING FEEDBACK

Conscious and Subconscious NEW
Positive Patterns Are
Reflected in Speech
and Actions with
Vigorous Health
Anything's Possible
I Can—I Will—I Do—Etc.
Materialization of Your
Programmed Goals

NEW SUBCONSCIOUS PATTERNS

Philosophy—Ethics—Moral—
Religion—Patriotism
Integrity—Wisdom—Creativity—
Problem Solving
Positive Emotions—Love—Affection
Positive Mental Attitude—
Self Confidence
Vigorous Health—New Self-Image—
Goals—Will Power
Expectation—Faith—I Can—I Will—I Do
Anything's Possible—Etc.

NOW TURN TO CHART NUMBER 3.
NOW STUDY CHART 3 WITH ME.

MENTAL FILTER DECISION

We are made in such a way that all thoughts and feelings reach our conscious through our "five senses." Notice that thoughts and feelings must first pass through a "mental filter" which may be called "free agency," to be analyzed by conscious, critical inquisitive, and analytical thinking. Facts must be collected. Evaluations, estimations, opinions, and experiences have to be weighed. The conscious is your director, selector, chooser and decider.

Finally through willpower and obedience to physical, moral and mental laws, you can make your decisions. These decisions are represented in the small upper circle of the conscious faculty marked as "deliberate new positive affirmations and goals."

The Way to Reach the Subconscious—the New Method:

In a relaxed state of mind, your subconscious can be influenced or programmed with self-suggestions, positive affirmations, imagination and mental picturing for new goals.

Listen to what J.S. has to say. "Thanks to the simple method of 'Standard Relaxation,' I have learned in an incredibly short time to program my subconscious and work with these immense powers."

Keep on reading, you will be introduced to Standard Relaxation in Part I, Chapter 3.

THIS IS THE MISSING LINK

Your thoughts, wishes, goals, and resolutions have to be expressed on a "positive mind track," to influence your subconscious. The very simple formula is:

```
                I WANT IT
               I EXPECT IT
          I AM GOING TO HAVE IT
            I KNOW IT IS MINE
```

This mind formula has to be interwoven with your goals and activities. One of my students applied this mind formula in the following manner:

Promoted Through Programming:

"*I want* to be promoted in my company. I have prepared myself and I am ready for this promotion. *I expect* to be known to the executive making the decision for my promotion for the best of all concerned. *I am going to have* this change in my occupation. *I know the promotion is mine* because the position is open and I have prepared myself and I am ready for it." (He was promoted.)

DAVID AND THE FIVE STONES

The Prophet Samuel Taught Us a Great Lesson

"David chose him five smooth stones out of the brook and put them in a shepherd's bag. And David put his hand in his bag and took a stone and slung it, and smote the Philistine in his forehead." (I Samuel: 17:40)

Why five stones if he needed only one? We can apply this to our "Mind Track Formula" and give every stone an assignment. *I WANT IT—I EXPECT IT—I AM GOING TO HAVE IT—I KNOW IT IS MINE—EVERYTHING IS POSSIBLE.* Or with the second formula: *ENTHUSIASM—BURNING DESIRE—MENTAL PICTURING—IMAGINATION—EXPECTATION.*

The stone David chose was the right mental attitude, the absolute assurance that he would succeed. There was no room for doubt or fear in his mind. He had faith in himself and in his God. The modern "Mind Track Formulas" will give you self-confidence that your programmed goals can be achieved.

Repetition Is The Key!

The subconscious computer wants to be sure that you really expect this thing and mean it; that you want it above everything else. This is why programming must be repeated over and over again. Cicero said: "Repetition is the mother of learning of all arts." Repetition is imperative. You must, "see it coming and hear it humming."

Let it Work Undisturbed

Your subconscious will bring things about in its own way. As soon as your desires are programmed you must cultivate a positive state of mind, believing that your goals are already accomplished.

Burning Desire

Your subconscious doesn't react to words alone. Its language is the complete "positive mind track." The words—our wishes—our goals must be emotionalized with "ENTHUSIASM, BURNING DESIRE, IMAGINATION, AND MENTAL PICTURING AND EXPECTATION."

The Positive Mind Track

The diagram shows a half-circle with an arrow representing "the positive mind track" for programming established goals into the subconscious computer. The lower circle in the subconscious represents the subconscious computer. The computer of your subconscious is like any computer; it is automatic and impersonal; it sifts, screens, and scans through stored facts until it finds the solution to the problem, any problem. This computer in your subconscious is unique and highly sensitive to your emotions, wishes and expectations.

Once programmed into the subconscious it must be left undisturbed. Let me explain it to you with the following story:

FLOWER SEEDS

We bought our little girl an assortment of flower seeds, which she carefully planted in the garden. Soon we discovered that little Susi went out secretly, day after day, digging up the seeds to see what had happened. We explained to her that she was interfering with the process of growth and that she must leave the seeds undisturbed so they could germinate, take root, and finally sprout into beautiful flowers.

It is the same with our minds. The Subconscious Mind is the fertile soil. After we decide on a goal or idea with our conscious faculties, we have to program or plant the seed or thought in our Subconscious Mind, where it will then develop beyond our perception. Just as the seed has the capabilities to grow and needs only to be planted in the soil and receive water and sunshine, so must an idea first be accepted, then programmed with expectation into our subconscious, where it will grow to abundance all by itself. The unique ability of our subconscious will collect all the missing facts, make the necessary corrections and move heaven and earth to create the end result. Doubts and fears hold back the forces of the dynamic mind power at work. Like the digging up of the seeds, doubts interfere with the process of growth and creation.

Let us all learn from this story that the good we have done with a positive, affirmed thought mentally pictured, and programmed must not be nullified minutes, hours or days later by doubts.

A Word of Caution: Do Not Be an Overtime Worrier

Your positive mental attitude will be suppressed, blocked, congested or distorted when you are overwhelmed with negative mental attitudes such as overconcern, stress, fear, doubt, anxiety and frustration. The Universal Law of doubt and failure acts when your mind is filled with such questions as: I WONDER WHEN IT WILL COME? I WONDER WHERE IT WILL COME FROM? I WONDER HOW IT WILL COME? This will nullify the good you have previously done with positive programming. This must be avoided like a contagious disease!

Negative and Positive Patterns Lodged in the Subconscious

Deeply lodged in the subconscious are: mental blocks, complexes, grudges, the inability to forgive, hate, habits, self-image, positive and negative patterns, character traits, feelings of love, positive and negative emotions; your total life experience. Notice the faded circles in the graph of the subconscious. They represent all the numerous negative and positive patterns lodged in your total subconscious. NOW TURN TO CHART 4.

COMPELLING FEEDBACK INTO YOUR DAILY LIFE AFTER POSITIVE RE-PROGRAMMING

Now let's end this explanation and study of the mind with the most important consideration: the FEEDBACK into YOUR daily life.

Positive or Negative Compelling Feedback from YOUR Subconscious

You can see in the drawing (Chart 4): "What Your Conscious Faculty Can Conceive, Expect, and Believe, Your Subconscious Will Achieve For You." Really, everything is possible for you if you *Really Expect It!*

In the past when unexpected positive, pleasant, happy feelings suddenly overwhelmed you, you probably took them for granted, and simply enjoyed the positive compelling feedback. Did you give it some thought? Were you thankful for it?

4.

COMPELLING FEEDBACK FROM YOUR SM
AFTER POSITIVE RE-PROGRAMMING

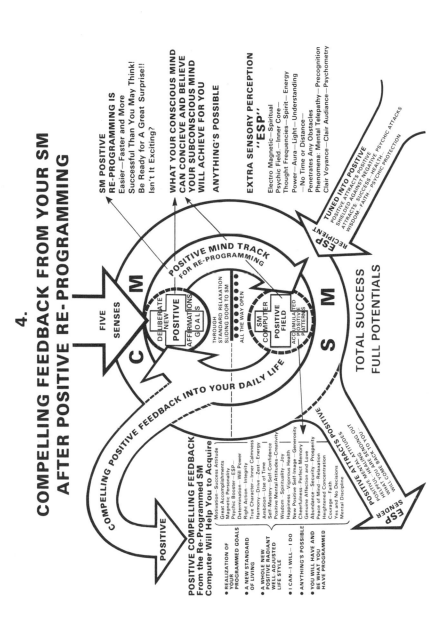

SM POSITIVE RE-PROGRAMMING IS
Easier—Faster and More
Successful Than You May Think!
Be Ready for A Great Surprise!!
Isn't It Exciting?

WHAT YOUR CONSCIOUS MIND CAN CONCEIVE AND BELIEVE YOUR SUBCONSCIOUS MIND WILL ACHIEVE FOR YOU

ANYTHING'S POSSIBLE

EXTRA SENSORY PERCEPTION
"ESP"

Electro Magnetic—Spiritual
Psychic Field—Inner Core—
Thought Frequencies—Spirit— Energy
Power—Aura—Light—Understanding
—No Time or Distance—
Penetrates Any Obstacles
Phenomena: Mental Telepathy—Precognition
Clair Voyance—Clair Audiance—Psychometry

TUNED INTO POSITIVE
POSITIVE ATTRACTS POSITIVE
SHIELDED AGAINST NEGATIVE
ATTRACTS: SUCCESS, HEALTH, PSYCHIC ATTACKS
WISDOM, FAITH—PSYCHIC PROTECTION

ESP RECIPIENT

POSITIVE MIND TRACK
FOR RE-PROGRAMMING

FIVE
SENSES

C M

DELIBERATE
NEW
POSITIVE
AFFIRMATIONS
GOALS

THROUGH
STANDARD RELAXATION
SLIDING DOOR TO SM
ALL THE WAY OPEN

SM
COMPUTER
POSITIVE
FIELD

ACCUMULATED
POSITIVE
PATTERNS

S M

TOTAL SUCCESS
FULL POTENTIALS

COMPELLING POSITIVE FEEDBACK INTO YOUR DAILY LIFE

POSITIVE

POSITIVE COMPELLING FEEDBACK
From the Re-Programmed SM
Computer Will Help You to Acquire

• **REALIZATION OF YOUR PROGRAMMED GOALS**

• **A NEW STANDARD OF LIVING**

• **A WHOLE NEW POSITIVE RADIANT WELL-ADJUSTED LIFE STYLE**

• **I CAN—I WILL—I DO**

• **ANYTHING'S POSSIBLE**

• **YOU WILL HAVE AND BE WHAT YOU HAVE PROGRAMMED**

Motivation—Success Attitude
Great Accomplishments
Magnetic Personality
Psychic Booster—ESP—
Determination—Will Power
Right Action—Integrity
True Character—Inner Calmness
Harmony—Drive—Zest—Energy
Ambition—Use of Time
Self Mastery—Self Confidence
Positive Mental Attitudes—Creativity
Wisdom—Spirituality—Joy
Happiness—Vigorous Health
New Positive Self Image—Generosity
Cheerfulness—Perfect Memory
Genuine Affection and Love
Abundance—Security—Prosperity
Peace of Mind—Relaxation
Heightened Concentration
Courage—Faith
Yes and No Decisions
Mental Discipline

POSITIVE ATTRACTS POSITIVE

POSITIVE MENTAL ATTITUDES
POSITIVE MERLDS YOU SENDING OUT
HELPFUL VIBRATIONS TO OTHERS
WHAT COMES BACK TO YOU
WILL COME BACK POSITIVE

ESP SENDER

On the other hand, if unexpected negative feelings made you suffer with feelings of fear and anger, tension, and worry, you probably interpreted the forces as coming from the outside. You felt them to be none of your own doing. You felt you were not the cause and blamed others. *You were not aware that such feelings were the result of feedback from your own negatively-programmed subconscious.* You had allowed your subconscious mind to absorb negative statements and attitudes, creating in you a negative self-image and a negative mental attitude, triggering negative emotions.

FIJI ISLAND HOT-STONE WALKERS

Have you heard about the Fiji Island Hot-Stone Walkers? The Fiji Chief selects men from his tribe for the ceremony. For the chosen ones and their families this is a great honor. These favored ones must live in solitude for a period of time in their huts, separated from their families. There the priest programs their minds with belief, faith, a positive mental attitude, and a passionate desire to walk on the hot stones without burns or pain. Fear and doubt is eliminated.

Scientists, doctors and investigators have examined the feet of these men for special preparations or coatings before the performance, and for blisters and burns afterwards. They found none. The only explanation was: complete faith, and a total absence of fear and doubt. The programmed minds of the fire walkers created a protective shield of energy and chemical and physical changes in their bodies, so that the extreme heat of the stones did not harm them. Don't you think that such a demonstration of Dynamic Mind-Power should convince us that, as Hamlet said, ''There are more things in heaven and earth than are dreamt of in your philosophy.''

Very few of us would want to learn how to walk barefoot on a bed of hot stones. Why not analyze this phenomenon, however, and find the secret of such programming, such incredible faith and expectancy. You may have already guessed the secret. Let's spell it out. You can do anything you want to do if your mind is completely imbued and programmed with the white heat of a burning desire. As Dr. William James said: "What the mind can conceive and believe it can achieve."

Mental Telepathy

E.S.P. will work in your favor now. You are tuned in.

Positive E.S.P.

Positive will attract positive. This "psycho-electro-magnetic-energy-thought-field" will bring you total success—health and wisdom. Remember, what you are sending out will come powerfully back into your life, bringing rich rewards. All your programmed goals will be realized in your life. A new standard of living will emerge. A change of your self-image will bring you a whole new life-style. You will be a great help to others because you are sending out positive thoughts, attitudes, and "good will."

Read and study Chart 4 over and over until you have a complete understanding of the material. Enjoy the new understanding. Rejoice about the new beginning of the rest of your life.

Success Will Be Yours

You can now have success. Your full potential will unfold. You will have and will be and will do what you have programmed into your subconscious. *It should always be positive.* This is all you need to know before we begin with our "Standard Relaxation" for programing positive affirmations and goals into your subconscious.

Don't try to analyze the working methods of your subconscious; just assign it; do it; and enjoy the success.

Twilight State of Mind

It has been found that the subconscious functions best when the conscious faculty is by-passed, pleasantly occupied or in a twilight state. NOW TURN TO THE NEXT CHAPTER, CHAPTER 3 STANDARD RELAXATION.

PART I
CHAPTER 2
SUMMARY

There is a better way: Find it.
What your Subconscious Mind can do for you
The Spiral
What does ESP stand for
Chart I—The Negative Vicious Cycle
Chart II—Mental Guard Stop
Chart III—How to Re-Program Your Subconscious
Chart IV—Positive Compelling Feedback from Your Subconscious

PART I
CHAPTER 3

Standard Relaxation

The Tornado

Any Type of Relaxation Will Help You
On Your Way to Total Success

Students Remarks

Standard Relaxation S/R Exercise in Four Steps

Relaxation Response to Hypertension Diseases

Deep Breathing

Story: Relaxed Fluid

Can You Unwind?

THE TORNADO

"Hurricanes, tornados and typhoons are cyclonic storms. Winds blow spirally inward toward the center of the system. The reason for this phenomenon is that the pressure is always lower at the center of the system than at the margins. In cyclones there is usually a central 'CALM' known as the 'Eye of the Storm.' "

The cyclone derives its devastating power from its calm center. You derive your driving energy from the calm inner core, your Subconscious Mind. This calm inner core can be reached with "Standard Relaxation." Out of this relaxation will then come energy, zest, endurance, drive, vigorous health, wisdom—a total new positive lifestyle.

ANY TYPE OF RELAXATION WILL HELP YOU ON YOUR WAY TO TOTAL SUCCESS

Any Type of Relaxation and Meditation Will Help YOU to Cope With Stress and Anxiety. You Will Feel Superior at Whatever YOU Do in Life

Thousands are involved with TM (Transcendental Meditation—Yogi Maharishi Mahesh), RR(Relaxation Response—Dr. Benson), DM(Diet Meditation—Dr. Solomon), RM(Reducing Meditation or GURDJIEFFIAN techniques, Silva Mind Control, Alpha Dynamics), just to mention a few of the many leading philosophies of relaxation, and approaches to Meditation and Motivation.

All relaxation approaches seem to be effective and helpful and contribute to the health and well being. Research has proven the various relaxation techniques are just about equal in terms of physical and mental benefits.

I came to the conclusion that it is absolutely necessary to choose and then use a specific approach or method for a period of time. You have to mature, experience, experiment and finally find your own individual way of relaxation and meditation.

After studying methods of relaxation in different parts of the world, I have developed my own "Standard Relaxation" approach, a natural anxiety, fear, stress and negative mental attitude reducer.

I recommend that you stick to it faithfully for a while until you are able to modify according to your own feelings, emotions and needs. For instance, a student of ours reported in class one day that she was starting out with "Thank You" mouthed slowly, humbly and with great emotion, three times and more expressing this attitude toward Diety.

This would be similar to the idea of using a "MATRA."

I teach the "Western Style" and leave the non-essential, oriental, more complicated schemes alone. When you come down to the basic elements of relaxation, you will find that there is no unique, single, secret or "only" method of relaxation and meditation.

Some prefer a set of prepared, memorized prayers; others pray whatever comes in their minds, and still others say: "I pray not at all. I talk and listen and have a real COMMUNICATION with God." My technique and the related mental exercises, will bring many benefits into your life, such as tranquillity, peace, restfulness, serenity, healing and calmness. You will feel placid, still, cool, composed and unruffled. Counting up from zero to six at the end of every relaxation exercise will give you, at the same time—all in one exercise—energy, ambition, vitality, vigor, pep, liveliness, zest and inner drive (explained in Part II Chapter 1).

In doing the exercises for years myself, I sometimes have not been able to tell whether I was praying, meditating, relaxing or exercising. It is all one to me. There should be no difference for you either.

REMEMBER: It is Not the Form or Technique You should be concerned about. Your Interest Must Be The End Result—How It Makes You Feel; How It Is Affecting Your Daily Life, and Your Health. It Must Bring You A NEW POSITIVE LIFESTYLE: A NEW POSITIVE SELF-IMAGE. IF You and the People Around You Notice a Change in You—then You Are Doing it Right—Then You are in the Correct Way. You Should DO it Regularly! Never Stop Again!

One Learn to relax and meditate. You will have less psychosomatic reactions and problems, fewer ulcers, colds, flu attacks, headaches, or any of the respiratory sicknesses, and overcome insomnia.

Two It is not the stress which makes you sick—It is how you react toward it. Depleted, you will not be able to handle the daily accumulative stress, you will suffer under the consequences and break down under the strain of daily living.

Three With every Relaxation Exercise you will fill up your energy reservoir and feel psychically recharged.

Four Relaxation practiced daily will give YOU the ability to handle any stress, anxiety and the heavy burdens of life—the energy drainers.

Five I would like to hear your experiences and how you applied the suggested exercise to your personality and requirements.

It is not the number of books you read, nor the variety of sermons you hear, nor the amount of religious conversations in which you unite, *but it is the frequency and earnestness with which you dwell on these things* till the truth in them becomes your own and part of your being, that ensures your growth.—*F.W. Robertson*

STANDARD RELAXATION

These relaxation and meditation exercises can be used by any one, without violating the creed of any church doctrine or system of beliefs. The Standard Relaxation and all the other mental exercises attached are independent and non-denominational. These mental exercises will afford you a higher awareness of your own particular religion and philosophy. Many have been side-tracked from real meditation and prayer in relaxation and lack close communication with God.

Students Remarks

Students have said: "It gives me a pleasurable state of mind, I can pull myself together. I have a feeling of being charged up. I have an assurance that I can accomplish my specific programmed goals."

"In all my years, I cannot remember anything that has had such an immensely exciting influence on my life."

"You have to become habituated to Standard Relaxation and all the other mental exercises. They are not an escape—they are a means to an end for a specific purpose."

"The exercises will not take a lot of time, but they will bring priceless rewards into your life."

STANDARD RELAXATION
EXERCISE IN FOUR STEPS

Step 1.

You should be where you will not be disturbed, with the lights dimmed, and the room as quiet as possible. Sit down comfortably, your feet flat on the floor and your back against the back of the chair, or you may rest comfortably in a reclining chair. Preferably, lie down comfortably on a flat surface with your legs slightly apart, and your arms resting loosely on your thighs, or at the sides of your body. Loosen any tight clothing, and take off your shoes. Wiggle a few times and shift your weight, until you are really comfortable.

Close your eyes and keep them closed. You can mentally picture and concentrate better with closed eyes. Take a few deep breaths and relax for a moment. You are about to start an adventure that will richly reward you for the rest of your life.

Step 2. Next, Tense, Stiffen Up, and Stretch Out Your Arms and Legs Three Times

FIRST TIME: Tense, stiffen up and stretch out your arms and legs, pull in your abdomen and *suddenly* let go.

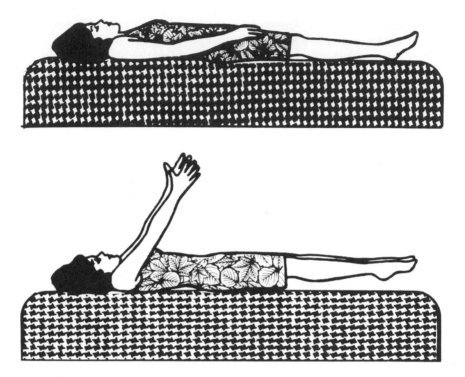

SECOND TIME: Tense, stiffen up and stretch out your arms and legs, pull in your abdomen and *suddenly* let go.

THIRD TIME: Tense, stiffen up and stretch out your arms and legs, pull in your abdomen and *suddenly* let go.

NEXT: Take Three Deep Breaths. With each breath you take, concentrate on the inhalation. Feel the air passing through your nostrils, moving down your throat, and filling your lungs to capacity. Deep breathing charges and vitalizes the whole body with "Vital Energy."

Step 3. Take Three Deep Breaths, Focusing Your Closed Eyes on the Tip of Your Nose

INHALE ON THREE COUNTS. HOLD YOUR BREATH FOR THREE COUNTS. EXHALE ON THREE COUNTS. YOU MAY INCREASE THIS IN TIME UP TO SEVEN COUNTS.

Inhale Your First Deep Breath

Bring the air deep into the lowest lobes of your lungs, using the

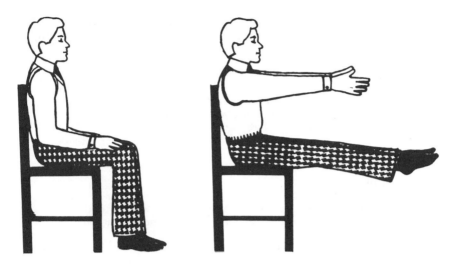

strong abdominal muscles and the powerful diaphragm, at the same time focusing your eyes, while closed, on the tip of your nose; keep your eyes closed, hold your breath—and then exhale slowly, forcing all of the air out of your lungs.

Then Inhale Your Second Deep Breath

Bring the air deep into the lowest lobes of your lungs, as before, at the same time focusing your eyes, while closed, on the tip of your nose; keep your eyes closed, hold your breath, hold it longer, longer—then slowly exhale, letting all the stale air out of the lungs.

Then Inhale Your Third and Last Extra Deep Breath

Fill your lungs to capacity. Bring the air deep into the lungs, at the same time focusing your eyes, while closed, on the tip of your nose; keep your eyes closed; hold your breath extra long——hold it—————longer—————hold it—————then s-l-o-w-l-y exhale at the same time, counting down from six to zero. 6-5-4-3-2-1-0. Then relax and keep your eyes closed. Let go and feel limp all over. Just let go, and remain relaxed. You are now calm, relaxed and at ease.

Step 4. To Arouse Yourself

Many of our students use the "I AM" formula in connection with this exercise and arouse themselves by counting up from zero to six. Use one sentence with every count. Imagine the "I AM" formula will then be programmed into your subconscious every time you count up.

Counting Up From Zero to Six
Count Zero: I AM BECOMING MY OWN BETTER SELF, THE NEW ME, THE POSITIVE ENTITY WITHIN MYSELF.
Count One: There is no one in the whole world like me.
Count Two: I like myself. I have self esteem.
Count Three: I am a worthy, humble person, Whatsoever I desire of good is in me.
Count Four: My Positive Entity in my Subconscious Mind will supply all my needs.
Count Five: Blink Your Eyes.
Count Six: Open your eyes and be wide awake and feel wonderful, full of dynamic energy, very vigorous and enthusiastic.

You will always awake clear headed, and full of enthusiasm. A wealth of New Positive Compelling Force is then in your Subconscious Mind from this time forward. *IF YOU ARE INTER-RUPTED DURING YOUR EXERCISES, IMMEDIATELY COUNT UP FROM ZERO TO SIX AS EXPLAINED ABOVE.*

What Breathing and Counting Will Do For You

The counting down from six to zero is a conditioning process for relaxation. Counting up from zero to six will always end the relaxation and awaken you fully, giving you pep, vitality and new energy. This too is a conditioning process.

Looking at the tip of your nose will create heightened concentration and help you to avoid mind-wandering. The breathing is a MENTAL EXERCISE which will educate you to become a deep-breather. At the same time, all the vital organs will receive a gentle stimulation and more oxygen will be brought to the lungs and heart. Concentration on deep breathing seems to be the simplest way to develop the ability for heightened concentration.

After you have used this "Standard Relaxation Exercise" several times you will reach an even deeper level of relaxation; a level which is best for the programming or re-programming of your subconscious mind.

In the following chapters you will be taught mental exercises which will be attached to this "BASIC STANDARD RELAXATION." Take your time and practice this fundamental "STANDARD RELAXATION" thoroughly.

RELAXATION RESPONSE TO HYPERTENSION DISEASES

Hypertensive cardio-vascular diseases caused by high blood pressure (hypertension) trouble close to fifty percent of the adult population. Hypertension in its early stages has very few symptoms but untreated will lead to Arteriosclerosis (hardening of the arteries), Cerebral Vascular Accidents (strokes), Myocardial Infarctions (heart attacks) Arteriolar Nephrosclerosis (kidney disease) and other related conditions. Almost half the deaths in the U.S. have their origin in hypertension. Other statistics indicate that those having hypertension can lose their life by the time they are in their early 50's.

What can be done to avoid these dreadful conditions? Medical science claims that there is a direct relationship between hypertension and mental stress.

Through meditation and relaxation, the blood pressure, heart and respiratory rates can be greatly reduced. It stands to reason therefore if negative emotions and mental stress can produce hypertension, then positive emotions, relaxation and meditation will decrease stress the cause of hypertension, and bring the blood pressure down.

Imagine! By simply changing one's thoughts and attitudes to positive in all situations, hypertension and all related conditions can be avoided.

DEEP BREATHING

The great prophets of the Orient and the Yogi centers are teaching meditation and physical and mental exercises as well as deep breathing. A famous psychic healer in the Phillippines told me: "Deep breathing is health. Deep breathing is life. Deep breathing is the best medicine." (Dr. Perry S. Lim)

Breathing is the great purifier, flushing the blood with oxygen. The lungs not only remove carbon dioxide but also other waste matter from the body. Deep breathing exercises reach lung areas ordinarily neglected and improve oxygen absorption, which enhances circulation and metabolism. Shallow breathing creates oxygen deficiency, hastens fatigue and decreases your efficiency. When you are physically and mentally tired and depleted deep breathing with total relaxation will restore your vigor and energy. Biologists have discovered that the average person uses about one-third of his lung capacity. The result is oxygen starvation. Ordinary breathing is usually too weak and ineffective to throw off the waste matter from the lungs. The inhalation and exhalation of a shallow breather takes only three to five seconds. But a healthy breather will increase this span to seven, even ten seconds.

The following exercise should be done three to five times daily in fresh air. Inhale, taking three to seven counts to do so; hold the breath for three to seven counts, then take three to seven counts to exhale. You can program your subconscious to change your breathing so that it is automatic, controlled. Deep, healthy breathing is a must for Subconscious Mind Training and controlled health.

RELAXED FLUID

I read about a "non-Newtonian" fluid which becomes thicker the more it is used. You can roll it like a ball of clay between your hands, but when you stop the motion, it turns into a fluid again like milk of magnesia. If this type of material is under "stress" and has, so to speak, "no time to relax" it acts like solid material. But if the same material is "left alone" and no "stress" is added, it remains in a liquid form.

This chemical phenomonon interested me. It can help us to understand the functioning of our minds and bodies in a new and better way. If we work or perform under imagined mental stress we become stiff, rigid, awkward. The mobilized adrenal and pituitary glands discharge hormones into the bloodstream which are not needed by the body for "fight or flight." These excess hormones play havoc with the body, creating all kinds of psychosomatic sicknesses. We become rigid just like the chemical and we cannot perform at our best. But if we free ourselves of tension and relax in body, mind and emotions, then we are flexible, calm and serene. As the chemical changes from solid to liquid by taking time to relax, so we can change from a feeling of stress to one of ease by taking time out to relax.

You know that when you have been relaxed, everything has gone smoother! New ideas have emerged! You have been happy, energetic and full of inspiration. The only trouble is that it does not happen often enough. Let me assure you that it doesn't have to be that way. With Standard Relaxation you will be able to create a relaxed state of mind or mood anytime and anywhere; even under severe mental stress. An effective programming to accomplish such a state or mood would be: "I will always stay calm, serene and relaxed. Everything will turn out all right."

CAN YOU UNWIND?

Every day I hear people say, "I am a bundle of nerves. My family upsets me. I can't stand noise any more. Every little thing bothers me. I am so irritable that I could cry about everything. I fly off the handle whenever someone criticizes me." These are common complaints. Let's take a situation for illustration.

Sometimes when I turn off the ignition key of my car, the motor fails to stop, and continues to idle. The cause is carbon deposits which come from the use of low-grade gasoline. When I switch to a different brand of high-octane test fuel the difficulty is corrected.

Let's compare this to our daily lives. All day long we have to run, be on the ball, concerned and usually quite keyed-up. Finally when the time comes to relax, we cannot "turn off." The nervousness and tense feelings persist. This is quite harmful and becomes the cause of many psychosomatic sicknesses and complaints.

We should take time out for relaxing at least three times during the day. Try this method from time to time: Exhale, then inhale slowly, to the count of three, through your nose, just as you would smell a beautiful rose. Hold the breath for three counts, then exhale through your mouth to the count of three. Repeat this several times. Then sit, or if possible, lie down, close your eyes, and count slowly down from sixty to zero. Follow by counting up from zero to six, and then open your eyes. The result is unbelievable, incredible, and marvelous. Every time you do this you become refreshed, vigorous, energetic and at the same time calm, clear-headed and more highly aware of the duties at hand. These exercises will prevent the accumulation of stress, just as the accumulation of carbon can be prevented by the use of the right gasoline.

PART I
CHAPTER 3
SUMMARY
STANDARD RELAXATION AND MEDITATION EXERCISE

1. Get Comfortable
2. Three Times—Tense Up
3. Three Deep Breaths
4. Arouse Yourself Counting Up from Zero to Six
5. Stories

NOW YOU TOO CAN ENJOY GREATER PEACE OF MIND,
ENERGY, HEALTH, AND TOTAL SUCCESS BY LEARNING
HOW TO RELAX

Mental Training for Focused, Heightened Concentration and Mental Command Mental Picturing Exercises

Conscious and Subconscious Concentration

The Egg of Christopher Columbus

Suggestion: Work Exercises With Another
Person the First Time

Chart for Pendulum Exercise

Pendulum Exercise

Conscious Swinging of the Pendulum

Subconscious Swinging of the Pendulum

Magnetized Finger Exercise

Light and Heavy Arm Exercise

CONSCIOUS AND SUBCONSCIOUS CONCENTRATION

We *all* admire and envy people who have the ability to concentrate. Perhaps you, too, have tried to focus your attention on one matter, and found that it wandered. Our mind manifests itself in two ways, the conscious and the subconscious. Our concentration has two faculties: conscious and subconscious concentration.

Let's compare concentration with a car. Turn the key in the ignition and the engine starts running. Starting the car puts quite a strain on the battery because a great deal of energy is needed. The automatic transmission will shift from lower to higher gears, according to the speed we drive. There is no drain of energy from the battery any more. The generator produces more electricity than is needed to run the engine. The battery will recharge in the process.

It is the same with our concentration. Conscious concentration should be applied as a starter only, because it uses a high amount of energy, it is tiring and quickly causes fatigue. Conscious will power with focused concentration will start the wheels, so to speak.

No one would try driving the car with power from the starter only. The battery would soon be dead and the car stalled. If we apply will-powered concentration for too long, we do exactly that. By holding on to conscious concentration, we try to *make* it work instead of *letting* it work. We have to allow a shift into automatic subconscious concentration, which means we must be absorbed or obsessed by the thing we are doing. Then concentration will be effortless. Creative ideas will flow into your mind. Doing it right will and must bring success; doing it wrong will bring failure. Use the following concentration affirmation: "What I am reading, studying and memorizing right now will be permanently absorbed in my subconscious and readily recalled whenever I need it."

CHRISTOPHER COLUMBUS AND THE EGG

Columbus had the absolute conviction that the earth was round. No one believed him. Everybody thought it impossible to sail around the world. The world was flat, they believed, and ships might sail over the edge. The Queen of Spain believed Columbus and gave him three ships.

Columbus returned with the great discovery of the West Indies (America). His ships were loaded with precious stones, gold, silver and herbs. The council of Lords and Noblemen honored him. But a jealous courtier said, "Anybody could have done what you did." Columbus said, "Bring me a raw egg." He challenged all the highborn patricians, aristocrats and distinguished gentlemen to balance the egg on one end. Some tried, but nobody could do it. They all said, "It can't be done!" Columbus replied, "Again you say it is impossible!" He placed the egg on the table, crushing and flattening the shell slightly at the end where the air bubble is located. The egg stood on one end.

Beginning mental exercises, you might think, "It is impossible!" Don't let yourself be deceived. There is always a better way and you will find it. Whenever you think, "It can't be done," remember this story.

SUGGESTION

In practicing the "Mental Picturing Exercises," the first time it is advisable and helpful to have another person present to vocalize the progressive steps of the exercises for you and watch your performance.

PENDULUM EXERCISE

MENTAL TRAINING FOR FOCUSED AND HEIGHTENED
CONCENTRATION AND MENTAL COMMAND.
MENTAL PICTURING WITH THE PENDULUM EXERCISE

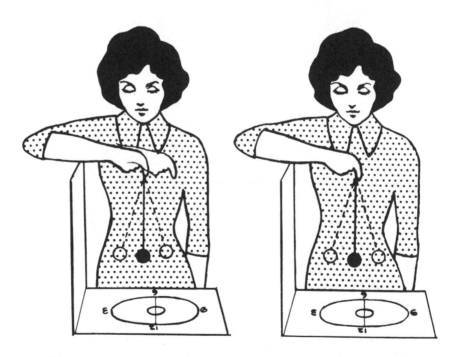

This is a mental exercise to train yourself to create a mental picture and to obtain focused, heightened concentration.

The Procedure is as Follows:

Step One: Make yourself a pendulum: a ten-inch long chain with a 1/8 inch ball. You can also use a long, thin necklace with a pendant or ring on it. (See Page 92 for pendulum chart.)

Step Two: Put the chart from your book on the seat of a chair, facing you. Stand upright in front of the chair, feet together, and body relaxed as much as possible. Hold the chain with the pendulum between the thumb and forefinger, chest high. The other arm should hang loosely at your side. The pendulum should hang straight down over the center of the chart. Then move your hand, swinging the pendulum back and forth between the numbers twelve and six. *By this you are actually programming your subconscious for the expected effect:* "The swinging of the pendulum automatically through the power and influence of your subconscious."

Step Three: Then keep your arm and hand absolutely still. Again fix your eyes exactly on the center ring, so that the pendulum hangs straight and steady over the center of the bullseye. Concentrate easily and effortlessly. Look at the object as if you wanted to look through it. Then begin to move your eyes back and forth along the line. At the same time, let the subconscious formula go through your mind as follows:

I Want My Subconscious To Swing the Pendulum
I Expect the Pendulum to Swing
I am Going to Prove That My Subconscious
Can Be Programmed
I know the Swinging of the Pendulum Through the
Power of My Subconscious Is Mine

Don't make it work! Let it swing through the influence of your subconscious. Mentally picture the pendulum swinging. See the pendulum swinging back and forth. Imagine the performance. Move your eyes along the line. All other thoughts vanish. Your mind will be locked around your desire. This will create focused and heightened concentration.

Expect the outcome, the action of your desire. This is expectation fulfilled. Just watch it happen and enjoy your accomplishment. Watch the pendulum swing all by itself.

You will find that the pendulum will swing according to your mental picture, according to your desire, and according to your expectations. Why is this so? You established selective thinking and focused concentration. You allowed the suggestion, the wish or idea, to be transformed to subconscious mental ACTION. You by-passed the critical and analytical faculty of the conscious mind and established automatic thinking and acting by your Subconscious Mind, although you may at first have wondered if it could be done.

After you have done this several times, change your mental picture to the center of the chart and stop the pendulum swing mentally by command. Change your mental picture then from 9 to 3, 3 to 9, left and right. Let your gaze travel left and right along the line, and the pendulum will again obey your thoughts, and focused concentration, guided by your mental picture. Enjoy this phenomenon. Again, change your mental picture with a command to stop and let the ball rest above the bullseye. Follow this with a mental picture of a clockwise movement, swinging around the circle.

After a while bring the pendulum to a halt by your mental command and change your focused concentration and mental picture, your eyes gazing around the circle counter-clockwise. According to your concentration and imagination, through your mental picture, the pendulum again will obey your concentrated command. You may do this exercise between any numbers of the chart in the same way.

You may concentrate on the center point again, and the pendulum will obey your focused concentration and command and come to a stop. If it does not work on the first try, don't be disappointed. Let your mind rest and start all over again with the success formula: "I want it, I expect it, I am going to watch it happen, I know it is mine."

The chief requirement for success is focused concentration without conscious effort or will power. The action must come from the subconscious with the attitude:

"LET IT WORK. DON'T MAKE IT WORK"

Do this exercise also with your eyes closed. You actually have to open your eyes from time to time to see whether the pendulum is swinging or not.

The Spiral Effect

The pendulum exercise will help you to stimulate, develop, and train the faculty of your subconscious for "focused and heightened concentration" and "mental picturing ability." The rewards are immense. Day by day you will find yourself reaching higher levels of thinking and concentration. (Read again "The Spiral" Part I, Chapter 2.

You will experience more self-confidence, self-mastery, and creativity. A chain reaction will be triggered in your subconscious and focused concentration will follow. You will also learn to hold one thought at a time, as long as you want, until you change it consciously.

Remember: What You Concentrate on, Becomes Real. You Will Always Find and Achieve What You Expect.

The concentration mechanism in the brain has been isolated on top of the brain stem and in the lower thalamus. Tests have demonstrated that mental exercises cause this part of the brain to grow larger, and your ability to concentrate increase. Any constantly repeated action or thought will bring about through the stimulating programming effect and method, a chemical, physical, and psychic alteration on the end of certain receiving and sending nerve fibers. When more and more alterations of its kind are formed, the "message," "impulse," or "habit" (positive or negative) will then again be transmitted more easily and forcefully transformed into automatic action.

You Should Repeat This Experiment Often

Do it over and over again, constantly in different ways. Be creative, experiment as much as possible with it.

This is your first training for focused subconscious concentration and mental picturing ability. Do it right! Do it Often!

You will be surprised how this will influence your daily life. You will experience more focused concentration. This heightened, focused concentration emanates from your subconscious. It will manifest itself to you in reading, listening to lectures, and conversations, studying, memorizing, in tests, and examinations. You will feel its help in playing golf, basketball, football, bowling, skiing, or in any other of the competitive sports.

This is the first step toward your "New Positive Lifestyle."

Now you understand the purpose of the pendulum exercise.

It is a means to accomplish your goals.

After you have found that you can program your subconscious to swing the pendulum according to your conscious mental command, expectations, concentration, and mental picturing, then it stands to reason that you can program any goal into the Automatic Computer Faculty of Your Subconscious Mind.

You can be assured that what you desire from your subconscious, will be accomplished in your daily life. You become what you think and concentrate on. What your conscious can conceive, believe and expect, your subconscious will achieve for you.

PARENTS: THIS IS AN EXCELLENT EDUCATIONAL GAME TO AWAKEN IN YOUR CHILDREN AS WELL AS IN YOU, "HEIGHTENED CONCENTRATION" AND "MENTAL PICTURING ABILITIES."

MAGNETIZED FINGER EXERCISE

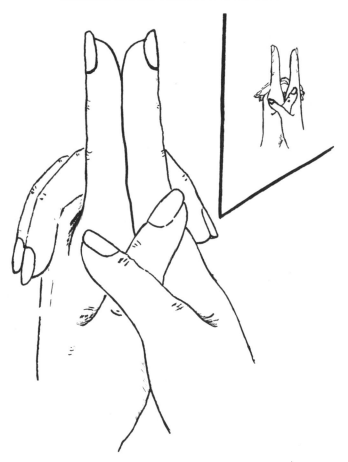

Mental Picturing Training Exercise

Interlock your hands and fingers in front of your face. Open your forefingers and hold them apart. Consciously close and open them three times. Then, keeping them apart, hold your hands in front of you. Look between the separated forefingers. Then imagine that your forefingers are magnetized to each other; accept the idea and believe it. Let it sink deeply into your subconscious.

By opening and closing your forefingers consciously three times, you have already programmed your subconscious. Now turn the exercise over to your subconscious; expect the subconscious to take over. *THINK:* I want my fingers to draw together. I expect this phenomenon. I am going to have my forefingers drawn together.

To Your Surprise, This Will Be Done By Your Subconscious Mind. It Stands to Reason That If You Can Assign Your Subconscious Mind to Magnetize Your Fingers, Then You Can Ask Your Subconscious Mind For Anythng You Want.

LIGHT AND HEAVY ARM EXERCISE

Mental Picturing Training Exercise With Your Subconscious

Stand erect. Stretch both arms out in front of you. Turn your right hand, palm up, facing the ceiling, fingers together. Your left hand, palm vertical, fingers together, thumb extended. CLOSE YOUR EYES.

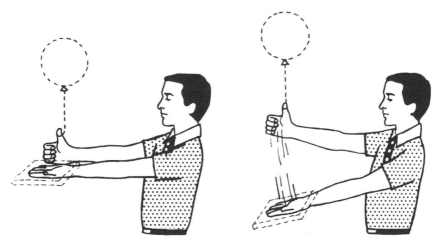

Picture in your mind's eye that a heavy book is placed on your right hand. On the thumb of your left hand, a string with a balloon is fastened. Keep this mental picture strong and long enough in your conscious until it is accepted by your subconscious. Soon you will feel the compelling force of your subconscious making your right arm heavy coming down, down, down, heavier and heavier. Your left arm is getting lighter and lighter, the balloon, pulling your arm up, up, up. Think and experience it for a while, and then open your eyes and see what you have accomplished with imagination.

IF YOU CAN BRING YOUR SUBCONSCIOUS MIND WITH FOCUSED IMAGINATION TO PRODUCE THE PHENOME-NON THAT ONE ARM IS HEAVY AND THE OTHER IS LIGHT—THEN YOU CAN ASSIGN YOUR SUBCONSCIOUS MIND TO OBTAIN ANYTHING YOU WANT.

PART I
CHAPTER 4
SUMMARY

1. Make yourself a Pendulum
2. Put the Chart in Front of You
3. Move your arm and hand consciously to swing the pendulum. (You are programming your Subconscious)
4. Focus the pendulum again over the center of the chart and hold it steadily
5. Move your eyes in the direction you want the pendulum to swing and expect performance from the subconscious with the compelling feedback. Let the Mind Track Formula go through your mind—"I want it—I expect it—I am going to have it—I Know it is mine."
6. Enjoy the phenomenon
7. Will the pendulum to stop and change the direction

8. IT STANDS TO REASON: IF YOU CAN PROGRAM YOUR SUBCONSCIOUS TO SWING THE PENDULUM, THEN YOU CAN ALSO LEARN TO PROGRAM ANY GOAL INTO YOUR SUBCONSCIOUS, AND EXPECT PERFORMANCE.

9. Mental Picturing Training Exercises
   a. Magnetized Fingers
   b. Heavy and Light Arm

PART I
CHAPTER 5

Positive Mental Attitude

POSITIVE THINKING AND ACTING AND CHANGE OF
YOUR SELF IMAGE WITH THE HELP OF YOUR
SUBCONSCIOUS. A TOTAL CHANGE—
NOT A PATCH UP JOB

THE GAME OF LIFE

Life is a great game of experiences of learning and striving to
achieve. Everyone can and should be a winner. But he has to know
and keep the laws and rules and understand all forces which
determine success or failure. The forces are our thoughts. Every
thought is a reality. It builds up or tears down something in our
future, our destiny.

Pay attention for a moment to what you are thinking right now.
What are your thoughts? How do you feel? Are they uplifting or
depressing, full of love or hate, positive or negative? If we know the
direction of our thoughts, we know our future.

We are the result of our thoughts. Our life's circumstances are
the end result of our dominant dreams. This is the key to success or
failure in life. Thought reigns over matter and over circumstance. If
we want to improve our circumstances, change ourselves, become
happier, healthier and more successful, we have to follow the rules.
First, we have to see ourselves in our minds-eye in better
circumstances. We must think health and prosperity. In this way we
create the foundation for their realization. Think big about
yourselves. It is our reponsibility and destiny to activate these forces
and strengthen them so we can obtain success.

THE BASKETBALL GAME

It was quite rewarding for me to watch a coach train, condition
and program his team for a basketball tournament. "Avoid weak
points and dwell on your strengths," he told them; "be aware,
watch the others around you; concentrate on teamwork and have as
your one and only goal to get the ball in the basket. Overcome
failure by dwelling on your successful shots, and duplicate those
actions. Practice your dribbling. Keep your fouls down." The coach
pepped-them-up physically, psychologically and emotionally. He
created the right frame of mind and a mental picture of winning
the game.

I saw a parallel with life in this. We have Fundamental Laws of Right Thinking and Living to follow; fixed rules to obey in order to succeed. We can learn by analyzing our mistakes. Our conscious faculty uses its reason and judgment to tell us when we have done something wrong; when we are off course. No one is perfect. From time to time even successful and well-adjusted people are sidetracked. If the goal-striving automatic faculty of our subconscious is programmed for the ultimate goal that we desire, this power will guide us back, will correct our course and straighten us out. Just as a guided missile reaches its ultimate goal by constant corrections in its course, we will arrive at our goal by correcting our course from time to time.

Our minds have the ability to duplicate mistakes as well as successes, automatically. We can choose to dwell on our mistakes or our successes. We continually face new problems. We need not accept defeat in anything. Life has a design for health, financial independence, love, and creative self-expression.

You will find the following affirmation very helpful: "The right idea and plan will be revealed to me. All negative influences will be dissolved."

BLOOD TRANSFUSION

In every city across the country, the Red Cross maintains a central blood bank. Most hospitals have an additional emergency blood supply. People are encouraged to go there and donate blood.

The four main blood types or groups are O, A, B, and AB, with additional sub-groups. By the RH factor, the rhesus monkey serum, the four blood types are again divided, into Negative and Positive.

A person has to be generally in good health before his blood will be accepted by the bloodbank. It should not be donated more often than every three months. Just imagine, four times a year you can save another person's life by donating your life-sustaining blood.

As all of this went through my mind, I pictured the many ways we can transmit positive, uplifting thoughts daily to our family, friends, neighbors, clients, customers, or strangers. A transfusion of disease bearing blood, or the wrong type blood, could be fatal to the receiver. Before the Rh factor was discovered, many people died because Positive and Negative types were mixed. Daily we mix positive and negative thoughts and suggestions which can lead ourselves and others astray. Just as a medical staff has to make sure

NEGATIVE MEANDERING LIFE
VS
HOW TO ACHIEVE YOUR GOALS WITH THE HELP OF YOUR PROGRAMMED SUBCONSCIOUS

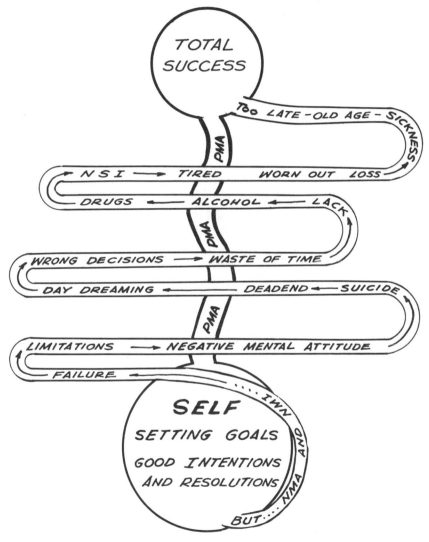

that the right blood type is used, so we must learn to control our thinking and speaking. We can think and mentally picture anything we want, but the human mind can not stop thinking. Every hour we have an opportunity to pause and become interested in the worries and problems of others. Sometimes a few words of encouragement can change the attitude and the self-image of a depressed and discouraged person. Well-directed words expressed with honest feelings can create a new mental outlook and cause an immediate change from a negative to a positive outlook on life.

TOTAL CHANGE VS. PATCH UP

Subconscious Positive Thinking Formulas and Exercises in Five Steps:

Formula 1:   A mental exercise which conditions you to shift from a negative mental attitude to a positive mental attitude with positive thoughts and actions to achieve total success compelled by the power of your subconscious mind.

> "POSITIVE THINKING PROGRAMMED INTO MY SUBCON-
> SCIOUS BRINGS ME A POSITIVE MENTAL ATTITUDE—A
> NEW POSITIVE LIFESTYLE, AND A NEW SELF-IMAGE—
> SELF-MASTERY—SELF-CONFIDENCE—CREATIVITY—
> WISDOM—SPIRITUALITY—JOY—VIGOROUS HEALTH—
> AND SUCCESS, COMPELLING ME TO RIGHT ACTION WITH
> INTEGRITY, SO THAT ALL THINGS GOOD FOR ME WILL BE
> REALIZED IN MY LIFE."

Formula 2:   The "I AM" formula develops the real "YOU," your positive entity. A new self-image.

> I AM
> (MY SUBCONSCIOUS—MY INNER CORE)
> I AM BECOMING MY OWN "BETTER SELF" THE "NEW ME,"
> THE "POSITIVE ENTITY" WITHIN MYSELF.
> THERE IS NO ONE IN THE WHOLE WORLD LIKE ME.
> I LIKE MYSELF: I HAVE SELF-ESTEEM
> I AM A WORTHY, HUMBLE PERSON. WHATSOEVER GOOD
> I DESIRE IS IN ME.
> MY "POSITIVE ENTITY" IN MY SUBCONSCIOUS, WILL
> SUPPLY ME WITH ALL MY NEEDS.

Alternate each formula, using Formula No. 1 one day, and Formula No. 2 on the following day. Or use both formulas together. After you have memorized both formulas, you are ready for programming them into your subconscious.

EXERCISE IN FOUR STEPS
NIGHT EXERCISE

Step 1:

Find a comfortable position on your bed, your legs slightly apart, and your hands resting loosely on your thighs. Wiggle a few times and shift your weight until you are really comfortable. Then close your eyes and take one deep breath, exhale and relax. KEEP YOUR EYES CLOSED.

Step 2:

Proceed with "STANDARD RELAXATION" fully explained in Part I, Chapter 5, *WITHOUT COUNTING UP FROM ZERO TO SIX AT THE END*. Counting up is the "ENERGIZER" but what you want after this NIGHT EXERCISE is sleep—*So do not count up!*

Step 3:

You are calm, relaxed, and serene. Repeat four times the formula for conditioning your subconscious for "Positive Thinking" and the "I AM" Formula, for a new self-image. In order to create a "New Positive Lifestyle" think every word of the formula very slowly, silently, mouthing the words with your lips. Create a vivid, happy mental picture of yourself as having already accomplished it. See yourself acting positive in different real-life situations. This exercise should take you about five minutes.

Step 4:

To keep track of the four repetitions, mouth the formula once, and then let your right arm slide down from your thigh. Mouth the formula a second time and then drop your left arm from your thigh.

Mouth the formula a third time, and then lift your right leg and let it drop suddenly, just as though someone had taken a pin from your hip. Mouth the formula a fourth time, creating a vivid mental picture of yourself as having already accomplished it. Now lift your left leg and let it drop suddenly. The movement of arms and legs will help you to stay in a twilight zone, just enough for you to stay awake, so that the formula can drift into the subconscious. The dropping of the arms and legs will enhance the deepening process of your relaxation. Be sure you always do this, s-l-o-w-l-y. This exercise should take you approximately five minutes. Mouth every word of the formula effortlessly, with positive emotions and a burning desire and expectation of achievement, seeing yourself already having attained this healthy, happy, and positive attitude, a "Positive New Life Style."

THIS IS NOT A LONG CONDITIONING PROCESS: EVERY STUDENT WILL EXPERIENCE A POSITIVE CHANGE IN THE FIRST FEW DAYS AND THAT CHANGE WILL BECOME STRONGER AND STRONGER DAY BY DAY.

Under no circumstances should you let yourself fall asleep before you have completed the four repetitions. After you have completed your assignment, you may go on with the formula until you fall sound asleep. *This exercise must be absolutely the last thing you do before you fall asleep.* As you fall asleep, the suggestion and the formula will simply drop into your subconscious. While you are sleeping peacefully, the formula will be worked on by your subconscious, producing the results which you are seeking, without any effort on your part.

Through the breathing exercise, you create a state of relaxation of body, mind and emotions. Through the repetition of the carefully selected formula, the subconscious becomes programmed with all the positive ideas from the formula.

During the day and in any situation, the subconscious computer will feed back into your consciousness, self-mastery, self-confidence, creativity, wisdom, and whatever else you are in need of. It will guide, compel, and impel you to act positively in daily life. It will develop self-esteem, uncover your "better self;" "your positive entity." It will find all your needs and give you a NEW POSITIVE SELF-IMAGE. It will surprise you to find that an incredibly strong influence this will have on you. *YOU SHOULD DO THIS EVERY NIGHT.*

In my lectures I explain this programming state of the Conscious Mind Faculty with a drawing like this:

The "one cross bar" in the Conscious Mind Faculty depicts: Deliberate relaxation of mind, body, and emotions; a twilight state of mind accomplished by "STANDARD RELAXATION." This opens the

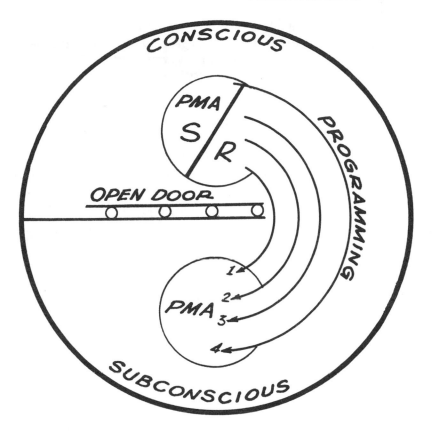

"DOOR" figuratively speaking, to the subconscious for programming. The formulas can now be programmed into the subconscious computer. Your subconscious has to be indelibly impressed and nourished with these new formulas to create a strong conviction. This conviction must be a request, a trust, or a prayerful statement. "Delight thyself also in the Lord, and He shall give thee the desires of thine heart. Commit thy way unto the Lord; trust also Him and He shall bring it to pass." (Psalm 37:4-5)

WHEN THE FIRST request reaches the Subconscious computer it will look up, figuratively speaking, and say: "You have had other fads before; you have pretended before and you did not follow through. Therefore, I am not willing to react."

Then the SECOND request will arrive. The computer will say: "Do you really mean it this time?"

Then the THIRD request will arrive even more enthusiastically.

The Subconscious will react: "You have finally made up your mind. Congratulations! In the past you fell asleep every night and gave me nothing worthwhile to do—I can hardly wait to PROVE to you how willing and anxious I am to serve you."

Then the FOURTH request comes through forcefully loaded with expectation, mental pictures and a burning desire; the subconscious will push every button and open every channel, bow down like a Genie, and say, "Master, your desires will be fulfilled. Your wishes and expectations are my command. Your request shall be granted. You can depend on me. Thank you for letting me be your partner, your servant and Genie."

The Sleeping State of the Conscious Mind Faculty
After the Programming Exercise

The "double cross bar" in the Conscious Mind Faculty represents: "S-L-E-E-P." The "Door" to the subconscious is then closed. The subconscious was previously programmed with the formula or a prayerful statement and can now work with it undisturbed. It will ponder on it, creating new ways to accomplish it and bring it to pass in its own way; a way your conscious may not know. Your subconscious is all-wise; hot-wired, so to speak, with Infinite Intelligence. Your

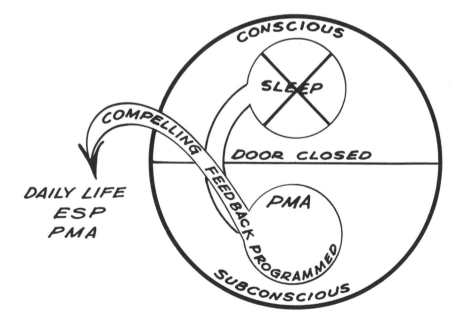

DAILY LIFE
ESP
PMA

subconscious will respond spontaneously according to your belief, faith and expectation and will compel you to right action at the right time at the right place.

DAY EXERCISE FOR FORMULAS I & II

During the day, carry the printed card with you and read the formula as often as possible. Better still, memorize and say the formula with enthusiasm, many times during the day. Create a vivid, happy mental picture of yourself as having already accomplished it.

See yourself acting positively in real-life situations. Through this, you are reinforcing the process you are programming every night.

There is magic power in the enthusiastically spoken word. Say the formulas aloud often to yourself while driving your car, or performing other automatic activities.

A WORD OF WARNING FOR THE
NIGHT AND DAY EXERCISE

Do not yet speak to anyone about these new mental training exercises. Other people might be skeptical and critical. This might tend to undo the benefits you have programmed in your subconscious mind.

You must leave the programming undisturbed, just as the farmer has to leave seeds undisturbed in the soil. *I can promise you a great surprise.* Very soon, your friends and relatives will notice the great change in you and will actually ask you what is going on. Then is the time to speak up with great enthusiasm.

SIMPLE BUT VERY EFFECTIVE EXERCISE TO CHANGE FROM A NEGATIVE TO POSITIVE MENTAL ATTITUDE:
IF YOU CATCH YOURSELF SPEAKING OR EVEN THINK-ING NEGATIVELY, YOU SHOULD IMMEDIATELY SAY 'NO' AND MOVE YOUR LEFT HAND FORCEFULLY DOWN, REPHRASE THE THOUGHT IN A POSITIVE FORM AND LIFT YOUR RIGHT HAND UP, SAYING, 'THANK YOU,' AND MOUTH OR SAY ONE OF THE P.M.A. FORMULAS.

For instance, if you should say or think: "I am poor, unhappy, unloved, sick, cannot pay my bills, worried, tense, depressed, angry," you are only reinforcing those negative statements, still lodged in your subconscious.

Positive thoughts expressed and sent out will join with positive thoughts from others and return multiplied and magnified, creating a newness of life in you.

POSITIVE THINKING

As a young adult I was a salesman for a big steel company. My work was pleasant and gratifying, the territory substantial in size, and the salary above average. In a sales meeting one day, the general agent announced that a new territory in France, bigger than ours, would be opened and a director chosen for this territory. I had been trained from youth to think positively, so I felt this would be the opportunity of my life. I probably was not the most technically-qualified man in the company, but I had prepared myself for an opportunity like this. I was able to picture the potential and importance of such an influential position as General Agent, Director and President of one of the largest steel companies of Germany.

I got the promotion and in a short time my company was leading all others. In board meetings, I was asked many times, "what is your secret?" I had trained all my employees, the janitors, the office and plant manager, the crane operators, truck drivers, workmen, salesmen and office personnel, to think big, to think positively, which meant never to accept the words "impossible," "defeat," or "failure." We programmed our minds "to stand tall, to think tall, sell tall and serve tall." My positive mental attitude was contagious and was picked up by every employee, and even by our customers. During a time of war, uncertainty, hatred, envy and mistrust; despite being in an occupied foreign country with employees from two different nations, we built in this industry an island of peace, understanding and success seldom realized before.

I challenge you to work in the same spirit and change the world around you.

THE 31-DAY METHOD: LIVING A 31-DAY PLEDGE TO YOURSELF

It is an established fact that doing the same thing for 31-days will cause a habit to be automatically programmed into the subconscious. There it will be accepted as the truth, as a goal and then re-enforced with the subconscious' infinite power. The subconscious computer will then feed the idea back into the conscious mind and cause it to become materialized in your daily life.

Following this is a sample worksheet for the 31-day programming method of the "Positive Mental Attitude Formula Number 1" and the "I AM" formula Number 2.

Keep track every day. Be honest with yourself.

Remember, if you promised "YOURSELF" that you will do this exercise for 31-days without fail, You will be unable to break your pledge. You may have broken promises to others but you can NEVER break a promise to yourself. This 31-day pledge is something from which you cannot retreat. You can't escape from yourself. You must keep the pledge. If for some reason you have failed to complete the 31-day method without interruption, then you must start all over again from the beginning. When you have finally completed the 31-day process, continue at least once a week or more times as needed.

I promise you that this technique will work for you. Thousands have used it before you and have changed their attitudes, their self-images, their marriages, their work habits, even their lives. I promise you success, based on a natural, universal, irrevocable mental law.

Even if you practice nothing from this "Mental Workshop Book," than these two formulas with the 31-day method, you will be richly repaid for your efforts. You will become a "level-headed" positive person with sustained "Go-Power."

After you have successfully applied this "31-day I Pledge To Myself" mental exercise for the "Positive Mental Attitude," and the "I AM" formula, you may want to use this method to overcome undesirable habits or achieve positive habits. Make up a worksheet for yourself, and word it like the sample.

DON'T LET ANYBODY MOVE YOU INTO NEGATIVE THINK-ING AND ACTING ANYMORE!!

IF YOU FEEL THAT YOU ARE STILL SUFFERING UNDER COMPELLING NEGATIVE FEEDBACK, MAKE PLUS (+) SIGNS ALL OVER THE HOUSE (MIRRORS, REFRIGERATOR DOOR, ETC.) IN YOUR CAR AND PLACE OF WORK.
THIS WILL REMIND YOU TO THINK AND ACT POSITIVELY.

I CAN   **I WILL**   **I DO**

I am Programming my Subconscious For This Pledge. I Pledge Myself that for the next 31 days I will: PRACTICE THE PMA AND I AM FORMULA EVERY NIGHT AND MANY TIMES DURING THE DAY. AFTER 31 DAYS, I WILL PRACTICE THESE FORMULAS AS MANY TIMES AS I NEED TO, BUT AT LEAST ONCE A WEEK.

Date: _____   Signature:_____

	YES	NO	Remarks		YES	NO	Remarks
1.				17.			
2.				18.			
3.				19.			
4.				20.			
5.				21.			
6.				22.			
7.				23.			
8.				24.			
9.				25.			
10.				26.			
11.				27.			
12.				28.			
13.				29.			
14.				30.			
15.				31.			
16.							

I WANT IT—I EXPECT IT—
I AM GOING TO HAVE IT—I KNOW IT IS MINE

PART I
CHAPTER 5
SUMMARY

1. Formula I
2. Formula II
3. Memorize both formulas
4. Night Exercise
   a. Find a comfortable position
   b. Proceed with Standard Relaxation
   c. Have hands resting on your thighs
   d. Mouth formula four times
   e. Say it additionally as often until you fall asleep
5. Night Exercise Explained with two drawings.
6. Day exercise: Say the formula aloud as often as possible with enthusiasm
7. Word of Warning
8. Thirty-One Day Pledge to Yourself with Record Sheet.

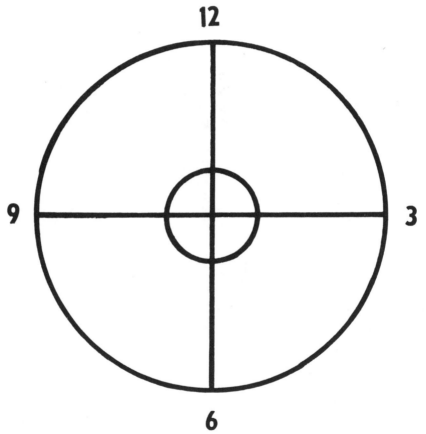

PART II

PART II
CHAPTER 1

Hand Levitation Exercise

HAND LEVITATION

Are You Climbing Molehills?

How many times have you had negative days, days when you just couldn't win no matter how hard you tried? Then have you had positive days when everything went smoothly and fell into place? You may have had days when you felt that you were battling unconquerable foes or climbing insurmountable peaks. This feeling may have persisted for days, weeks, even months without a change. Later you found that these psychic mountains were only molehills.

Let us hear what a student has to say about Hand Levitation.

"Before I heard about you I had read every book on the subject of the subconscious, positive thinking, motivation, and E.S.P., that came my way, but I still didn't know how to reach my subconscious. No one could have been more willing than I was, but no one explained it to me in a down-to-earth way, so that I could achieve all that was promised in the books.

After you introduced me to "Hand Levitation," a new world of understanding and accomplishment opened up for me. I needed proof that the subconscious can be programmed and I received it. I couldn't believe my eyes at first when I saw my own hand raising by itself, after using your simple method to program my subconscious. I finally comprehended what mental picturing meant, and was able to reason out how to transfer this method into daily experiences for achieving my goals. From then on I knew without any doubt, that I could assign my subconscious, my Genie, to obtain anything I wanted to have.

My private and business life has changed for the better in an unbelievably short time. I can only praise and recommend this method.

I am borrowing a phrase from you, Mr. Schneider, which I have heard so often: 'if you learn nothing else from this Subconscious Mind Training than Hand Levitation, you will be on the easy road to success.'

I hope 'Hand Levitation' will help many others to understand and achieve mental picturing, for it is an eye-opener for me."

Other students had the following to say about this highly effective mental exercise, "Hand Levitation":

—"This was the great proof for me that I have a Subconscious Mind."

—"I thought I had reason to doubt the Subconscious, but Hand Levitation made a believer out of me."

—"I can now assign my Subconscious."

—"It is the most effective exercise to reach the Subconscious."

—"It is much easier for me now to program and influence my Subconscious than I ever thought possible."

—"In my opinion, Hand Levitation is the best exercise for learning Mental Picturing, the language of the Subconscious, as I understand it now."

Means to an End

Please keep in mind that Standard Relaxation and the Hand

Levitation plus all the other mental exercises taught in this self-help book are a means to an end. The end is mental preparation for meditation and programming the subconscious for all the good life has in store for you.

Overshadow Negatives With a Positive Mental Attitude

For most of us, life is a chain reaction of anxieties, like: "Can I pay my bills?" "Will my health last?" "Will I have enough money to retire on?" "Will I close this sale?" "Am I respected in my church, community, job, and family?" "Am I loved and appreciated?" "Can I lose weight?" "Will I be lucky?"

They Are Not Blind Promises

How many would like to achieve a more Positive Mental Attitude with Self-Confidence, Self-Mastery, a Better Memory, Heightened Concentration, a Positive Self-Image, A Magnetic Personality, more Happiness, Vigorous Health, Zest, Energy, Vitality, Constructive Use of Time, more Productivity and Success: (See Appendix 1)

YOU CAN BE WHAT YOU WANT TO BE,
HAVE WHAT YOU WANT TO HAVE,
ACCOMPLISH WHAT YOU WANT TO ACCOMPLISH

PLEASE: READ THE ENTIRE EXPLANATION OF THE MENTAL EXERCISE A FEW TIMES BEFORE STARTING TO PRACTICE ON YOUR OWN.

Step One:

Sit down comfortably, your feet flat on the floor, and your back resting against the back of the chair. Have both hands palms down, resting easily on your thighs, your arms at an angle. Now choose the hand with which you want to make the exercise. Be sure you have a ring on one of the fingers of the hand you have chosen. If no ring is available, make a mark on one of the fingers. Now look at the ring or mark easily and effortlessly. Concentrate. Do not take your eyes away from the ring. Look nowhere else. This will condition and train you for heightened concentration, comprehension, reading and memorizing. The mind is always occupied with something. If you are not consciously directing your thoughts with heightened concentration or planned programming, your mind is allowed to wander. (Picture A)

Step Two:

Now lift up your hand slowly and consciously, touching your nose or any part of your face. (Picture B) Keep your eyes on the ring or mark. Bring your hand down again. Do this three times.

Do you know what you just did? You programmed your subconscious mind faculty for "Hand Levitation." In other words, you impressed your subconscious computer, your Genie, with a mental picture, that you want to have realized. Some of you may say, "Wait a minute. How can this be possible?" Just relax and go on reading. You will find out.

Step Three:

Now, with this suggested wording, let the "Mind Track formula "Number 1" go through your mind. (See Part I, Chapter 2)

"I want my subconscious to lift up my arm and hand in the same fashion I have just programmed consciously."

"I expect my subconscious to start to lift up my hand."

"I am going to have this performed by my subconscious as a proof to me that I can do what I want to do, have what I want to have, be what I want to be, with the help of my subconscious."

"I know that this Hand Levitation technique is mine. I am ready to experience this psychic phenomenon. I am ready to experience mental picturing."

This is what will happen—observe all of the sensations and feelings in your hand.

FIRST: The fingers will start to jerk, spread apart, arch up and one by one will rise from your thigh. Watch which of the fingers move first. Finally the whole hand will lift. Don't be surprised if the hand sways a little to the right or the left. As your fingers and hand rise you will notice that your arm will start to rise. (Picture C)

SECOND: The hand will become cool. It may turn pale. It will feel as light as a feather, independent, rising higher and higher; as if connected to a balloon. Do not take your eyes away from the ring or mark.

Think about your other hand. That hand will stay warm, resting heavily on your thigh, feeling the texture of your clothes. One hand is cool while the other hand is warm. Quite a phenomenon! If anyone had told you this, you might not have believed. Now you experience it for yourself. Everyone can do it. Don't be concerned if your hand does not rise all the way up to your face during the first exercise: Remember, "Practice makes Perfect." This is a conditioning process. Your hand will come up next time or the time after that, for sure. Even an inch of levitation will give you proof of the working method of your subconscious.

Your hand will feel light and buoyant. It may have a tingling sensation. It will act as if it no longer belongs to you. Keep watching your hand. You will hardly believe what you see. Your eyes will become watery, heavy, and tired. But do your best to keep them open. These effects may seem strange. But they are absolutely natural.

You will receive proof that your subconscious can be programmed. You may have been looking for this for a long time. You might have read many books about Mind Power and still not have been able to practice it. Now it will be yours.

> IT STANDS TO REASON THAT IF YOU CAN PROGRAM YOUR SUBCONSCIOUS FOR "HAND LEVITATION," THEN YOU CAN PROGRAM IT FOR ANYTHING ELSE YOU NEED OR DESIRE.

Step Four:

To conclude this exercise count in your mind from zero to six and think with every count as outlined. When you think "six," your hand will touch your face and you will close your eyes and your hand and arm will fall back on your thigh.

Suggestions on What You Could Think During Counting:

1. My hand and arm are getting lighter and lighter.

2. My hand and arm are moving upward. (Do your utmost to keep your eyes open, even when your eyelids are getting heavy and your eyes are watering. Don't take your eyes away from the ring or mark.)

3. A buoyant, serene feeling is creeping over me and is taking hold of me.

4. My hand is floating up, up, up. (Keep your eyes open, until your hand touches your face.)

5. My hand is only a short distance away from my face. (You are still looking at the ring or mark.)

6. My hand is moving all the way up. It is touching my nose or face. Now I am relieved. I can close my eyes and my hand will fall down on my thigh. (Keep your eyes closed. You are then in a meditating and programming state of mind, which you can use in different ways.)

WHAT TO DO AFTER YOU ARE IN RELAXATION

1. If you like to meditate or pray, you may clasp your hands together as you are used to in praying. Your conscious, critical and analytical mental faculty is bypassed and you will experience a closeness with Infinite Intelligence. You will begin to understand that "All things are possible to him that believeth." Your inner self can be in communication with God. Your ability to have faith and expectation is enormously increased. A great new understanding, spirituality and harmony will envelop you. You can bridge the gap between you and Infinite Intelligence. You can expect intuitions, promptings of the spirit, answers to your prayers and to the problems you have been working on. Let your mind be free. The answers will come. It will be the truth. This is good preparation for positive E.S.P. (Extra Sensory Perception).

2. You could start a motivation tape at the beginning of the exercise and listen to it at this point, in deep relaxation, meditation and a programming state of mind. It is advisable to have an empty run on your tape first, or use a timer to start the tape after you are relaxed deeply enough with Hand Levitation.

The programmed ideas will go directly into the computer part of your Subconscious Mind. Through this motivation programming an attitude of alert preparedness will eliminate the garbage, the accumulated negative statements, the false concepts and the negative self-image lodged in your subconscious. All negative traits can be erased and reprogrammed through NEW POSITIVE IDEAS.

3. You can use this Hand Levitation exercise to overcome insomnia and go to sleep faster and deeper. (Always state the time you want to wake up before you start the exercise.) During the day you can use it for "cat naps."

4. There is really no end to the ways you can use this exercise. Be creative; be inventive. I would appreciate hearing from you on ways you have discovered for yourself.

5. Always end this exercise by counting up from zero to six.

As You Arouse Yourself, Mouth as Follows:

One: Day by day in every way I will feel better and better. I have made contact with my subconscious, my inner-being, and with Infinite Intelligence.

Two: Today starts the rest of my life; a life of expectation that all things good for me will now be realized in my life. I am feeling buoyantly well.

Three: I will never let myself become discouraged again. I will be positive and optimistic. I am filled with a feeling of comfort and security.

Four: I blink my eyes and begin to awaken.

Five: I am awakening (Open your eyes). I am wide awake, alert, and ready for action. I am feeling fine. The relaxed and meditating state of mind is ended.

Six: I am happy about my performance. It stands to reason that I am now able to be goal-directed, greatly assured, and full of self-confidence. I can now expect the best in every situation. Say aloud or silently: "TODAY AND EVERY DAY I EXPECT THE BEST IN EVERY SITUATION."

YOUR SUBCONSCIOUS WILL BE YOUR FAITHFUL PARTNER FROM NOW ON IN ALL LIFE CIRCUMSTANCES

RE-READ THIS EXPLANATION MANY TIMES
BEFORE YOU ATTEMPT TO PRACTICE THIS
EXERCISE FROM MEMORY
When practicing "Hand Levitation" the first time, it is
advisable and helpful to have another person present
to speak the progressive steps of the exercise for
you and watch your performance.

SUMMARY OF THE EXERCISE

Basic Steps of Hand Levitation

1. Sit quietly. Choose a hand. Mark the chosen hand with a ring or mark.
2. Consciously move the chosen arm up three times and touch your nose or any part of your face with your hand. This is conscious programming; telling the subconscious what you want to have performed. Let the "Mind Track" formula go through your mind. "I WANT IT. I EXPECT IT. I AM GOING TO HAVE IT. I KNOW IT IS MINE."
3. Anticipate the subconscious movement of fingers of the chosen hand. Finger by finger it will arch up, rise and finally the hand will lift. Let the hand and arm soar upward in an uninterrupted flow to touch your face. Keep your eyes focused until contact is made. Then close them and let your hand and arm fall down.
4. Use this relaxation exercise for any chosen purpose.
5. Wake yourself up by counting up from zero to six.
6. IT STANDS TO REASON THAT IF YOU CAN PROGRAM YOUR SUBCONSCIOUS FOR "HAND LEVITATION" THEN YOU CAN PROGRAM YOUR SUBCONSCIOUS FOR ANYTHING ELSE YOU NEED OR DESIRE.

A   B   C

Relaxing Exercises with Fourteen Benefits

ENERGY BUILDER

NEW MENTAL EXERCISE—COUNTING DOWN FROM SIXTY
TO ZERO WITH THE CONDITIONING WORD *DEEPER*

By now you should have experienced results from practicing
"STANDARD RELAXATION" and "HAND LEVITATION."
Conditioned by these exercises you will be able to enjoy further
benefits. Even if you feel that things all around you are starting to
crumble and collapse, this exercise will be a fabulous help for
you.

ENERGY BUILDER
NEW MENTAL EXERCISE

This Simple Exercise Will Bring You Fourteen Benefits:

1. Mental Tranquilizer
2. Energizer
3. TIME Becomes Abundant
4. TIME Element
5. HEALTH-PSYCHIC HEALING
6. Revitalization of the Aura
7. Finding Lost Articles
8. Intuitions, Promptings, Psychic Guidance
9. Forgive and Forget
10. Suspended
11. Leveling to the Best Depth of Relaxation
12. Psychic Alarm Clock
13. Interpretation of Dreams
14. *WINNERS' CIRCLE*

DEEP SEA DIVER

Research experts have found in studying commercial divers, who
are trained to work at very great depths in the sea, that the depth,
pressure and cold slows the heart rate and decreased touch sensitivity.
Grip strength becomes weak. Memory is impaired. The divers do not
remain mentally alert. The capacity to solve problems is sometimes
diminished. Mental functions are deceitful. What a handicap this is for

these commercial divers, looking for off-shore oil, or treasure.

When I read this, I thought: Daily we have to "dive into life" and the pressure is sometimes unbearable, the emotional temperature around us extremely cold. No wonder its effects on our mental functions accumulate. The pressures of life get stronger all the time. We live today under greater stress than ever before. Unfortunately, we have not learned to live under such pressure. It would be fatal for deep-sea divers to be unprepared. How can we expect to be well adjusted under political, business, community and family pressures? No wonder people are memory- and concentration-impaired, near nervous breakdowns and unable to solve their problems. The Fundamental Laws of Right Thinking are the only answer. Man is capable of standing much emotional turbulence, yes, even more pressure than our society is causing us today. We are born with the ability to protect ourselves. All we have to do is to apply the ingenious gift of our Subconscious.

Would you dive miles under the sea without any protection and preparation? Certainly not! Then why not learn a few mental exercises to shield and protect yourself from emotional pressures and blows before diving into life?

Are You A Leader, or a Follower?

Have you ever wondered why so many people have failed in life, why they are fatigued, always sick and have a negative mental attitude? At the same time, others seem abrim with energy, health, and creativity? We call the latter "born leaders," but in truth, they are not any more gifted than you are. They have learned to take care of themselves. They free their innate abilities with mental exercises. They work with the higher powers, with E.S.P., knowingly or sub-consciously.

"A Winner Never Quits, and a Quitter Never Wins"

The great coach Vince Lombardi of the Green Bay Packers said: "Winning is not a sometime thing; it's an all-the-time thing. You don't win once in a while, you don't do things right once in a while, you do them right all the time. Winning is a habit. Unfortunately, so is losing. It is and always has been an American zeal to be first in anything we do and to win and to win and to win."

Repeat to yourself often: I CAN'T LOSE FOR WINNING!

I invite you to step into the Winners' Circle with the following exercise and be victorious in all you do.

THE BATTERY

You have probably known the frustrating experience of turning the ignition key of your car only to hear the dragging noise of the starter telling you that your battery is dead. It always seems to happen when you have one thousand, two hundred and three different things to do!

Could it be your fault? Many times, yes! You could have had too many things drawing on the battery: starter, lights, air-conditioning, radio. You forgot to turn off the lights. You should have checked the battery and the connections. Is it too late now for a remedy? Fortunately not! Sometimes your mechanic can restore the battery to full efficiency, just like new.

Perhaps you have guessed what I am driving at. Sometimes we do not start the morning vigorously and in health. We feel dizzy, sluggish, tired, empty, depressed and worried. Too much energy was used and not enough restored and accumulated. We burn the candle at both ends. A checkup by your physician will find what you have neglected. If you heed his advice, you can soon be on the road again. But what can you do to prevent a setback like this? I have good news for you.

You can develop sound sleeping habits by learning to apply deep-relaxation exercises a few minutes each day. You can accumulate new health and eliminate nervousness, and pep yourself up, while you become calm and serene.

THE PLUNDERING OF OUR MIND ENERGY

Today science is rightfully concerned about the plundering of the resources of our planet. They are used up millions of times faster than nature can restore them. It is like filling up a reservoir drop by drop while the water gushes out through the open gates.

The world burned more oil in one year than nature had created in 2.83 million years. It is frightening how we are depleting the earth's capital.

Many of us work, act and live our daily lives in this way, burning the candle at both ends. Body and mind can stand the abuse for a short time. Most of us don't even get enough sleep to recuperate from our daily tasks. Ernst Basler said: "Our economic development is one million times faster than the evolution of nature." And so is the relationship of the expenditure of our psychic energy in proportion to its replacement.

Many live against their better understanding and judgment. They act like the man responsible for the switches of the railroad tracks. He sees two trains speeding toward each other, and hopes for a miracle that would stop them in time. He does nothing himself to avert the disaster. He could prevent a tragic accident by simply throwing the switch.

The outlined mental exercises and short relaxation periods for body, mind and emotions will stop the depletion of our mental and psychic energy and recharge our vitality again.

EXPLANATION OF THE EXERCISE

Read this explanation a few times, and then start to practice. This very simple Mental Exercise is done as follows:

1. Standard Relaxation (See Part I, Chapter 2)

2. After the completion of the relaxation program; just let go—be relaxed and at ease. To maintain this state of relaxation and meditation, think or mouth *"RELAX"* when you inhale and *"DEEPER"* when you exhale until you achieve the desired effect. Do this easily, without any effort. You may want to concentrate on your breathing without doing, thinking, or mouthing anything.

Teachers of Relaxation and Meditation all over the world have found it helpful to count down or count up to maintain the state of relaxation and meditation, and create through this a time limit. I practice and teach counting down from sixty to zero, *inhaling* with every "COUNT DOWN," exhaling with the conditioning word *"DEEPER." "DEEPER" means, "I am moving to another level of relaxation,"* or until the expected response is achieved.

FOR EXAMPLE:

INHALE—"S-I-X-T-Y," EXHALE—"D-E-E-P-E-R"
INHALE—"F-I-F-T-Y-N-I-N-E," EXHALE—"D-E-E-P-E-R"
INHALE—"F-I-F-T-Y-E-I-G-H-T," EXHALE—"D-E-E-P-E-R"
INHALE—"F-I-F-T-Y-S-E-V-E-N," EXHALE—"D-E-E-P-E-R"
INHALE—"F-I-F-T-Y-S-I-X," EXHALE—"D-E-E-P-E-R"

And so on all the way down to Zero.

Mouthing or thinking the count-down and the conditioning word "DEEPER" will increase the depth of your relaxation and meditation. Your Conscious mind is slightly occupied and cannot interfere with the working method of the Subconscious Mind.

Thinking and mouthing every count down and the conditioning word "Deeper" will help you to stay partially awake.

Breath slowly, evenly, and regularly during this exercise. Exhale with the word "DEEPER." This is very important. The relaxing exercise should continue for five minutes. As soon as you reach zero or achieve the desired response, blink your eyes and simply count upward from one to six. This will awaken you, clear headed, full of energy, happy, healthy and well-adjusted. Every time you count up from one to six, you will end your relaxation and wake up full of energy.

Someone said: "That which you persist in doing becomes easy, not that the nature of the thing has changed, but your power to do has increased."

THE FOURTEEN BENEFITS WHICH
THIS SIMPLE EXERCISE WILL BRING YOU.

1. Mental Tranquilizer

This mental exercise will act as a mental tranquilizer. Body and mind and emotions will become composed and serene. Jittery, high-strung, nervous feelings will vanish.

It is impossible to be upset, angry, worried *and relaxed* at the same time. All negative emotions and reactions will leave and you will become calm, alert, happy and creative. You will see every situation in a new light, with a positive mental attitude. You will be able to think clearly and evaluate every situation positively.

HARD WORK NEVER KILLED ANYONE, BUT FAILURE TO DEAL WITH STRESS KILLS. TENSION AND STRESS ARE CULTURAL SYMPTOMS WHICH COME FROM WITHIN US, NOT FROM WITHOUT.

Some of My Students Had Interesting Statements About This Miraculous Exercise

"I can now stand the strain of daily living."

"I am very calm now, and I don't lose my temper any more."

"I was on the verge of a nervous breakdown, but now these frightening feelings have left me."

"My employees and my family say that it is much easier to get along with me now, and I am getting along with them much better."

"We are not shouting at each other anymore. A great new harmony and love surrounds us."

2. ENERGIZER

This provides a mental "ENERGIZER" for you, a built in "MENTAL PEPPER-UPPER." During this exercise, body, mind, and emotions will be powerfully invigorated. It will act as a "MENTAL BOOSTER." You can make two days out of one. Every time you follow this mental procedure, you gain energy from your own inner core. I recommend doing this exercise at noon, when you need help to finish the other half of the working day. It is good to do this exercise in the early evening, before going out for work or pleasure, to be alert, energetic and "on the ball" for any activity.

Practice this "energizer" two or three times daily and you will never be tired. Dragged-out, exhausted, fatigued, depressed and worn-out feelings will leave you. You can expect to feel on top of the world again immediately. We all need this extra psychic booster. "Lack of pep is often mistaken for patience." Kim Hubbard

3. Time Becomes Abundant

With increased energy and better health, you will be surprised how much more you can accomplish. You will use time more constructively. A heightened sense of the value of time will make you more effective in your daily work.

IT WILL SEEM AS IF YOU ARE MAKING TWO DAYS OUT OF ONE.

Have you wished before that you could ask a "Genie" to give you more hours? Your subconscious is Your Genie!

4. Time Element

This exercise will take approximately five minutes, depending on your counting speed. This time span will be essential for your next mental exercise, "How to Program Your Positive Affirmations and GOALS Into Your Subconscious." (Part III, Chapters 1 to 4)

All fourteen benefits are yours by practicing this mental exercise several times a day.

5. Health

Modern hurry-scurry living causes the accumulation of poisonous substances in our bodies. It blocks the automatic healing powers in our subconscious. During a relaxation period, we give free reign to the subconscious and have time to eliminate toxic chemicals from the body through the bloodstream. You will experience renewed health, more vitality and zest and an all-around better feeling.

Your State of Mind Has More to do With Illness Than We Know

I have witnessed psychic healing not only in the Philippines but in my own family. Many students of mine have told me of their healing experiences and improved health. In order to believe you must encounter it, and practice it yourself.

Today starts the rest of your HEALTHY NEW LIFE. You will soon look and feel younger than your chronological age. A wrinkled skin may make you look older, but a wrinkled soul and mind does so much more. This exercise will iron out physical and psychological wrinkles. It is a psychic facial.

Do Not Be Surprised if Your Positive Mental Attitude Brings About Positive Healing

By relaxing and expressing positive affirmations you are creating positive emotions, causing a positive mental attitude. This process strengthens your defense against disease. A physical curative process takes place through mental or psychic healing.

Negative thinking and a negative mental attitude can lead to all kinds of psycho-somatic diseases.

FATIGUE, if not relieved by relaxation can lead to exhaustion, nervous breakdown, and disease.

MISDIRECTING PSYCHIC ENERGY into negative channels over a period of time can lead to severe illness.

POSITIVELY DIRECTED PSYCHIC ENERGY will lead to vigorous health.

THE HEALING POWER IN US

Many times in our lives we have seen people who were very ill or had broken bones. After a time, these people are up and around again and living normal lives. Because this happens around us daily, we take it for granted. We don't even consider that we can use this marvelous, incredible, creative healing power for the prevention of illness and injury as well. We worry about our health and aging, and worry is detrimental to our built-in healing power. We are biochemical, electrical beings made up of living cells which are directed and governed by our Subconscious Mind.

We have a healing center within us with a pharmaceutical factory, a dispensary and a skilled staff so to speak, who know what to do in each and every case of illness. These living cells have to be recharged daily by sensible living and a positive mental attitude based on the

Fundamental Laws of Right Thinking. This healing center can be commanded by our minds. It can work negatively, as well as positively. Unfortunately, some of us dwell on sickness with negative expectations which are realized. By Subconscious Mind training we can educate ourselves to mentally picture our bodies as healthy and whole. Our powerful thoughts applied in total relaxation with a burning desire for health and youthfulness will spur the brain centers involved to send forth new energy and health, to shield and protect, and to heal. It really pays off in health to spend a few minutes in deep relaxation and meditation every day. Re-enforce with this affirmation: "My body is now charged with purifying and healing energy."

6. Revitalization of the Aura

Reinforcing the psychic energy of the Aura around you is of great importance. Many around you are a burden on your strength and energy. You become depleted. With this marvelous exercise you will never lack energy again. You will have energy to spare. (For more information about the Aura, read Part II, Chapter 3.)

7. Finding Lost Articles

Have you lost or misplaced anything lately? What would you give for a way to find it? Some individuals place a low value on the powers and abilities of their mind, but the subconscious is all-knowing. With this simple mental exercise, you can use your own subconscious and find any lost article. You can succeed in finding lost articles, remembering forgotten names, or telephone numbers.

EXERCISE FOR FINDING LOST ARTICLES OR
REMEMBERING NAMES WITH THE HELP
OF YOUR SUBCONSCIOUS MIND

First: State your problem before you start with the exercise.
Second: By the breathing, thinking deeper and the counting down from sixty to zero you occupy your conscious mind faculty and you will consciously forget all about "your lost article." Meanwhile, the subconscious can work uninterruptedly on the problem, and in its own time flash the solution up into your conscious.
Third: As soon as you have received the answer, stop counting down immediately and count up from zero to six for awakening and alertness. Express your thankfulness for the prompt service and

answer. Lift up your right hand and arm, and say three times: "Thank you, thank you, thank you."

8. Intuitions, Promptings, Psychic Guidance

Why are so many cut off from intuitions, promptings, spiritual guidance, personal revelations, or answers to prayers? Many individuals pray, but live in spiritual darkness and receive no answers. There are many dark tunnels and corners in the minds of men.

With this exercise you are exploring your mind. There are many doors which have never been opened. You are shedding new light into these dark tunnels, opening the doors, to find new ways.

What is the Reason?

First: Many don't spend enough time in prayer, meditation and relaxation.

Second: Many don't wait for an answer and instructions from the subconscious. Sometimes people act like a pilot approaching an airport in a blizzard, desperately asking the tower for landing instructions and help. Then he turns the radio off without waiting for an answer, goes in on his own to disaster.

Third: Many do not hear the guiding signals.

Fourth: Body, mind and emotions are not relaxed enough for meditation.

KEEPING YOURSELF IN A MEDITATIVE STATE OF MIND
LONG ENOUGH WILL OPEN THE PSYCHIC CHANNELS
OF POSITIVE E.S.P. FOR YOU.

"Meditation is the nurse of thought, and thought the food for meditation."
—C. *Simmons*

Simple Concise Exercises—"Western Style of Life" vs. Complicated Prolonged Oriental Yoga Exercises

In the Orient, I saw people in meditation for hours, practicing mental yoga or zen exercises. It is extremely hard for western people to do this.

We need not meditate for such extreme lengths of time. Most of us have neither the desire, reason, nor the time for such prolonged exercise. Short relaxing exercises appropriate for our "western style of life" will bring the spiritual and physical help we need. If some of you want to carry this mental exercise further and practice the physical and "mental yoga" meditations for your special purposes, there are many, many books available for study. However, you will be greatly rewarded by the simple and concise exercises as explained in this "Self Help Book."

9. Forgive and Forget

Because of the vital importance of this I would like to dwell on it. Forgive and Forget, it will free you from psychic enslavement. If you feel that you have transgressed religious, spiritual, social, moral or universal laws, this mental exercise can bring new light. It will help you in evaluating your problem with your subconscious mind. You will find creative new ideas, how to overcome sin, repent from past sins, and solve your problems. Countless people are suffering by not being able to "Forgive and Forget." If you think that you are one of them, please study the special chapter or hear our exciting tape on "How to Forgive and Forget With the Help of Your Subconscious." This tape exercise is tailor-made for practicing "Forgive and Forget." (Part IV, Chapter I)

10. Suspended

In the bible you read: Paul speaking to the Corinthians, "whether in the body, I cannot tell; whether out of the body, I cannot tell; God knoweth." (II Corinthians 12:2)

I am not talking about psychic traveling or about a state where the spirit leaves the body for a special witness and goes to another place, then returns to the body again, connected all the time with a spiritual cord for security. Para-psychologists have investigated this phenomenon and have some evidence that transcendental traveling is possible. I do not encourage anyone to engage in this practice yet. To do this, one has to be absolutely synchronized in body, mind, and spirit, have a highly trained moral, spiritual and social character and be in extremely good health. Very few individuals fit into such a category.

Don't Try to "Walk on Water"

I am teaching here only the bypassing of conscious feelings, a bypassing of the conscious mind to reach the subconscious mind. This is not unusual. Many writers, poets, artists, composers, inventors, religious leaders, men, and women of all ages and walks of life have witnessed this sort of experience and given testimony of it. The purpose of this experience is to find spirituality and psychic depth, and to gain greater knowledge and wisdom. Finding your place in the world and finding your destiny must be your goal.

11. Leveling to the Best Depth of Relaxation

Relaxation and meditation is a conditioning process. The first few times you practice this exercise you may not feel much different. But soon your efforts will be rewarded and day by day you will experience the deepening effect of your meditation. You will then level off at the most comfortable degree of relaxation for you. From then, every time you are relaxing, meditating, or praying, you will automatically drop into this level of relaxation, without any conscious effort on your part. Did you think that anything so important in your life could be so easily achieved?

12. Psychic Alarm Clock

If you feel that you have been cheated of natural sleep, then take "cat naps." State the time of awakening to your subconscious before this exercise, *but do not count up.* Stay in relaxation and natural "cat nap sleep" until the built-in "alarm clock" in your subconscious awakens you; *then* count up from one to six. You may practice the same procedure at night to over-come insomnia or to unwind and fall asleep. You never need to worry about not waking up in a case of an emergency. Your subconscious has the ability to sense danger and will notify you and wake you up if any problems arise.

13. Interpretation of Dreams

I would like to encourage you to take this matter very seriously. It will definitely change your life. Give it a chance. Practice this simple and concise exercise for four weeks consistently and you will often experience daily the power of your subconscious. (See Part II, Chapter 5 "How to Interpret Your Dreams.)

14. The Winners' Circle

The Winners' Circle is my "pet exercise." So many of my students have testified to complete success in changing their lives and others through the use of this exercise. (Read the special chapter on the Winners' Circle Part II, Chapter 4)

PART II
CHAPTER 2
SUMMARY

1. Begin with Standard Relaxation
2. Attach the Mental Exercise Counting Down from Sixty to Zero With The Conditioning Word DEEPER
3. Expect any of the Fourteen Benefits
4. Arouse Yourself By Counting UP From Zero to Six

THE MORE OFTEN YOU PRACTICE THIS MENTAL
EXERCISE, THE MORE ASTOUNDING, EFFECTIVE, APPARENT
AND RECOGNIZABLE ALL THE FOURTEEN
BENEFITS WILL BECOME.

The Human Aura

Explanation of the Human Aura and Its
Relationship to the Subconscious

The Kirlian Photography of the Aura
Discovery of Three Auras by Dr. W.J. Kilner
Pictures of the Aura—Picture 40, 41, 42
What You Can do to Increase Your Psychic
Energy—Your Aura with the Help of
Your Subconscious

Explanation of the Human Aura and Its Relationship to the Subconscious

"Let your light so shine before men, that they may see your good works and glorify your Father which is in heaven." (Matt. 5:16)

Experiments and studies at leading institutes and universities here and abroad have found that there is an energy field or glow which radiates from all of us and all living things.

This LIGHT, this glow, called the Aura, is an energy-field surrounding our physical bodies, often seen around the heads of holy men and great masters. All have noticed that you can feel warm right away with one person and get a chilly, cold feeling from another. This is the Aura. Even animals can sense the Aura. Our Aura which changes according to our negative or positive attitudes and moods will effect the Aura of others around us.

Your Aura Has to be Protected, Directed and Constantly Recharged

The Aura literally broadcasts energy to other people around you and influences them and your environment. This energy is received directly from the universal energy storehouse and increased by the living of a physically and mentally clean life, by being helpful to others, by being spiritual and striving for higher levels of knowledge and wisdom. You have to want it, expect it, claim it and it will be yours, provided of course that you put effort into obtaining it. The Universal Law is: "What you send out will come back multiplied to you." The teaching of the Great Master, "Give and you will receive" is the basis for recharging your Aura.

I daily meet people who are energy-depleted. Why? Because they suffer from mental and physical illness, are too materialistic. They are inconsiderate, angry, and live under constant stress. They may be overworked, eat an unbalanced diet, have insufficient sleep, or ignore relaxation exercises.

What Would Happen to Your Car if You Left the Lights On?

Soon the battery would be dead! The car would be all right. The motor could be perfect, the transmission in working order, the tires flawless, but still there would be no power, no energy to start. You would need a booster before the battery could recharge itself. So with you, if you are depleted, you need a psychic energy booster.

I always recognize this need when I teach and give personal motivation treatments to energy depleted people. I must first recharge their energy by arousing and adjusting their psychic centers. The positive flow of energy is jammed and blocked and has to be freed. Remember when the plumbing in your home was clogged? The same thing can happen to the positive flow of energy. In such a case, the energy centers are working but not in unison with each other. After the positive flow is re-established the person will feel revived in body and mind, the positive emotions reinstituted.

How Your Aura can Recharge

This is a "Workshop Book" for you. You can learn by the mental relaxation exercises outlined here, to re-establish physical, mental, spiritual and emotional harmony. This book will teach you how to recharge yourself for the drive, vigor and zest you need.

Kirlian Photography

Semyon and Valentina Kirlian from the Kazakh State University, Alma-ata, Kazakh, U.S.S.R. have discovered a method of photographing the human Aura. It is called after them: Kirlian Photography.

By their methods, the right forefinger placed on a Polaroid film exposed to a high frequency electrical current will record energy discharged from the body on the film in color or black and white without the use of camera.

The CORONA, a halo-like aura, surrounds the fingerprint. The Corona appears in a variety of colors, intensity and forms. The light, the glow which radiates, is the energy with which we live.

This is a new and strange process. Researchers predict that Kirlian photography has a great potential. It is beginning to get the attention of science. Other researchers concluded from this work that even people's characters can be identified.

The Colors of the Aura or Corona

White—energy and health; *Blue*—energy related to spirituality, harmony and peace of mind; *Red* or *Orange*—sickness, anxiety, tension and fear.

In a particular experiment I was called by a doctor to relax a lady who was suffering physically and mentally. Pictures were taken of her Aura and mine before and after I had worked with her. First her Aura was depleted. The film was dark; no color at all was visible. After I had worked with her for an hour, a picture was taken again, and her Aura was then slightly visible. The strange thing was that *my* Aura had improved considerably, following my work with her. "What you are sending out will come back to you, multiplied."

Some Can See the Aura with Their Naked Eyes

Some people have the ability to see the Human Aura. The late Dr. W. J. Kilner of England invented a filter through which one can see the Aura and then can condition his eyes through the chemicals (dicyanin) on the filter to see the Aura later on without this help. He showed that we have three Auras. The inner Aura is located about one to two inches close around the body. The middle Aura is up to five to six inches away from the body. He claimed that this Aura indicated sick parts or organs of the body and could be a way to diagnose sicknesses. The third Aura or outer Aura reaches out apparently without limit. This supplies the energy you might have felt before, the psycho-electro-magnetic energy field imprinted from our emotions.

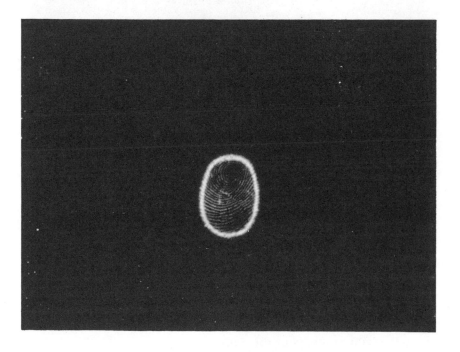

Happily married lady, age 39, well-adjusted, healthy, spiritual, singer, nine children. Picture taken 5:00 P.M. after a long day of many activities, and with a tired, light headache, worried and tense.

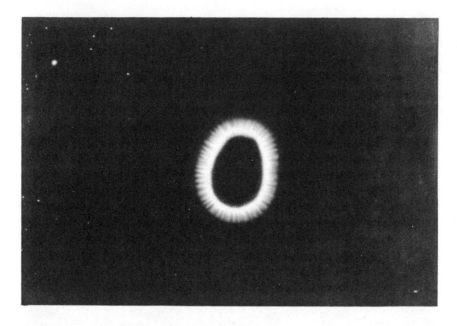

*Same lady. Picture taken same day 5:45 P.M. after Standard Relaxation
followed up by exercises counting down from sixty to zero and Winners' Circle,
marvelous proof for the energizing effect of these mental exercises.*

Our Five Senses Have Limited Faculties of Perception

Once while flying from San Francisco to Tokyo on China
Airlines, I conversed all night with a Chinese Yoga mind teacher. In the
morning, I looked out the window and said, "Look, Master, nothing
but water as far as our eyes can see!" After a few seconds he replied:
"Remember that you are seeing only the surface. It is like the mind.
The depth of the mind is in the Subconscious. It is the deep well of our
energy, wisdom and spirituality."

I only touch on this subject. For most readers it will be enough.
Others may not be satisfied until they investigate further. There are
many books written about the Aura.

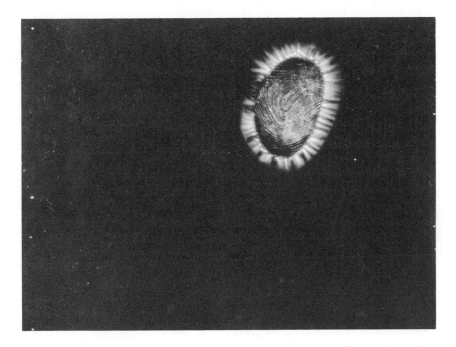

Man age 51
Spiritual, but lacks energy.
Aura broken in several places.
Mentally unstable.
Burned orange in the center of the Aura signifies sickness, and tension.
Psycho-somatically sick.
WHITE = ENERGY
BLUE = ENERGY RELATED TO SPIRITUALITY
ORANGE OR RED = SICKNESS

PART II
CHAPTER 3
SUMMARY

YOUR AURA WILL BE DEPLETED BY
ANGER, TENSION AND ALL NEGATIVE
EMOTIONS AND NEGATIVE THINKING AND ACTING.

YOUR AURA WILL BE RECHARGED EVERY TIME
YOU PRACTICE: STANDARD RELAXATION,
EXERCISE COUNTING DOWN FROM SIXTY TO ZERO WITH
THE CONDITIONING WORD "DEEPER,"
WINNERS' CIRCLE, MEDITATION AND PRAYER

Explanation of the Human Aura
Pictures No. 40, 41, and 42
Exercise to recharge the energy of your Aura.
Standard Relaxation, Part I, Chapter 3
Counting down from 60 to zero
with the conditioning word DEEPER, Part II, Chapter 2

The Winners' Circle

The Ideal Help

Graph of the Winners' Circle

Winners' Circle Exercise in Seven Steps
A. For Recharging Yourself (Inner Circle)

B. To Help Others (Outer Circle)

Pictures Explaining the Hand Movements

What You are Sending Out Will
Come Back to You Multiplied

Your Prayer Seen in a Graph

To the Best of All Concerned

Case Histories: PD $20,000. DH Collect $10,000

My Broken Ankle

Flight From San Francisco To Tokyo

A Business Friend

The Baritone

THE SUPER SUBCONSCIOUS

Research in the past few years has led some leaders in mind-power to suggest the existence of a supra, or super conscious. They see the mind as:

1. Conscious Mind—the center of thought
2. Subconscious Mind—the control center for all involuntary body functions.
3. The Super Conscious—or perhaps better THE SUPER SUB-CONSCIOUS—since it is not under conscious control—but has to be approached and handled in the same way as the subconscious.

This SUPER SUBCONSCIOUS seems to be in continual contact with Infinite Intelligence and appears to be able at will to communicate with others, and exercise all the vast range of mind power known as the E.S.P. faculties.

When you program your subconscious for problem solving, or the Winner's Circle, it is this SUPER SUBCONSCIOUS that comes into play, and reaches out to change the world about you for your good.

Actually it makes little difference whether you envisage this separation into subconscious and *super* subconscious or treat your subconscious as one magic, wonderworking, all powerful entity. The programming of the subconscious is unchanged by these discoveries. After all I have repeatedly told you not to be concerned *how* it brings about these wonders in your life, just be sure that what you consistently imagine and believe, your subconscious, or your super subconscious will bring about in your life.

THE IDEAL HELP

Let me share another story with you. A mother told me that she and her family had lost communication with their son. They just could not reach him any more. The more they tried to correct him, the wider the communication gap became, and eventually the boy left home. The parents were stunned because they had always considered themselves to be well-adjusted, open-minded and liberal.

Fortunately the parents heard and read about Dynamic Mind Training and how people could benefit through mental telepathy (Winners' Circle). Many case histories have shown that parents can communicate with their children through mental telepathy to change their attitudes, and encourage and help them.

These parents had everything to gain, so in an attitude of relaxation, meditation, prayer and a burning desire, they created a mental picture and imagined the ideal situation for their son. They thought harmonious relations between them, and encouraged him to communicate with them. In this state of mind they actually talked with their son. They assured him of their love and created the blueprint of a harmonious, joyful and successful life for him. They knew their son was on a dead-end street, and they felt that they could find a better way for him, if he would just communicate with them. After a very few sessions, their son called them. The mother said that she *almost* reacted as before—"where are you? Why haven't you called sooner? You've put us through hell with worry for you." Instead she reported that she felt calm, and happy to hear from him—concerned—but she didn't pry into his business) she was just glad to hear from him. (If she had acted "normally" his defenses would have immediately gone up.) She told him that she was glad he was all right; happy that he had called. Of course he was welcome to come, if he wanted. She said: "It took a lot of effort not to cry and plead with him to come home, but I didn't and I felt good about it!"

About ten days later, he called again. This time she was again prepared with a calm attitude. She told him that she was glad that he had called. He asked if he could come home and told her where he was, and what he had been doing. He added that he was amazed at her calm and concerned attitude, it gave him the comfortable feeling he needed to ask her if he could come home. Of course she was thrilled to have him return.

In an incredibly short time, there was a great improvement in his life and their relationship. The boy became interested in his education again. New and better friends entered his life, and he became involved in sports. This family knows the Winners' Circle works!

It is a law that what you send out comes back to you.

WINNERS' CIRCLE EXERCISE IN SEVEN STEPS

A. USE THE FOLLOWING EXERCISE TO STEP INTO THE INNER WINNERS' CIRCLE FOR RECHARGING YOURSELF, FIRST.

1. Standard Relaxation (Explained in Part II, Chapter 1).
2. With your eyes still closed, lift both your arms up and make

WINNERS' CIRCLE

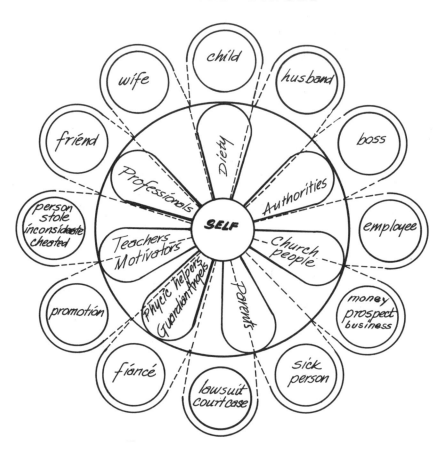

a circle, ending with your palms facing up in a receiving position (see picture). At the same time, think and mouth: "I am thankful that I am permitted to be in the Winners' Circle. I am thankful to be a winner. I wish to recharge myself through my subconscious."

3. "I wish to draw in good thoughts, wisdom, knowledge, effectiveness. Then mention your specific needs and from whom you wish to obtain your help. (Such as Diety, parents, husbands, wives, speakers, motivators, sales people, executives, buyers, organizers, doctors, lawyers, church leaders, BE SPECIFIC). Then state that you are thankful that you can be with all these good

people in the Winners' Circle. This is accomplished with Mental Telepathy—the so-called "Sling Shot" or "Boomerang Method."

You must *want* results. You must *expect them.* Then you will be recharged, rejuvenated and informed.

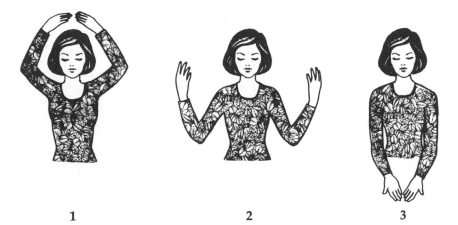

| 1 | 2 | 3 |

B. HOW TO HELP OTHERS WITH THIS EXERCISE USING THE OUTER WINNERS' CIRCLE.

Now you can begin to help and influence others because you have been helped yourself. This is accomplished with the so-called "Sling Shot" or "Boomerang" method (graph outer circle).

Your highly concentrated thoughts will reach the specifically chosen person through mental telepathy. Now say, "I am thankful that I am created this way; that I have the gift, power and talent to help others. I will reach out to influence people for the good they need." If you are used to praying, do this exercise in a prayerful attitude.

How to Solve Arguments Immediately

When reaching out to a special person, imagine that the individual is in front of you. Start a conversation with him or her and mouth every thought. With great emotion and feeling, play-act the whole situation with you playing the part of both persons in the drama. This is the best method of handling arguments, differences of opinion, and misunderstandings. It is a great help in handling your children. One of the advantages is that *the person in question cannot interrupt you*, and you can positively change an unpleasant situation.

What You Send Out Will Come Back to You Multiplied

Peace, love, and serenity govern the time you spend on this exercise. Only good comes from practicing this exercise. You will not be influenced negatively, nor harmed in any way. The Winners' Circle acts like a boomerang. Every thought and wish you send out, *good or bad* will come back to you multiplied many times. Therefore, what you send out must be good, positive and the best for all concerned. Remember! If you send out good you will receive good. If you send out bad thoughts, they will fall back upon you, multiplied many times, as consequences of your actions.

"GREAT MEN ARE THOSE WHO SEE THAT SPIRITUAL FORCE IS STRONGER THAN ANY MATERIAL FORCE: THAT THOUGHTS RULE THE WORLD."—RALPH WALDO EMERSON

Your Prayers Seen in a Graph

One student, a church leader, related to us one day in class: "I have prayed all of my life, but this is the first time I have comprehended what I was really doing. I can now visualize my prayers. I know now that the "boomerang" method is used every time I am in solitude prayer to God. My prayers will be much more effective from now on."

Evaluate the Day

Let the whole day, hour by hour, pass by again at night. Express your thankfulness for all good things which have materialized. Neutralize all negatives and give them a new direction. If there was a misunderstanding or harsh argument, smother it, forget it, for the best of all concerned; always repeating over and over again the arm movement forming the winners' circle.

For the Best of All Concerned."

When you have completed all aspects of this exercise, you close with another arm movement of the Winners' Circle and mouth: "I seal this exercise for the best of all concerned. Thank you." This means that you expect all of the expressed desires in the exercise to be granted for the good of all concerned. Finish the exercise by counting down from sixty to zero with the word DEEPER. After reaching zero, immediately count up from zero to six. Counting up from zero to six is the ENERGIZER. This exercise will bring you the added benefits mentioned in the Chapter on "Counting Down Exercise From Sixty to Zero with the word DEEPER" (Part II, Chapter 2).

The Whole Secret of Success Is Expectation

If you let your mind dwell on "How, When, Where or What," success will fly away from you. With expectation, faith and trust you will attract victory to yourself. All good things will then be materialized in your life and in the lives of others. "Nothing comes from nothing—nothing ever will."

Don't try to make it work, JUST LET IT WORK. Sit back, so to speak, and turn it over to HIGHER POWERS. I invite you to practice the exercise several times daily. I promise you that it will change your life and the lives of your loved ones, friends and acquaintances. Try it out. It is a powerful mental exercise, based on an universal law.

To show you how effective this exercise has been for others, I will relate some actual experiences.

$20,000 ANNUALLY

A young student, newly graduated from college, had a part-time job in an advertising company. The working conditions and pay were not ideal, and he decided to work a few times daily with the Winners' Circle, so his ways would be crossed with a person who could offer him a better position. He expected earnings up to $20,000 or more a year.

Shortly thereafter he met a forgotten friend on the street who offered him a challenging job. He reported to the class that after only four weeks, he was well on schedule with his commissions. He was very happy and planned to get married.

Isn't it exciting what people can do, after they make up their minds and set goals? You, too, have probably heard the advice, "Make Up Your Mind." But how do you make up your mind? Most probably no one has ever answered that question for you. Don't hesitate to use this mental exercise. Today starts the rest of your life. You too can be a Winner.

COLLECT $10,000

One of our students, a distributor for a nationwide company, had to collect a long overdue account of $10,000. His employees had tried many times without success. Everyone thought that it was impossible. My student had just attended our Seminar, and decided to give the Winners' Circle exercise a try. He needed the money badly. He had heard me say many times, "What the conscious mind can conceive and believe, the subconscious can achieve for you."

He reported to the class: "I really was obsessed by this mental exercise. I had no doubt. That is why it worked for me. I collected all the money." The customer told him: "Do you know I could never have met my obligation to you now if an unusual, unexpected deal had not suddenly come through!"

A coincidence? No. It was a typical chain reaction started by the Winners' Circle through the subconscious. It always works for the best of all concerned. It involves lives and circumstances in different areas so *everyone* will benefit from it.

Let me tell you some of my own experiences.

MY BROKEN ANKLE

Every disadvantage has the seed of greater advantages imbedded in it. Once I was in Stuttgart, Germany. War had been declared. The city lights were dimmed at night. I was standing on a traffic island waiting for a street car, when a soldier came running toward me. He ran into me, and hit my left foot with one of his heavy army boots, breaking my ankle. My first reaction was anger. My plans would be stopped. I was very busy. A heavy workload rested on my shoulders. I had just become engaged and my fiancee was waiting for me!

A policeman was kind enough to drive to her home and tell her of my accident. He said, "I have to tell you that your fiancee is in the hospital." She was very shocked, but recovered enough to ask: "What happened?" "He broke his foot," he retorted. She sighed with relief and murmured joyfully: "Thank you very much!" This was too much for the officer! He left and muttered to himself about how crazy some people are.

Do you know why Charlotte acted this way and was even thankful? She sensed the advantage immediately. The broken ankle stopped me from being drafted into the Hitler Army and kept me from military life throughout the war. I had used the mental exercise of the Winners' Circle regularly so that I wouldn't have to go into the Nazi Army and fight the Allies. See the peculiar way in which the subconscious works? I was able to work however and advanced rapidly to be a special representative in my company. See how much this disadvantage brought into my life?

FLIGHT: SAN FRANCISCO—TOKYO

Our son, who was flying for an airline in the Orient, invited us to take a study trip. This was during the energy crisis. We were supposed to fly with Japanese Airlines but couldn't get reservations. They recommended China Airlines. I called China Airlines and was informed: "We only fly twice a week and we are sold out for the next six weeks." At that moment I had a precognition that we would be able to get on China Airlines.

It was Friday and we had to catch a plane on Sunday in order to meet our schedule. I said to the Chinese lady over the telephone: "Please make reservations for Mr. and Mrs. Kurt A. Schneider for Sunday, Flight #2." She exclaimed: "Didn't you understand me? We are sold out." I answered: "Yes, I understand, but *please* write my name down on your waiting list." She replied, "Sir, it's useless!" Again I pleaded, "Will you trust me please? I know you will have two seats for us."

My wife had been listening to this strange conversation and wondered: "Don't you think you are going a little too far? I trust your precognitions and promptings, but this takes more faith than I've got."

I began to do the Winners' Circle exercise immediately. We packed for our trip to the Orient, and flew to San Francisco that Sunday. Without a doubt in my mind, I approached the counter of China Airlines. I gave them our passports and asked for our reservations. The clerk excused himself. After a few minutes he came back and asked me: "What section please, smoking or non-smoking?" I replied "non-smoking, please," and the tickets were issued!

We were the only Caucasians on the plane! Maybe the couple who originally had had our seats had decided to stay in the United States a while longer. Who knows? I had conditioned this situation for the best of all concerned." You can do the same thing and achieve success and harmony through the Winners' Circle exercise.

A BUSINESS FRIEND

I had just come back from extensive travel in the Orient. At that time I was still in the Insurance business. During a visit with a business friend in his office, he asked me nervously, "Have you paid my premium?" I said, "What premium?" "The cash I gave you to pay for my accident policy," he replied. "I had an accident and the policy had better be in force."

He described in detail how, when and where he had paid me.

He had not, of course. I had been in the Orient at that time! I stayed calm but assured him that I had never received anything from him. He became so upset that he pushed me forcefully from his office.

I hurried back to my office and put him in the Winners' Circle. I had a psychic conversation with him just as though he was present. That way he couldn't become angry with me, nor even interrupt! I poured my heart out to him, asking him to call me up and tell me the truth. Moments later, my wife called to say, "A man called. He seemed upset and gave me this number for you to call." I knew immediately who it was.

The Winners' Circle always works? I called his office. He asked me to forgive him, saying, "I don't know what came over me. I wasn't myself. You know that isn't like me at all!"

You can bridge the communication gap with your partner, your children, friends or customers or even enemies. There is no limitation; the Winners' Circle exercise is a marvelous mental tool.

Imagine knowing how to influence and help others for the best of all concerned.

THE BARITONE

Let's discuss the case of my friend Bill. This man has an extraordinary, deep baritone voice. He said to me one day, "I wished I had not missed my chance as a young man. I had an appointment to audition for a great bandleader who had his own TV show. He was impressed with my voice, and gave me an opportunity to sing before his audience. 'Shall I hire him?' he asked the audience. 'Yes,' they roared, and applauded enthusiastically. 'Come back later with a toupee,' I was told by the director. Accordingly, I shopped around for the right toupee. I had a difficult time because there were not many places to choose from. When I finally came back, after two months, with my custom-finished hairpiece the position had already been filled by someone else. I see now that I should have tried earnestly for another chance, but I was discouraged. I had too little self-confidence. I forgot show business. Many have said to me, 'With a voice like yours, so much better than others who have succeeded, you should be in show business and thrill thousands with your singing.'

Let us analyze Billy's life:

1. He did not recognize the "once-in-a-lifetime chance" soon enough.
2. He should have gone back periodically to check with the bandleader.
3. He should have looked for a manager or tried another bandleader.
4. He did not have the determination and fortitude to press forward and follow through. He lacked the knowledge to make things happen through programming, and hang on until he finally succeeded.

At age 53, he still has a chance. All he needs is a positive mental attitude and the knowledge of the Winners' Circle and his subconscious .

His ways can still be crossed by the right person to discover and promote him. Is he too old? No. Is it still possible? Yes.

PART II
CHAPTER 4
SUMMARY

1. Proceed with Standard Relaxation
2. Lift up both arms and describe a circle and express thanks that you are permitted to be in the Winners' Circle (see Pictures 40, 41, 42)
3. Recharge yourself from Higher Powers, from people you admire and like to emulate.
4. Help others with mental telepathy. Form a new circle for each person or case.
5. Close with another circle and seal everything you did with the wording "for the best of all concerned." End the meditation by counting down from sixty to zero with the conditioning word DEEPER.
6. Arouse yourself by counting up from zero to six for psychic energy.

How to Interpret Your Dreams

Have you been fascinated, amazed, sometimes even frightened and baffled by your dreams? Now you can learn to interpret your own dreams with the help of your subconscious mind.

HOW TO INTERPRET YOUR DREAMS WITH THE HELP OF YOUR SUBCONSCIOUS MIND

Dreams are projections from your subconscious. *You are best qualified to interpret your own dreams.* Don't rely on others. Learn to interpret the language and projections of dreams, they are messages from your subconscious.

Have you ever seen the small stenotype machine that court stenographers use to record the procedure? It can be compared to the language of the subconscious, the dream. You simply have to learn the symbols and relate them to your daily life.

Prayer, meditation, and relaxation are the means to an understanding of your dreams. *Relaxation* is the way to tune in. *Prayer* is speaking to God. *Meditation* is listening to God who reaches you through your subconscious mind.

The dream may be the answer to questions which you have mulled around in your conscious during the day. The dream is a blueprint, a precognition, which precedes reality. Lack of understanding of the working method of the subconscious, lack of interest, materialistic attitudes, and impurity of body and mind are the reasons many people cannot interpret their dreams.

WHAT ARE DREAMS?

What are dreams? Everyone dreams. Psychologists claim that we dream several times every night. You might say: "Why be concerned about a dream? Of what importance is dreaming anyway?"

Dreams are vitally important to our health and well-being. Dreams have messages which we should heed and interpret for our own happiness, protection and success. Dreams can shed light on the mysteries of life.

Think of it this way: Dreams are a reflection of the general nature of our subconscious mind. Dreams intensify our inner awareness. Dreams are the symbolic language, the projection of the subconscious, which speaks in mental pictures, symbols, emotions and desires, the only language it knows. Your dreams are communications between the subconscious and the conscious mind. Why don't most people remember their dreams? They do not pay attention to them. Dreams are mental pictures which will fade if we don't pay heed to them. When you awake, you should seek to remember your dreams even if at first they are hard to hold on to. There may be a message of great importance hidden somewhere in them.

Be guided by your subconscious mind. This inner mind knows far more than you are consciously aware of. Just reflect on any important issue and then turn it over to your subconscious. *Everything in your dreams concerns you, your future and your environment.*

Conditioning Yourself to Respond to Dreams is Easy

Always keep a notebook on your nightstand so that you can immediately record your dreams. From time to time apply this mind-track formula before you fall asleep:

I want to dream, be guided, warned and receive solutions to my problems. *I expect* to dream and receive creative ideas, spiritual understanding, and all the phenomena of E.S.P.
I am going to have positive and meaningful dreams for me and for others. *I know* uplifting and helpful *dreams are mine,* for the best of all concerned.

In a dream you get the guidance of your subconscious. With mental telepathy you can be tuned to others who need you or whom you need. God can reach you in a dream, when your conscious mind is at rest.

It is interesting to read what Job had to say about this: "For God speaketh once, yea, twice, yet man perceiveth it not, (consciously too busy with activities during the day to hear God). In a dream, in a vision of the night, when deep sleep falleth upon men, in slumberings upon the bed, then he openeth the ears of men, and sealeth their instructions. Job 33:15-16. (Conscious relaxed, even asleep—subconscious can't sleep.)

DREAMS ARE THE BEST PROOF THAT THE SUBCONSCIOUS NEVER SLEEPS

You dream when you are asleep. Your body needs natural sleep and must have this rejuvenation. Start to program your subconscious. Give it assignments and expect promptings, intuitions, guidance, protection, warnings, information, and solutions to your problems. You will experience greater dream activity.

After awakening in the morning, while a dream is still fresh and vivid in your mind, ask for an interpretation. *This is IMPORTANT.* You must learn to understand the language of the subconscious. Dreaming is a higher form of symbolism than we are used to. It seldom shows pictures relating directly to your real life situation, but gives you ample clues to the solutions to your problems.

LET ME GIVE YOU TWO EXAMPLES:

The Insurance Case

It looked promising, but suddenly things went sour. I thought I had lost the account. (Salesmen know how terrible it feels to lose an account after you've worked on it for months!) Matters looked pretty bleak. Then I had a dream: two hoodlums cornered me in a dark alley and tried to stab me in the back—to kill me. Miraculously, I escaped. What had this dream to do with my case? I asked for an interpretation and received an answer: "You are surrounded on two sides (the two men) by men who are dishonest and unfair (in the dark alley); the fight is not business-like. (They may try to stab you in the back.) New facts and new solutions are coming up; don't give up; hang in; fight! (My miraculous escape? You will win the case.) I won the case.

Interview on a Two-Way Radio

A Disc Jockey related a dream to me which he had had repeatedly over the years, though he paid little attention to it. In his dream he entered a beautiful castle. He saw many precious things and was told that there were fabulous jewels and treasures in the basement. Every time he entered the spiral staircase, he found himself moving through spider webs, rats, and mice. He had almost reached his destination several times but he always became frightened and ran out of the castle. He asked me, "what does the dream mean?"

I paused to let the right impression come to me. A strong feeling came and I told him: "You are afraid of life, afraid to change your job; afraid even to get married." (I did not know that he was single.) "You have not yet learned to make decisions. If you do decide on something, you don't follow through because you are afraid." He said, "You're right! I can see it now. You have accurately read my life."

Recurrent Dreams Show That Your Subconscious Wants to Instruct You

"Please listen and act before it is too late."

See how easy it is? Everyone can do it. You can train yourself to interpret your dreams. You have a built-in Genie. Your subconscious is wise and powerful. Just keep reading, and you will learn how to interpret your own dreams.

FIVE STEPS TO INTERPRET YOUR DREAMS WITH THE HELP OF YOUR SUBCONSCIOUS MIND

Follow the Five Easy Steps:

The First Step:

Want and *Expect* dreams to warn you and help you make decisions in your daily life.

The Second Step:

Recall your Dreams in Detail. If it seems meaningful to you, make a mental exercise immediately, DON'T WAIT. *Do this by bringing back every detail of your dream. Don't be concerned about the meaning yet. Just see your dream in your mind's eye again and again, just as it was.*

The Third Step:

Ask for the Interpretation. Ask in relaxation for an interpretation when the dream is still vividly in your mind whether in the middle of the night or in the morning. State through your subconscious that you would like to know the meaning of the dream. "Has it any meaning for me? What do I have to do? If it is not my concern, for whom is it then? What can I do?"

The Fourth Step:

Standard Relaxation. Proceed with Standard Relaxation. (Part I, Chapter 3)

The Fifth Step:

Count Down—Relax—Listen. Count down from sixty to zero with the conditioning word DEEPER (Part II Chapter 2). Why should you count down? So you will *consciously* forget your dream. Don't try to make anything work! Just let it work. During this easy relaxed counting, with the word DEEPER, you may expect the answer. Flashes of interpretation—clairvoyance—precognition, the whole scale of E.S.P. will work for you. As soon as you have an impression, stop counting. Arouse yourself by counting up from zero to six and *act according to the promptings.* Don't hesitate. Just do what you are told to do. Don't waiver—*A C T!*

Did you think something so good could be so easy? It works! I promise you it will work for you.

Let me share with you some experiences of mine.

CHARLOTTE'S DREAM AND MY ESCAPE

At the end of the Second War, my wife and I lived in the Black Forest in the French occupied zone. One day I was arrested right in front of my home. French soldiers took me away as a prisoner of war.

A curfew had been set which I had not heard about, and I arrived home just a few minutes too late. The French soldiers forced me into a truck while my wife watched from the window. Nobody was able to do anything about it.

For weeks I starved in a French prison camp. Once the guards accused the prisoners of having poisoned the commanding officer. We were assembled on a field, surrounded by machine guns, and threatened with death if the officer should die. Fortunately he survived and we were marched back to the camp.

After four weeks we were herded to the railway station. I sensed through E.S.P.: "They will transport us to France to work for them at hard labor," which proved later to be their plan. I meditated on an escape plan. Since many soldiers were guarding us with machine guns, there was no escape by running away. I was clearly informed by clairaudience (as if by a voice in my ear) not to act hastily. I would be prompted later as to what I should do.

In the railway station, the soldiers pushed us with their rifles into open freight cars, like a herd of cattle. I became a little nervous. I thought, "This is carrying this a bit too far." I looked up and thought, "God, do you want me to be killed or taken away from my family?" Then a passage of the Old Testament flashed into my mind: "Have not I commanded thee? Be strong and of good courage, be not afraid, neither be thou dismayed; for the Lord thy God is with thee whithersoever thou goest." (Joshua 1:9) Other encouragements from the Bible flashed up in my mind, such as: "Let not your heart be troubled, neither let it be afraid." (John 14:27).

I received a direct assurance through this, since Bible verses were the last things that normally came to my mind. Suddenly, the spirit commanded me to jump from the car. It was as if I were pushed by a higher power. Soldiers with machine guns came running from all directions. I stood straight and unafraid. Then I pushed them away. They lowered their guns, which had been pointed at me. My actions stupified those grim-looking soldiers. The looks on their faces indicated fear and respect. I spoke English to them, I don't know where it came from: "I am in the service of America. I am on an important mission." One of the officers understood my English and called the station commander. I told him my story in a more forceful manner, with strong body language. He released me! Then I was escorted into the town where the French Captain in charge was stationed. I related my story to him, and I was set free immediately.

During the ordeal, I had lost thirty pounds, and grown a long beard. Before I returned, my wife saw me in a dream, coming up our driveway with a beard like a sea captain. She was assured that all was well with me. Because there was no public transportation I had to walk home. It took me two days. When I finally walked up the driveway, Charlotte looked out of the window and saw me coming just as she had seen me in her dream.

EMIGRATION TO THE UNITED STATES

It had long been my wish to emigrate to the United States of America, but I realized that wishing was not enough. So I started to arouse belief and expectation with the help of my subconscious to fulfill my dream. Even when it seemed hopeless, I constantly believed and programmed and had full expectation that my goal would be fulfilled.

After World War II, a truce was signed, and I collected

testimonies from people I had helped, to offer them to the U.S. Consulate so that we could obtain our passports and emigration papers. It seemed I might realize my goal. The time finally came for us to make the long trip to the American Consulate, located 200 miles away in Stuttgart, Germany. When we arrived there, we were passed from one office to another until we ended in the office of the Vice Consul, a sober and stern woman. She was thumbing through my 1½" thick file, with an attitude of "I couldn't care less!" Suddenly she looked up at me, piercingly and said, "You were a member of the Nazi party, weren't you?" I said, "Yes, I was required to be. You can see from my file I was President of a large steel company. However, I did use my influence to work secretly for the underground." She interrupted me in a loud, unpleasant voice: "Don't give me all those excuses! It's a bunch of nonsense! You cannot emigrate to the U.S.A." She forcefully closed my file, and with extreme hostility in her voice, ordered us to leave.

I could have turned her attention to the many testimonies found in my application. I could have told her about the Jewish people I had saved from concentration camps by smuggling them into the safety zone. How I had helped many a young man to avoid the draft into the Hitler army. How I had freed many French employees from the Gestapo after they had been caught listening to the "Voice of America." I had testimonies that I had provided steel to small businesses and factories, who were manufacturing for private economic needs only and not for the "Hitler Army." Page after page testified that in such incidents I had risked my life, and my family's, and would have suffered badly had I been caught.

This passport refusal was devastating. But at that very moment a still small voice, call it E.S.P. advised me, "don't say a word. Just say, 'thank you' and leave quietly." That is exactly what we did, with tears in our eyes and a lump in our throats. The dream of a lifetime had vanished. We couldn't believe it. We had been so sure we would receive our passports this day. I was upset, desperately upset. Depressed, disappointed, we drove home.

That night I prayed as I never prayed before. I felt like Jacob, wrestling with the Lord. I pleaded with the Lord, crying: "If you want us in America, please do something. Otherwise, tomorrow I will have to buy a house and stay in Germany." Sometime during the night I began to dream. I saw myself in a certain Office Building in America, being guided across all the marble floors and being introduced to the Authorities in their mahogany paneled offices. I was congratulated for my achievements, and for my decision to come to America. When I awakened in the morning, the dream was so vivid in my mind that I asked for an interpretation. Clearly I felt the instruction, "Go back to the consulate again; you will receive your passport. Your place is in America."

When I told my wife, she said: "I had begun to doubt your intuitions and promptings, but if this comes true, you are my Hero again!"

We drove the long road back to Stuttgart and started all over at the Consulate, beginning this time at a different desk. At last we were ushered into the office of the same Vice Consul. As we approached her desk I saw that she was so involved in reading my file, that she did not notice our entrance. We stood there silently. She read page after page. Finally she looked up, walked around her desk toward us, reached out and shook hands. She smiled and enthusiastically proclaimed: "Congratulations, you are welcome with your family in America. We need people of your courage in our country. Please go to room 202 and receive your passports."

This time tears of joy and thankfulness filled our eyes. We stood in the hallway in front of room 202, hugging and kissing each other, expressing our excitement and gratitude. Sixty minutes later we were on our way home with our passports.

When we arrived in Salt Lake City, a close friend invited us for a sightseeing tour of the city. He didn't know of my dream. He took us to an office building where he had his own office as an interpreter. There he introduced us to some of the Authorities. We saw the mahogany-paneled offices, marble floors and stairway in the office building that I had seen in my dream.

If we ever needed confirmation of the power of prayer, or proof of the value of subconscious mind training, we now had it. What you think, concentrate on, decide, desire, pray for, expect and accept thankfully in advance, your subconscious will materialize with the help of the universal power in your daily life. We are limited only by the boundaries set by our *own* minds and imaginations.

I hope you will catch a spark of the possibilities that are in the realm of the mind. They can enable you to master your life with mental discipline and faith. Are you thinking: "I am too busy. I can not devote time to mental exercises, meditation, and prayer." If so, you are living the hard way. Don't try to conquer life with will alone. "Let it work." Just turn all your problems over to the subconscious. Wait for promptings and intuitions and then act accordingly. It will work for you, too.

BUYING TRIP TO THE STEEL MILLS

The term E.S.P. was not used much in my youth, but the psychic phenomena it describes were very much in evidence. Clair-audience, clair-vision, precognition and mental telepathy were experienced by mind teachers and students alike. Their teachings encouraged me to want and expect these psychic gifts. I educated myself to be alert for all sorts of psychic experiences.

During the second World War, I was president of a large steel company at Strassburg. Even though I was young, I had been given the responsibility for building a warehouse, a harbor, an office and guest building. Almost everything was rationed, and steel was hard to obtain in any form during the war.

One night I had a dream that I should drive to a certain steel mill to buy the materials I needed for customers. The war was on, but France had not yet been invaded by the allies. The heavy bombing had not yet begun. In accordance with the dream, I went to this mill, anxious to know what the outcome would be. I represented a well-known, highly-respected business name in steel and was therefore very well received. What I needed was not available, but the executives were friendly. I was disappointed because my dream-precognition, which had been so clear and forceful, seemed to have failed me. I decided to leave empty-handed.

By this time it was late afternoon and my chauffeur said, "It is too dangerous to drive at night." We decided to spend another night in that city. That night I had another dream in which I saw myself back in the mill again, getting a huge amount of steel. In the morning, I told my chauffeur, whom I had educated to help me in my business, that we would go back to the mill again. He asked: "Why? They said they didn't have anything for us." I replied, "I don't know, but I was told to do so." "Did they call you last night?" he asked. I answered, "Not by telephone, but by mental telepathy."

When we entered the office of the manager, he was dumbfounded. He couldn't believe it was us again. He exclaimed: "Do you know that I have been thinking about you all night? I was sure that you had left and I had no way to get in touch with you." I said, "You did." When he inquired how, I replied, "With mental telepathy. It is faster and cheaper than the telephone."

He said, "I have something to offer you." I excitedly replied, "O.K." He took us out in a field and showed me his surprise. There were tons and tons of heavy, large, thick steel plates stacked in odd sizes. I questioned, "What in the world do you expect me to do with this material?" He said, "I don't know, but you may have it without steel ration stamps and at half price. He said, "I don't know why I thought of you, but I couldn't get you out of my mind."

I stood there, doing my mental exercise to solve this problem. The dream and precognition flashed back into my mind and this time an answer came to me: "THIS IS IT. BUY IT!" I thought, "Do you want to get me fired? Nobody will ever buy it!" The clairaudience came through loud and clear to me again, "BUY IT!" I turned and said to the manager, "It's a deal. I'll take all of it." He couldn't believe his ears and said, "Are you sure? All of it?" I said emphatically, "YES."

Three large canal boats full of the heavy odd-sized steel plates arrived two weeks later in my harbor. It was much more than I thought. What a sight! I was the laughing stock of my colleagues. To make it worse, the big boss of the Cartel announced a visit with many other leaders of the steel industry to see the new buildings and harbor. I would have liked to disappear into a hole, and take the hole with me!

The big boss was accompanied by three other leading steel tycoons and their secretaries. He wanted to brag about my building program, even with a war going on. When they saw the enormous stacks of steel, approximately three hundred feet long, ninety feet wide, and fifteen feet high, they just about passed out. I will spare you their curses while they were inspecting the steel. Would you doubt your own E.S.P. in such a case? But I persisted. I pleaded: "Please give me time. I will prove to you that my decision was right." I didn't know why, but I had faith in my E.S.P. I had accomplished much in the past. I had earned the trust of my employer, and he knew this was not the first time I had done something unusual.

Two months later, the heavy bombing started in Germany. Bridge after bridge was destroyed. Every construction company cried for heavy steel plates to repair the damaged bridges. Who do you think had these heavy steel plates? Any and all prices were offered. We sold them all over the country like hot cakes! Praise came from all sides, and best of all, I received a big raise.

PART II
CHAPTER 5
SUMMARY

1. How to interpret your dreams?
    a. Bring your dream vividly back again into consciousness.
    b. State that you would like to have the interpretation and be informed about the meaning
    c. Proceed with Standard Relaxation
    d. Expect the Interpretation
    e. Follow up with the exercise counting down from sixty to zero with the word conditioning word DEEPER to forget all about your dream
    f. As soon as you are informed about the meaning, stop counting down and arouse yourself by counting up from zero to six to recharge your psychic energy at the same time
    g. Act on your answer right away. Don't put it off!

PART III

How to Program Your Subconscious Mind with the "Positive Affirmation Card Method" for Weekly Short Term Goals

The Funnel
Almost
Mental Exercise in Eight Simple Steps
THANK YOU Method
How to De-Materialize Intruding Negative Thoughts
Digging Ditches "AS IF" Method

THE FUNNEL

From Nuremberg, a large modern, industrial city in Germany, comes the story of the "Funnel of Knowledge." A man had a funnel which he used to pour knowledge into the minds of people. He had a flourishing business. People are always interested in finding a shortcut method which does not involve personal effort. Would you be interested in such a funnel? Of course.

Something like that really is available to us. It is not a funnel, or any other sort of gadget, but it is the proven, successful method of programming the subconscious.

It may appear too good to be true, but thousands of case histories have shown that such programming is incredibly successful. "The proof of the pudding is in the eating." What is "Programming The Subconscious?" Your mind has a subconscious faculty, like a kind of computer. This computer, like any other computer, can be programmed for action. How can such programming help us? All our goals and ambitions, can be programmed into the subconscious. Learn to relax body, mind and emotions. Then with a burning desire and using mental pictures and imagination, the language of the subconscious, programming can take place. WHATEVER YOU PROGRAM WILL GROW TO ABUNDANCE IN THE SUBCONSCIOUS. You will experience a feedback, being compelled by your inner self to act and to complete the programmed ideas and goals.

Use the following affirmation: "Every day I will learn and experience something *NEW*. I can—I will—I do accomplish this."

ALMOST

If you want steam and boil water to only 211 degrees, you will get "almost steam." But if you heat the water just *one* more degree, to the boiling point, and keep it at that temperature, all the water will be transformed into steam.

I have met many a salesman who has *almost* closed a sale, and *almost* received the commission. Many marriages turned out *almost happy. Many students almost* made the grade, but quit too soon and dropped out. A miner was once told of a tremendous vein of gold and had his crew tunneling in the right direction. But after digging day after day, and month after month, he became discouraged. Finally, he gave up, sold the machinery and left. Someone else started over again, and after a few more blasts, struck the gold. The first miner *almost* did it.

How many of you have just missed an advancement in your work, have *almost* achieved a promotion?

Studying the lives of successful people and interviewing them, I found two reasons why people succeed: *first,* they selected a worthwhile goal and pursued it with great determination. They followed the advice of Dr. Napoleon Hill in his famous book, *"Think and Grow Rich."* A quitter never wins and a winner never quits.

Second, they have a happy-go-lucky attitude. Somehow luck steps in with great force and gives the person the last push. "Luck" is a Fundamental Law of Right Thinking, too. Basic rules obeyed will associate the right thoughts and can lead a person to his luck. These mental laws work independently of other laws. The following affirmation can produce the flow of luck prepared and created by the subconscious: "The genius in me will be released, and the design and plan of my life manifested to me. I will always be happy, and lucky going toward my goal."

NOTICE: THE FOLLOWING EXERCISE IS NOT DESIGNED
TO TAKE THE PLACE OR THE HELP OF A PHYSICIAN,
PSYCHIATRIST, PSYCHOLOGIST, OR PSYCHO-THERAPIST.
THE PURPOSE OF THIS EXERCISE IS TO ENABLE EACH
INDIVIDUAL TO BECOME WHAT HE OR SHE DESIRES TO
BECOME. MANY MINDS ARE CLOUDED, CONFUSED AND
UNSETTLED. I WISH TO MOTIVATE AND STIMULATE RIGHT
THINKING AND RIGHT ACTION.

MENTAL EXERCISE FOR PROGRAMMING YOUR
SUBCONSCIOUS. SHORT TERM GOAL METHOD:
FOR WEEKLY SHORT TERM GOALS

THE SIMPLE TECHNIQUE:

1. Write your selected positive affirmation on a 3 × 5 card. Sign it, date it, and brand the card with "Thank You."
2. Read the card five to six times—slowly—with GREAT expectation, and ENTHUSIASM.
3. PUT THE CARD ASIDE.

4. Create "Standard Relaxation" (Part I—Chapter 3)
5. Stay in Standard Relaxation approximately three to five minutes.
6. During this period DO NOT COUNT or consciously repeat the words on the card.
7. Don't make it work—let it work.
8. End "Standard Relaxation" and programming of your Subconscious by counting up from zero to six with the "I AM" FORMULA using each sentence with each count from zero to six.

(See #4 Appendix)

The Procedure is as Follows:

Step 1: Whatever your needs are, write an appropriate POSITIVE affirmation—a goal you want to achieve, or an undesirable habit you want to overcome on a 3 × 5 card. Word it *"POSITIVELY."* (It is VERY IMPORTANT that the affirmation IS ABSOLUTELY POSITIVE. See Chapter II for samples of Positive Affirmations)

Brand your card with your name, date it, write on the bottom of the card, "Thank you." "Thank you" means it is already accomplished and on the way to you.

Step 2: *Read the prepared card five to six times. Say it aloud to yourself or just mouth every word with enthusiasm and great belief, and a burning desire for accomplishment, or think and mouth it with the Mind Track Formula* (see following examples)

EXPECT the materialization. There must be no doubt in the conscious that whatever you program will be realized in your life. Although you can't see how it will be done, give your subconscious a chance. Assign this incredible force to bring it to pass. Do it with the attitude of the Mind Track Formula, I and II, and in conjunction with your affirmation (Mind Chart III).

Step 3: Proceed to create the programming state of mind with the Standard Relaxation.

THE SECRET

You are calm, relaxed, and serene, breathing evenly and regularly. Do Nothing. There is no counting with this technique. Stay in programming relaxation for approximately five minutes. Just stay relaxed, and let yourself drift away deeper and deeper into relaxation. Breath evenly and regularly. With every breath of air you exhale, you will experience a sensation of deepening your relaxation and finally leveling off into an appropriate state of relaxation.

Do Not Make It Happen—Let It Happen

Let the ideas from the card sink deeper and deeper into your subconscious. Don't try to make anything happen—let it happen. Don't try to remember the affirmation. Soon the phrase on the card will go round and round in your mind. You might see yourself as having already accomplished it. All kinds of real life situations may flash through your mind. You may see yourself as already being congratulated on your achievement. You may get the feeling of pride, joy and satisfaction of its accomplishment Whatever your experience is, enjoy it and greet it with confidence and thankfulness.

Let yourself by carried away by these positive experiences. Bathe yourself in feelings of faith, trust and expectation, that you can and will master the programming technique, and that success will be yours. Don't force anything. Don't do anything that requires any effort. Let the programming work and develop. Let it sink deeper, and deeper, and deeper into your subconscious. Remember, "WHAT YOUR CONSCIOUS CAN CONCEIVE, AND BELIEVE, YOUR SUBCONSCIOUS WILL ACHIEVE FOR YOU." *Everything is Possible!*

Step 4: End the programming by counting from zero to six, using a sentence of the "I AM" formula with every count. (Part I Chapter 3) All at once, you will feel that your predetermined time of five minutes is up. You will count up from zero to six; and blink your eyes, this will arouse you, and will end the relaxation and programming.

While in this state of mind, you will instantly become aware of anything in your surrounding which might require you to be alert. In such a case, you will instantly awaken. The subconscious has the unique ability of reckoning time and will arouse you when the predetermined period of time, approximately 5 minutes, has elapsed.

THIS IS NOT A LONG CONDITIONING PROCESS. EVERY STUDENT OF THIS EXERCISE WILL EXPERIENCE A POSITIVE CHANGE IN A VERY FEW DAYS.

Even when off guard or in trying situations, the subconscious will guide, compel and impel you to act positively and according to the programmed affirmation.

EXAMPLES FOR THE CARD METHOD: HOW TO THINK OR MOUTH WITH THE MINDTRACK FORMULA, THE CARD, *BEFORE* GOING INTO RELAXATION.

For instance, let's say you want to be POSITIVE.
"I Want to be Positive"
"I expect that I will be Positive in every situation."
"I am going to have this new Positive lifestyle."
"I know that this Positive Mental Attitude is mine."

Or for instance:

"It is necessary for me to have $5000. by . . . . *(date)*
"I want to meet this financial obligation."
"I expect $5000. by . . . . *."*
"I am going to have this sum of $5000. by . . . . *."*
"I leave it up to my subconscious to prepare the way and compel me to right action."
"I know the sum of $5000. is mine by . . . . *."*
"FOR THE BEST OF ALL CONCERNED."

For a Salesperson:

"I want to double, (or more if you desire) my sales and commission."
"I expect promptings, guidance and creative ideas from my sub-conscious."
"I expect a compelling force from my subconscious so that I can and will use my time constructively."
"I am going to up-grade my sales. I am going to be led to the right prospects who need my service, have the money, and can afford it. They will like me and I will like them."
"I know that this increase of sales, and commission—is mine."
"FOR THE BEST OF ALL CONCERNED"

For Parents:

"I want harmony, the best disposition from everyone in the family, love and affection to govern our home."
"I expect peace of mind, harmony, and love from and for everyone in the family."
"I expect that all good things, including financial security, will be realized in our lives."
"I am going to have all this and more for our family."
"I know this inner and outer peace is ours."
"FOR THE BEST OF ALL CONCERNED"

For Someone Who Wants to Find the Right Partner:

"I have prepard myself and want to find the right partner for life."
"This partner should be (name the qualifications you desire)"

"I expect that our ways will cross for the best for both of us. I expect that my future partner will be as well prepared as I am for marriage."
"I am going to have a great life, satisfaction, and security."
"I know that a happy, harmonious, and true marriage is mine."
"FOR THE BEST OF ALL CONCERNED."

You Must Claim It

When you do your programming exercise, you must actually "claim" the result, the goal, the realization for you. You must know that it is already on its way to you. "SEE IT COMING, AND HEAR IT HUMMING." The slightest doubt will postpone your success.

Remember: ASK—SEEK—KNOCK

EXERCISE CONSISTENTLY TWICE DAILY

Standard Relaxation and Subconscious Programming practiced twice daily will give you the wanted success, a feeling of serenity, and freedom from the environment around you. It will give you psychic energy, pep and vitality. It will enable you to calm down at the same time.

Set aside a quiet time each day, preferably at the same time, because the effect is accumulative and results are not obtained after one single exercise.

Many people will be willing to undertake Subconscious Programming when they discover the many benefits to be derived therefrom.

THANK YOU METHOD

You will always awaken happy from any programming exercise, full of zest and confidence, and with an assurance that from now on, the new affirmation will grow and grow until it is a part of you. As soon as your eyes are open, say aloud to yourself, "Thank You." "Thank You; Thank You." Thank you stands for: "it is accomplished." You are feeling the reality. This is the meaning of "believing you have received, and you will receive." Whenever the affirmation pops up in your mind later on, greet it with "Thank You." Lift your right hand upward and say "Thank You."

DON'T BE TEMPTED TO DOUBT OR LACK FAITH AND EXPECTATION. AVOID SUCH THOUGHTS AS:

I WONDER WHEN IT WILL BE REALIZED?
I WONDER WHERE IT SHOULD COME FROM?
I WONDER HOW IT CAN BE DONE?

PUSH YOUR LEFT HAND DOWN FORCEFULLY AND SAY "NO." ALWAYS KEEP YOURSELF IN A POSITIVE MENTAL ATTITUDE OF FAITH, SUCCESS, EXPECTATION AND HEALTH: THEN:

LIFT YOUR RIGHT HAND UP, MOUTH OR SAY "THANK YOU."
THINK OR SAY ALOUD:
I WANT IT, I EXPECT IT, I AM GOING TO
HAVE IT. I KNOW IT IS MINE.

During the Day

Say the positive affirmation from your card with enthusiasm aloud many times during the day. A good time for this exercise is while you are driving your car, or when you are involved in mechanical activities.

Always create a vivid, happy, mental picture of youself having already accomplished your desire. See yourself acting positively in different real-life situations. Read or say the affirmation from memory slowly with belief, and a burning desire for accomplishment. There must be no doubt in your conscious that the affirmation will be realized in your life. Do it with full expectation.

Select a New Card Every Week

Keep your cards in a file box for reference. If you feel that you are slipping back in any particular affirmation, use that specific card *in addition to your weekly card.*

YOU HAVE THE CHOICE
YOU NOW HAVE THE CHOICE EITHER TO REMAIN NEGATIVE, OR TO DO THIS SIMPLE EXERCISE, AND ACQUIRE A NEW SELF-IMAGE, A POSITIVE NEW LIFESTYLE WITH TOTAL SUCCESS.

It is not enough to suppress and submerge your negative thinking and attitudes. They have to be drowned in the depths and immediately replaced with a positive mental attitude.

"AS IF" METHOD

Dr. William James, the father of Psychology, harvested the great ideas of the philosophers, prophets and of the Master. He suggested that we approach our seemingly unsurmountable problems with the method, "as if." The great stumbling block is the word, "impossible," backed up with a negative mental attitude. Man is created that he must imagine, see and believe, before his hopes can become actualized. It is necessary for all of us to see an idea first, before it can be manifested for us.

A student of mine wanted to hear a special tape on Dynamic Mind Training, but didn't own a tape recorder at the time. She bought the tape in good faith and soon someone offered her a tape recorder. Another lady wished with great desire for a beautiful sewing machine in a cabinet. She embroidered a beautiful cover for the cabinet top. Soon afterward, such a sewing machine came into her possession.

We must prepare ourselves for the things we have asked for, even if there isn't the slightest sign in sight for actualization. Every day should be started with an affirmation like the following: "Today is the day of accomplishment. I am willing to do my part. I know my desire will be fulfilled. Miracle will follow miracle, phenomena shall never cease."

PART III
CHAPTER 1
SUMMARY

1. Write your selected positive affirmation on a 3 × 5 card. Sign it, date it, and brand the card with "Thank You."
2. Read the card five to six times slowly with great expectation and enthusiasm. Mind Track Formulas I and II, Mind Chart III (Part I, Chapter 2)
3. Put the card aside.
4. Create "Standard Relaxation" (Part I, Chapter 3)
5. Stay in Standard Relaxation approximately 5 minutes
6. During this period no counting—no conscious repeating of the words on the card.
7. Don't make it work—let it work.
8. End "Standard Relaxation" and programming of your subconscious by counting up from zero to six with the "MY I AM" formula, using each sentence with each count from zero to six. (Part I Chapter 5)
9. Do this exercise twice daily.
10. Select a new card every week.
11. File your cards for reference.
12. If you feel that you are slipping back, use this specific card in addition to your weekly card.

PART III
CHAPTER 2

Positive Affirmations

PRINCE BUDDHA AND THE "AS IF" METHOD

Our guide in Nakorn Pathom, Thailand told us the following story about Buddha at the foot of the world's tallest Pagoda.

In 1625 Prince Buddha was in battle with his army. A epidemic of scurvy broke out, and many of the soldiers were stricken. He prayed, and received the counsel to personally give every soldier a drop of water on his tongue, and to tell him that this was a holy medicine which would bring fast recovery. He did this. The soldiers believed, and it worked! His army won the battle and Prince Buddha became the Lord Buddha.

The placebo effect (a placebo is a harmless substance given to a patient *as if* it were a drug) is the phenomenon by which patients improve merely from a suggestion. What they receive is true healing. Healing occurs even though they actually take a powerless medicine. The effect is psychic healing.

Positive suggestion is powerful. This power has not been fully utilized. It has not even been touched.

To use it, first you have to believe and expect it to work. Act "AS IF" and you already have it. Your subconscious will serve you with whatever you request.

ABRAHAM LINCOLN

Abraham Lincoln said, "You can't help men permanently by doing for them that which they could and should do for themselves." With many stories I have repeatedly encouraged you to use positive affirmations. I cannot do them for you—but I can assure you that they work. Think, or even better, mouth these affirmations, with strong emotion, several times during the day, and especially shortly before you go to bed.

Don't challenge them. Don't look over your shoulder, and question whether they will work or not. The law of Doubt and Fear is nourished by your questions of "I wonder when they will come; where they will come; and how they will come." With such a negative, destructive attitude of mind, you are holding back the powers of your mind. Every time you allow your mind to vacillate, the forces of your mind are cut off. Whenever negative thoughts of how, when and where pop up, push downward with your left hand and say, "NO." "NO" means, "I can wait; I know the forces of my mind are at work." Instantly fill your mind with the law of faith,

success, and health. Then lift upward with your right hand and say with great emotion, "I want it; I expect it; I am going to have it; I know it is mine."

Program positive affirmations over and over again and trust in the infallible ability of your subconscious to engrave them into your life. Soon they will sound in your ears, and you will see them coming with your mental eyes. Stop and dwell on the affirmations with your powerful imagination; enjoy them, and be thankful for them; "AS IF" they were already a reality in your life.

You canot bring about prosperity by discouraging thrift.
You cannot strengthen the weak by weakening the strong.
You cannot help the wage earner by pulling down the wage payer.
You cannot further the brotherhood of man by encouraging class hatred.
You cannot help the poor by destroying the rich.
You cannot establish sound security on borrowed money.
You cannot keep out of trouble by spending more than you earn.
You cannot build character and courage by taking away initiative and independence.
You cannot help men permanently by doing for them what they could and should do for themselves.

—Abraham Lincoln

THE GOLDEN NUGGET

A German legend tells about a man who lost his vineyard to a swindler. This man felt very disappointed, depressed and desperate. He considered taking his life. While in this attitude of mind, he met a well-to-do-stranger, who recognized the frustration of this poor man.

The stranger offered him a golden nugget so he could buy another vineyard. With great appreciation and gratitude the poor man accepted the gold and hurried home. The possession of the golden nugget made him feel rich. His attitude changed. He started to believe in a successful future. No one knew about his gold. He never showed it to anyone. He never sold it. People suddenly came to him and offered all kinds of favors. Finally he gained back his vineyard. He prospered.

Years afterward he met a man who was in a situation similar to the one he had been in years before. He invited this poverty-stricken man to his office and gave him the golden nugget which he had kept all those years. Excited about his newly-acquired fortune, the man took the nugget to a jeweler to have it evaluated. The jeweler told him it was "Fool's Gold," and had no value at all. His hopes were crushed on the spot. His attitude instantly changed to lack, limitation, and misfortune. Unlike his benefactor, his hopes vanished because he thought he couldn't do anything without having money first.

Let yourself be motivated and stimulated. Don't be analytical. Dream a little; "as if" let little joys and happinesses change your life for the better. Be gracious toward others. Always have a word of encouragement and praise on your tongue. Accept the Fundamental Laws of Right Thinking and incorporate them into your life. "What I am sending out is coming back to me multiplied."

THE DETENTION HOME

I once had an opportunity to inspect a detention home. The purpose of my visit was to explain to the staff members and inmates how Subconscious Mind Training can change a negative mental attitude to a positive outlook on life. I was to tell them how a positive self-image can re-program a negatively programmed subconscious, so that a complete new reality acceptance can emerge. I tried to show them how to have love for oneself, and love and appreciation for others. I taught how the purpose of life can be programmed into the subconscious and how self-confidence and self-assurance can be established.

Most of these people had fallen for everything and were too weak to stand for anything. I showed them how a new relationship toward home, school, job and environment can be created; how undesirable habits can be overcome; and how new, lasting character traits can be sown into the fertile mind, and grow to an overwhelming abundance. Hemingway wrote: "Life breaks everyone, but afterwards many are stronger at the broken places."

It was a sobering experience to watch these children, and hear about their lives. Subconscious Mind Training is not a magical formula to solve every problem the first time it is used. Constant repetition is necessary. *After the conscious mind is saturated over and over again with positive affirmations, the seed will and must grow in the subconscious to produce good and desirable fruits.*

The following affirmation, applied in Standard Relaxation, with a burning desire to obtain help, should be used: "Forgetting those things which are behind and reaching forth for those things which are ahead, I press forward. Today starts the rest of a better and well-adjusted life for me."

READING WAS USED AS PROGRAMMING TO GO TO SLEEP

Many people have told me that whenever they have started reading to enlarge their knowledge and education, they have fallen asleep. Considering this problem, I came to the conclusion that in the past, they might have used reading to fall asleep more easily at night. Their subconscious became conditioned and programmed to induce sleep and took it as a command and proceeded accordingly. I recommend strongly that you avoid such an attitude.

You can read and study books which contain a wealth of information. Following a well-planned reading schedule, you can complete an education, or keep up with new developments, by budgeting your time and reading four pages from two to three different books daily. It sounds impossible but little by little, day by day, it will add to your knowledge.

Read with awareness. Mark the books and then give your mind time to weave the new knowledge into that which you have already accumulated. Soon your mind will absorb what you have read like a sponge, and will lead you into new fields. It is wise to work out a plan in what you read: e.g., scriptures, history, literature, motivation or professional books. Reading expands your mind and make you think in new dimensions. It will change your life and give you the strength to cope with your environment.

Let me give you a self-help. Before you start studying, read the following affirmation three times: "During the time I have set aside for 'study-reading,' learning and memorizing, my mind will concentrate and be aware. The new material will be effortlessly absorbed into the subconscious, together with the wealth of knowledge already there, awakening more creative ideas. When I want to recall this information, my subconscious will bring it forth."

SAMPLES OF
POSITIVE AFFIRMATIONS
FOR THE CARD METHOD

The following are examples of "Positive Affirmations" which you may use for the "Card Method." However, be creative and develop your own affirmations according to your personal needs. You know that silverware needs polishing regularly if you want it bright and shiny all the time. Otherwise it becomes tarnished and will be of little value. So it is with the exercise of programming Positive Affirmations and goals.

"KEEP THEM SHINY AND BRIGHT." Exercise twice daily. IT WORKS!

Positive Affirmations

I believe in my inner calling, and in what I am doing. This belief will release Dynamic Mental Energy, from my inner core. Persistency and determination will govern my activities.

This relaxing exercise will make me healthy and happy. It will bring new vitality and endless energy into my life. It will keep me young.

I instruct my subconscious now to give me ___ money, to give me great ideas; to lead me to people who can help me; to make me a success in every goal I am striving for.

Through this "Relaxing Exercise," I now set in motion all the mental forces to bring a steady flow of harmony, happiness, health, abundance, and creativity in my life.

I know that good things need time for materialization. I will not interfere with the developing process. I wait patiently, and expect that all good things will be realized in my life at the right time.

I remove from my thinking any negative aspects of the word "work." I look at it as "self-motivated activity."

I AM BOLD IN ALL OF MY CONCEPTS
I THINK BIG
I ACT BOLD

What my conscious mind can conceive, and believe, my subconscious mind will achieve for me.

My ship is coming in now loaded with abundance. I expect its arrival and I am preparing my life for it!

Thoughts of fear and limitations projected to me from others will now be nullified and transformed into positive vibrations for myself and others.

I will always identify with the positive characteristics of others. I will be guided to seek out interesting, positive and creative people. Successful and truthloving people will be my friends.

I believe in my destiny. Constant programming exercises will open the doors of the universal storehouse for me. I expect the best in every situation.

I want to be great in every way. I will dwell on great thoughts and high ideals. I will constantly seek out and be magnetized to people, books, situations and opportunities that can help me to realize greatness in my life.

With a thankful heart, I have paid my obligations. I expect now that obligations due to me will also be fulfilled.

My subconscious is in charge of healing. I expect now, during this Relaxation Exercise, that damaged and sick cells will be carried away through my bloodstream and will be eliminated. All feelings of sickness are leaving me. I will now be engulfed with radiant and perfect health.

I am thankful for the healing powers in me. I want perfect health. I expect perfect health. I am going to have perfect health. I *know* perfect health is mine.

My depressed condition is caused by a physical imbalance. All decisions are postponed until I feel up to par again. I am directing my subconscious to adjust me physically, mentally, spiritually, and emotionally. I want good health. I expect healing and the best health. I am going to have perfect health. I *know* this adjustment is mine.

I expect that my subconscious will cross my path at the right time with a person whom I can choose for a partner. I expect: friendship, understanding, companionship, tolerance, love, beauty, compassion, integrity, courtesy, intelligence (fill in your own ideas).

I am now neutralizing and undoing the harsh arguments with _____. I am now mentally changing this unpleasant experience and redirecting it to a pleasing situation for the good of all concerned. (For use with Winners' Circle).

I have the courage to face the truth.

Every adversity has the seed of greater benefits imbedded in it.

I can do it—because I believe in the way my mind works. I believe in belief itself. I believe in myself.

Day by day, in every way, I am getting better and better. I WILL DO IT.

I will act enthusiastically. Nothing great was ever achieved without enthusiasm, so I will be enthusiastic from now on!!

There is nothing to lose by trying, but everything to gain. By all means, I will do it now.

I STAND TALL—I SIT TALL—I THINK TALL—I LIVE TALL

I will face my problems in a calm, positive, controlled and intelligent manner. I will be more tolerant of faults in others. I will be more patient and understanding because I have learned how to relax.

I have learned a wonderful way to control my nerves and quiet my fears.

Nothing succeeds like success. I refuse to accept failure, so I am bound to succeed.

I am becoming more engrossed and absorbed in my work every day. The material I am about to study interests me, making deep, indelible, lasting impressions on my subconscious. It is becoming integrated into my personality. The material I have learned will flow freely into my mind whenever I need it. The facts that are stored in my subconscious are instantly released when I need them. They pop into my mind easily and effortlessly at my slightest wish.

I am able to talk and pronounce each word. I shall be able to do this better and better; under all conditions. I will make myself calm and peaceful when I am with people. I will concentrate on what I say rather than how I say it. I am determined not to be discouraged. If I have speech difficulties on any occasion, I will do better next time; I can; I will; I do speak better, day by day in every way.

My mind is infinitely great and powerful. I am determined to endure to the end. I will never turn back. I will never flee, nor will I tremble.

I fear not. I yield not, neither will I hesitate to trust.

I can enjoy driving my car only by obeying and sustaining all traffic laws.

All fear, nervousness, and excitement is leaving me. I am cool, calm and relaxed.

I shall develop unwavering courage, self-control, a keen sense of justice, powers of decision, and the constructive use of time.

My self-confidence and positive self-image is increasing day by day in every way.

There is nothing beyond my reach, or so hidden that I cannot discover it.

I THINK POSITIVELY, AND THEREFORE, I ACT POSITIVELY.

I practice the American zeal to be first in anything I do and to win, and to win, and to win!

That which I think today I will be tomorrow.

I will burn the bridges behind me, set my mind on a definite goal, and notice how others stand aside to let me pass.

THERE IS A BETTER WAY, AND I WILL FIND IT.

I AM AN AMERICAN. I PRACTICE THE LAST FOUR LETTERS, "I CAN."

The only thing I have to fear is fear itself. I am free of fear.

I believe in living each moment, and then weaving those moments together.

Problems are given to me to be solved. By solving problems I will grow. As I strive for higher goals, and purposes and as I associate with good influential people, I become a more successful and better person.

When my conscious accepts an idea, my inner creative power works to bring it to completion, whether I am consciously aware of it or not.

I give thanks that this is already created by my subconscious. I completely identify myself with it. I await with confidence receipt of the equivalent in my life.

I know that whatever is on the way for me can only be good. I give thanks in advance for all good things in my life whatever they may be, and from whatever direction they may come. I set no limits. I am not concerned with where, why, how or when good things will happen to me. I know that everything will come to me in proper order. I give thanks for all these good things in advance. Today and every day I expect the best in every situation.

Positive thoughts create positive emotions. From now on, my physical and mental powers will be awakened and freed in me. The ability to improve in every way is in me. Adversity is a temporary obstacle which I will overcome. I am able to solve all my problems.

Fear and the irritation and annoyances of everyday life will roll off me like quicksilver. I shall be self-assured and confident in every situation.

I feel happy, calm, and tranquil, self-assured, humble and at ease. I feel peace, serenity, tranquillity, and contentment. My body is now being charged with mighty currents of purifying and harmonious energy. My self-confidence is increasing day by day in every way. I am master of my fate. I am in the driver's seat. I am contemplating the future with optimism and security.

I believe I have power to attain what I really want, all that which is good for me. I expect the best and I will attain the best.

I am faithful, self-reliant, positive, and optimistic. I undertake my work with the assurance of success, magnetizing my condition.

Failure is only mental. I think VICTORY and I get VICTORY.

Affirmative thoughts release positive results.

I DO IT NOW!

I shall develop courage, self-control, a sense of justice, definiteness of decision, and definiteness of plans.

With the mighty, magnetizing power of my personality, I will draw to me _____ (use whatever you want)

Relaxation can make me well. I shall now relax. I find it easier every day to maintain a correct diet.

I am developing a distaste for those foods which I know are not good for me, and I am developing a definite liking for fresh fruits and vegetables and other items which I know are good for me.

THE BAT

I once witnessed an experiment wherein a robin and a bat were placed in a room with one open door for escape. The robin flew frantically around and bumped his head against the walls, while the bat, with its built-in radar system, flew around easily, detected the opening right away, and sailed through it.

I have seen people who would rather batter their way through a wall instead of finding the door. We have a built-in system in our subconscious for our guidance. This creative power in us works independently from our conscious faculties. Do we all have it? Yes. It is really only a function of exercise.

All men have the same basic gifts and talents together with the ability to decide between right and wrong, good and bad, positive or negative. To achieve success above the average, we have to apply the Fundamental Laws of Right Thinking. One of these basic laws is: If you constantly use a positive affirmation, a statement, a wish, or a prayer with a burning desire for its realization, you will activate creative faith and power. This in turn will bring what you want into your life. The bat does not have to learn to use its built-in radar system to fly. It knows! So do we! We can always use the powers of our subconscious. We are born with it; everyone has it. All we have to do is use it and apply it for the right purpose. This idea can be reinforced with this affirmation: "I expect that the "I AM," my positive identity, will emerge and guide me on the road to total success."

REDUCING THROUGH PROGRAMMING YOUR SUBCONSCIOUS

(Used as "Card Method")

From now on, my main objective is to LOSE WEIGHT. I eat only foods my body needs for nourishment. I CAN — I WILL and I SHALLY CARRY OUT THIS NEW EATING HABIT PLAN TO A SUCCESSFUL CONCLUSION. I am getting more satisfaction from less food.

I eat only at meal times, sparingly and properly. I reject all fattening foods. I dislike them.

I will stay strictly on the diet my doctor prescribes for me. (Include your specific diet here)

_____

_____

_____

_____

_____

_____

I eat from a smaller plate. I serve myself small portions—no seconds. I eat S-L-O-W-L-Y. I take small bites. I relish each bite as I chew it thoroughly. I take my time. Between bites I wait until I have completely emptied my mouth.

I always create a harmonious atmosphere and pleasant conversation at the dinner table.

I now weigh ____ pounds. I wish to weigh ____ pounds because I will feel much better, and be much more attractive. I am going to consume the excess fat from my body at the rate of ____ pounds a week. In ____ weeks I am going to weigh ____ pounds. Each week I consume ____ pounds of my OWN fatty tissue.

My measurements are now   ____, ____, ____, ____, ____.

I wish to measure: ____, ____, ____, ____, ____.

By this Date: _____.

I desire to be strong, vigorous and healthy. That desire is so great that it is easy for my subconscious to control my appetite and I will automatically eat only the foods that my body needs, in the quantities my body requires. I TURN THIS JOB OVER TO MY SUBCONSCIOUS, WHICH WILL AUTOMATICALLY CONTROL MY APPETITE.

In my daily work and activities, in walking and exercising, I am consuming the reserves of fat that have been stored in my body. This fat is being drawn from the entire body, but especially from the abdomen and hips, the upper arms, thighs, and legs. Soon my figure will be suited to my height and bone structure in an ideal physical form.

GOAL SHEET

Name _____ Date _____

Present Weight____ lbs.   Goal Weight____ lbs.   Goal Loss____ lbs.

Present Measurements: Bust _____ Waist _____ Hips _____

Goal Measurements: Bust _____ Waist _____ Hips _____

Date to Reach Goal_____

IT IS SUGGESTED THAT YOU MEASURE ONCE A MONTH AND
WEIGH ONCE A WEEK. THIS MAY VARY DEPENDING
ON THE AMOUNT OF WEIGHT YOU WISH TO LOSE.

	Date	Weight	Date	Weight	Date	Weight	Date	Weight	Date	Weight
1.										
2.										
3.										
4.										
5.										
6.										
7.										
8.										
9.										
10.										
11.										
12.										

First Month	Bust		Waist		Hips					
Second Month	Bust		Waist		Hips					
Third Month	Bust		Waist		Hips					
Fourth Month	Bust		Waist		Hips					
Fifth Month	Bust		Waist		Hips					

DIET PILLS

Dr. James L. Goddard, Food and Drug Administration Commissioner, stated in a Senate hearing: "No drug can safely control the problem of obesity. At best, their potential is secondary to the elimination of the cause of overeating. There is no easy, painless way for an over-weight person to eat anything and melt off excess fat by taking one or a dozen drugs a day." Does this mean that the obese people who have used drugs in the past are now at the end of their ropes? Certainly not! But it was never the right way to begin with.

If you have a burning desire to lose and control your weight and be well-adjusted, there is a natural way to regulate your weight and eating habits. Obesity is usually the end result of other undesirable character traits. Most people overeat because they are frustrated or depressed, disappointed or nervous, tired or over-worked, lonely or bored, or have failed in different endeavors. We cannot change such negative mental attitudes, or self-images by indulging in food. Food may give a temporary alleviation, but when the excess fat follows we become more upset. This is a vicious cycle. Willpower alone cannot overcome the compelling influence of the stream of negative forces from the subconscious.

First remove or neutralize that which has been negatively programmed into the subconscious. This can be done by positive affirmations programmed into the subconscious during Standard Relaxation and with a burning desire for achievement.

Affirmation: "Less food makes me satisfied. I will eat small portions and will chew thoroughly."

THINK THIN

In collecting interviews I found that Cary Grant the perennially-youthful movie star, had been asked many times his secret for staying slim. His term is, "Think Thin." All our actions originate with thought. Subconscious Mind Training and Programming of the subconscious is an essential technique for success in any endeavor. Thousands have used this new way of thinking and found a new way of weight control. These people picture themselves slim, at their ideal weight, according to their bone structure. In a relaxed state of mind they influence and command this built-in weight control, and program into their subconscious the diet and necessary exercises prescribed by their physicians. Later they will automatically choose the right food and drinks and will be satisfied with *less*. Thus they will reach their desired weight.

As well as being perfectly safe and healthy, this method has another advantage. It programs into the mind positive mental attitudes, new interests, and a new self image, together with self-discipline, happiness and emotional stability. A blueprint programmed into the subconscious will cut a habit-pattern in the subconscious which will echo back into the consciousness with compelling positive force. These four steps followed each day will help you become thin and accomplish anything you desire:

1. You must want it with a burning desire.

2. You must expect it beyond any doubt and believe in the power of your mind.

3. You must see, hear and feel it in advance just "AS IF" it were already reality.

4. You must give "thanks" in advance.

FOR SALESPEOPLE

I.   I will make all my demonstrations and sales as attractive, desirable, and appealing as possible because I want to be a sales success. I will increase my income, become financially independent, and win the esteem of my family, friends and company. I will always make Dynamic Sales-Producing Demonstrations.

II.   My subconscious will lead me to profitable connections. Day after day, I increase my ability to make Sales-Producing Demonstrations because I am inspired with great self-confidence and enthusiasm about my company and its earning possibilities.

III.   I know my business. I know the product. I have confidence in myself and in my company. I will sense sales resistance in the minds of my prospective buyers, and I will be able to answer their objections and questions before they are even expressed. I like people and people like me. By giving honest service, I will be prosperous in all my undertakings. All things good for me will be realized in my life.

IV.   My demonstrations are short but very convincing and geared to create the desire to buy. My personality, conduct and manners are so impressive that my customers always feel relaxed and at ease. Sales resistance is lowered or completely done away with, and all doubts are erased. Total success is a reality in my life.

"Every one gives by selling something."—Robert Louis Stevenson

THE WORLD IS FULL OF PROSPECTS

I. Every day assign your subconscious to furnish you with new leads to prospects. This may be programmed with the following affirmation: "I assign my subconscious to furnish me constantly with leads to new prospects whom I can give my service through _____. I would like to be compelled and guided to act, follow through, make most convincing presentations, and close the sale effectively." This affirmation should be used in Total Relaxation and said loudly many times to yourself during the day.

The leads may pop up during your Total Relaxation Exercise or any time.

II. Every evening program five or more such leads back into your subconscious. This may be done with the following affirmation: "I assign my subconscious the following names for whom I want to make effective presentations tomorrow. I expect that the place and favorable conditions will be prepared so that I can see these prospects in a relaxed, open-minded state of mind. They will like me; I will like them; and they will like my company and my products: _____. All good things are coming my way!!"

PSYCHIC ACCELERATOR

Psychic energy will now stimulate my mind and personality with ideas of how to re-program my subconscious with a burning desire for health, happiness, wisdom, spirituality, and financial independence.

Questions To Your Subconscious Before Relaxation
Is it harmful for me to take _____?
What steps can I take to stop forever _____?
How should I proceed to stop _____?
What benefit can I expect in the future? _____?

PSYCHIC ENERGY BOOSTER: My self-mastery and self-confidence are now so strong that I am able to overcome and quit forever this bad habit

I will
I now stimulate my higher psychic powers in me to give me the strength and courage to overcome my problems and live a normal, healthy, happy, spiritual and successful life. (Use additionally the 31-day "I Pledge To Myself," Part I Chapter 5)

Success Formula

I was a success in the past (Think what you have already accomplished).

I am a Success Now (think on that which you are doing now and what you are accomplishing).

I want to be a greater success from today on. (I want to be at least twice as good and successful or more as I am now.)

I will act according to the guidance from my subconscious.

POSITIVE QUOTATIONS FROM THE BIBLE

A Psycho-Somatic Medicine

For God hath not given us the spirit of fear; but of power, and of love, and of a sound mind. (II Timothy 1:7)

Forgetting those things which are behind and reaching forth unto those things which are before, I press forward. (Phillippians 3:13-14)

Let not your heart be troubled, neither let it be afraid. (John 14:27)

There is no fear in love, but perfect love casteth out fear; because fear hath torment. He that feareth is not made perfect in love. (I John 4:18)

Have not I commanded thee? Be strong and of good courage; be not afraid, neither be thou dismayed; for the Lord thy God is with thee whithersoever thou goest. (Joshua 1:9)

I can do all things through Christ who strengtheneth me. (Philippians 4:13)

If God be for me, who can be against me? (Romans 8:31)

As a man thinketh in his heart so is he. (Prov. 23:7)

Where there is no vision (goal) the people perish. (Prov. 29:18)

With men things are impossible but with God all things are possible. (Math. 19:26)

If thou can believe all things are possible to him that believeth. (Mark 9:23)

Therefore I say unto you, what things so ever ye desire, when ye pray, believe that ye receive them, and ye shall have them. (Mark 11:24)

Whatsoever a man soweth, that shall he also reap. (Galations 6:7)

For the thing which I greatly feared is come upon me and that which I was afraid of is come unto me. (Job 31:25)

But my God shall supply all my needs according to His riches in glory by Christ. (Phillippians 4:19)

The earth is full of the goodness of the Lord. (Psalm 33:5)

Be sure that you think on whatsoever things are true, whatsoever things are honest, whatsoever things are just, whatsoever things are pure, whatsoever things are lovely, whatsoever things are of good report, if there be any virtue, and if there be any praise think on these things. (Phil 4:8)

But others fell into good ground and brought forth from it, some an hundredfold, some sixtyfold, some thirtyfold. Who hath ears to hear let him hear. (Math 13:3-8)

Ask and it shall be given you. Seek and ye shall find. Knock and it shall be opened unto you. (Math 7:7)

Keep thy heart with all diligence; for out of it are the issues of life. (Prov. 4:23)

For I am not ashamed of the Gospel of Christ: for it is the Power of God unto salvation to every one that believeth. (Romans 1:16)

Thanks be unto God for His unspeakable gift. (II Corinthians 9:15)

Thou preparest a table before me—my cup runneth over. (Psalm 23:5)

If ye have faith and doubt not. (Mathew 21:21)

He that is slow to anger is better than the mighty; and he that ruleth his spirit than he that taketh a city. (Prov. 16:32)

Don't be a stumbling block (Romans 16:13)

If any would not work, neither should he eat. (Ecclesiastes 12:11)

Total change of self image vs patch up (Matth 9:16-17)

SMOKING

Daily I am approached by compulsive smokers with the question: "What can I do to stop smoking?" The Fundamental Laws of Right Thinking, Dynamic Mind-Training and the Programming Method for the Subconscious are *sure ways to stop smoking.* You may have tried to quit by will power. You may have quit for a short while, but started again. It is physically painful to stop smoking. You feel nervous and nauseated. You think the only thing that can make you feel good again is a cigarette. Why make it more painful to stop smoking than it need be? Proper use of the subconscious will make it a great deal easier to stop smoking.

Someone once said that he had quit smoking. It was easy; he had quit a hundred times!

Conscious will power is far too weak to stand up against the automatic compulsion to smoke which comes from the negatively-programmed subconscious. What is the best way to push your car? Put the transmission in neutral and release the brakes. It might not be easy to push the car alone, but eventually you will succeed.

My point is that we first have to release inner sanctions just like the brakes on the car. Years ago, you consciously or unconsciously programmed your subconscious for smoking. You smoked to relieve yourself of tension, nervousness or anger. Maybe you tried to overcome a depressed and frustrated state of mind or solve a problem by lighting a cigarette, cigar or pipe. The computer part of your subconscious accepted this practice as a command and method and faithfully repeated the action automatically whenever you were confronted with the same problems.

The subconscious has to be repeatedly re-programmed in total relaxation with the "burning desire" to quit smoking. This is not a hit-or-miss method. Subconscious programming is certain. An affirmation which is helpful: "I find ___ cigarettes a day to be plenty." Change the formula periodically, until you are down to one, and then make a decision as to what you want to be—a smoker or a non-smoker.

THE MOUSE AND THE ELEPHANT

A businessman revealed to me his inner despair. He said, "I am at the end of my rope. I smoke six packs of cigarettes a day; I drink. My nerves are jittery day and night. I lose my temper over every little thing that goes wrong. I am unfair and unconsiderate with my employees, and my family. I find myself throwing things around and slamming doors!"

This was quite a confession! He knew what was wrong with himself. He recognized his frantic way of life, but he still was not able to change. He went on to unload his burden, saying, "I've tried many times, but it seems I haven't got enough will power. I just can't change; I guess I'll have to live with it or kill myself," he said in bitter humor.

My friend is not alone in his misery. Millions are in the same situation. It doesn't have to be this way. You can change. It is not easy, but it is not too hard.

As an illustration, mentally picture a mouse standing before an elephant, and saying, "get out of my way." The elephant lifts his foot, squashes the mouse and goes his way.

Our friend, and all the other millions who are in the same situation, are like the mouse. Why? He said it: "I haven't enough will power." Our conscious will power is the mouse, and the inner negatively-programmed drive in the subconscious is the elephant. This marvelous, miracle-working, incredible power can be negative or positive. If programmed into the subconscious over a long period of time, deeply-rooted habits cannot be overcome by conscious will power. There is only one way to overcome. They have to be rooted out where they are growing, in the computer part, the automatic compulsive section of the subconscious. There is no reason to give up. There is always a better way. Learn it; live it; share it with others.

ORDER AND DISCIPLINE

Emerson said, "I don't know how many books I have read, or how many meals I have eaten. But I know they are all a part of me." Let me rephrase this. I don't know how often as a youth I was encouraged to clean my room, clear my desk, sort my books, keep myself neat and clean, and to check my looks and appearance carefully. I know all of this is now a part of me. It is now done automatically. It has become me.

We have to train ourselves to have order and neatness in our physical environment. This training will develop discipline and self-mastery. It will bring order and discipline to our thinking.

Physical discipline creates mental discipline. When we see that all our belongings are neat and orderly, then our mind tends to be orderly. All of our mental energy will be focused on the matter at hand.

Order and discipline is a marvelous Mind Training tool. Magnetic personality, leadership and salesmanship depend on order, discipline, and self-mastery. Great success in any field of endeavor comes by doing one thing at a time. This one thing at a time has to be done in an orderly manner, and with focused physical and mental discipline. Let's start today to have order all about us without going to extremes. Physical neatness and order is the blueprint and example for our minds. With this simple method we program the computer part of our subconscious for orderly, focused, disciplined thinking.

The following affirmation will be very helpful: "I enjoy order in the house, in all my personal belongings and especially in my work." This will create focused, orderly and disciplined right thinking and acting.

PART III
CHAPTER 2
SUMMARY

POSITIVE AFFIRMATIONS

After the conscious mind is saturated over and over again with positive affirmations, the seed will and must grow in the subconscious mind to produce good and desirable fruits.

WITHOUT PROGRAMMING YOUR SUBCONSCIOUS—
SOMETHING TERRIBLE WILL HAPPEN TO YOU
NOTHING

How to Start Your Goal Book How To Program Long Term Goals Permanently Into Your Subconscious Mind

PROGRAMMING YOUR SUBCONSCIOUS MIND BY MENTAL PICTURES DURING RELAXATION EXERCISES

You are now determining where you will spend the rest of your life.

THE MATERIALIZATION AFTER PROGRAMMING YOUR SUBCONSCIOUS MIND

Have you ever thought that something so powerful could be so easy?

Thomas A. Edison once was asked during a banquet, "what is electricity?" He replied, "I don't know. But it works!" So it is with mental exercises. No one actually knows how the mind works—but it does work! I have heard the late Napoleon Hill end his lecture by saying, "Please swallow it. Everyone who swallows it will be successful."

BLACK FISH

In the Gulf of Siam, I was diving with my son for beautiful, brightly colored corals. Suddenly we saw a huge black fish.

Extremely frightened, we swam back to our boat and climbed in. Later we were told that this fish was able to swallow other fish three to five times larger than itself, just as a python can swallow a whole pig.

So I say, just swallow this whole explanation. Involve yourself in programming. Just do it. I promise you it will work for you.

You too will experience the miraculous change in your life, but you have to program your subconscious first.

Remember: "Whatever you are by nature, keep to it; never desert your own line of talent. Be what nature intended you for, and you will succeed; be anything else and you will be ten thousand times worse than nothing."
—Sydney Smith

YOU TOO CAN ACHIEVE YOUR GOALS

Before I relate the success stories of some of my students, let's lay the cornerstone for a solid, successful life. Think of the many people drifting aimlessly through life without definite purpose. They are dissatisfied, frustrated with themselves, constantly struggling for financial comfort and happiness without making any head way.

Be honest with yourself. Can you clearly state your goals? Can you write down in detail what you want out of life? If not, you may have to do some soul searching. Planned goals are worth whatever the effort it takes. As soon as you are able to crystallize your goals, you will be on your way to achieving them. Then there will not be any boredom, unhappiness nor lack of financial security in your life.

IT IS NEVER TOO LATE

Setting Goals is natural to your subconscious.

Your subconscious is waiting for you to program goals with a burning desire. I promise that this time you will achieve your goals! It's easier than you think. Don't take my word for it. I shall teach you simple mental exercises and mental laws which will enable you to find and achieve your goals. Stick to them with the help of your subconscious. The feedback will compel you to act productively. This faculty of your mind acts as a "Magic Genie" for you, bringing you everything you assign to it.

SUCCESS STORY: LAKE TAHOE MOTEL

Following a seminar on the North Shore of Lake Tahoe, one couple decided to put into practice the principle of "programming the Subconscious Mind." They wanted to sell their property, a motel, containing twenty cottages. The deadline for their goal was three years. They programmed the time, the price and a beautiful big new home for themselves. In less than one year, the property was sold "for the best of all concerned." The deal closed right away. At the same time, a once-in-a-lifetime opportunity came along; a big lodge was available as a home for themselves. They were never without a roof over their heads. What was even more miraculous, the new property was almost next door to their former motel. The children didn't have to be uprooted. They could keep their friends, school, and even the private beach on the lake.

Programming will work for you, too, in all phases of your life!

THE DINING ROOM SET

A student of mine badly needed a dining room set. She went to various stores, but the prices were outrageous for the particular kind she wanted. She could not afford to spend $1,000.00 to $1,500.00 for a set of that kind. She started to program her subconscious for the fulfillment of this need.

One day her car stalled in front of a used furniture store. This was the last place she would have looked. In the show window she saw a beautiful dining room set. It was just like the one she had mentally pictured, and programmed her subconscious to obtain, and at a bargain price! When she tried her car again, it started immediately. She parked it and went into the store. Later on, we were invited to her new apartment and there stood the new dining room set. Truly beautiful! The set was worth $2,500.00 and she had bought it for $600.00. It looked absolutely brand new.

A coincidence? No. The result of programming? Yes. What a saving for a few minutes of exercising.

THE JET TAKE OFF

Each time I see jet airplanes roar down the runway, and rise skyward at incredibly steep angles, I stand in amazement. I was told that a jet has to be going 200 miles per hour before it can climb this way. To take off, it needs 12 to 15,000 pounds of thrust per engine, twice as much power and energy as is necessary after the plane has leveled off in flight. It is easy to understand why the jet is prepared and the throttle tested on the runway, letting the engines run fullspeed to warm up for the take-off. A power failure during takeoff would be fatal.

I have watched the take off of many salespersons, junior executives, proprietors starting a business, or students starting college. Many of these people were complacent, did not seem to have enough will power, desire and endurance to take off and soar. Just as a jet needs many times the engine power for takeoff than for level flight, so we need at least twice the vigor, energy, willpower, and endurance for every endeavor in life if we are to succeed. Later on, when we are succeeding, we can level off, and take it easier. Let me tell you how you can develop this extra energy for a good start:

1. Have a worthwhile goal.
2. Have self-confidence in your ability to reach the goal.
3. Have a burning desire to succeed.
4. Have the endurance to hold on until you achieve your aim.

How can you do it? You may have tried before and failed. Did you try with the programming method of your subconscious?

Join the ten percent who succeed, and start today to arouse the extra energy you need for a smooth and perfect take-off. Use the following positive affirmation: "It is a challenge to me when it gets rough. I expect the best. I think victory. I am positive and optimistic, arousing the extra energy for success."

THE VIOLIN

'Twas battered and scarred, but the auctioneer
    thought it scarcely worth his while.
To waste his time on the old violin,
    but he held it up with a smile.

"What am I bid, good people," he cried,
    "Who'll start the bidding for me?"
"One dollar one, one dollar two,
    two dollars, who'll make it three?"

"Three dollars once, three dollars twice—
    going and gone"—but, no!
From the room far back, a gray haired man
    came forward and picked up the bow.

And wiping the dust, from the old violin
    and tightening the loose strings,
He played a melody quiet and sweet,
    as the caroling angel sings.

The music died and the auctioneer,
    with a voice that was quiet and low,
Said, "What am I bid for the old violin,"
    and he held it up with the bow.

"One thousand dollars, one thousand, two,
    two thousand, who'll make it three?"
"Three thousand once, three thousand twice,
    going and gone," cried he.

The people cheered, but some of them cried,
    "We do not quite understand
What changed the worth of the old violin?"
    And his reply, "THE TOUCH OF THE MASTER'S HAND."

Now, many a man with life out of tune,
    and battered and scarred by sin.
Is auctioned cheap to the thoughtless crowd,
    much like the old violin.

A mess of pottage, a glass of wine, a game,
  and he carries on.
He's going once, he's going twice,
  he's going and almost gone.

And then the Master comes, and the foolish crowd,
  can never quite understand:
The worth of the soul, and the change that's wrought,
  BY THE TOUCH OF THE MASTER'S HAND.

Author unknown

THE VIOLIN

During a performance given by Florian Zabach, this famous musician mentioned that his violin is one of three famous Stradivarius and it is insured for $150,000.00. In the musical piece, *"The Hot Canary,"* which made Florian Zabach famous around the world, he struck tones, combinations of tones and sounds on his violin which were absolutely incredible.

I once visited the world renowned violin-manufacturing town of Mittenwald in Germany. These famous masters in the art of violin-building told me about their painstaking efforts to select wood from hundreds of specimens, and how this wood had to be aged, treated and finally handsawn and carved in a manner kept highly secret and guarded from one generation to the next.

Was it this famous violin of Florian Zabach that brought about these marvelous tones? Yes—and No. For many of us the violin would have been just another piece of wood. We couldn't have elicited one beautiful tone from it. It takes talent and years and years of practice, exhausting drills, repetition and untiring endurance to finally program the finger techniques, grip and musical structure into the subconscious. Such a groundwork is laid by self-discipline and unyielding self-mastery, born in a mind filled with determination and free of doubt, with a burning desire for outstanding accomplishment. Anyone can arouse the faculties of his mind power to such an extent that he has complete confidence in the power of his mind. You and I can become a Florian Zabach in our own field of endeavor if we are willing to pay the price. The rules are:

1. Find the talent.

2. Set your goal in accordance with your call from Infinite Intelligence.

3. Follow through with your plan obsessed with a controlled positive mental attitude, despite obstacles and criticism.

The reward is worth all the efforts.

MALE AND FEMALE

The subconscious and the conscious work in entirely different ways. We sometimes call the conscious a male, and the subconscious female. The conscious has to collect with hard work and willpower all the missing facts for evaluation. The working method of the subconscious is quite different. You only have to flash the mental picture of your goal on the screen of your subconscious. Then this incredible force will work in its own way to put all the missing facts, connections, opportunities, in motion and release from your inner core gifts, talents, capabilities, creativities, extra sensory powers and the inner strength for the accomplishment of the goal.

HOW TO START YOUR GOAL BOOK

HOW TO SET GOALS AND HOW TO PROGRAM THEM INTO YOUR SUBCONSCIOUS MIND WITH "STANDARD RELAXATION"

ANNUAL GOALS—LONG TERM GOALS—LIFETIME GOALS

Have You Set Your Goals?

Have you set your goals? Are they positive? Goals and wishes are controlling your thoughts. Thoughts are controlling your life.

HOW TO PREPARE YOUR GOALS

1. Start a Goal Book—Use a looseleaf notebook with dividers. Some of the basic goals of your life may involve: family, spirituality, community, finances, education, recreation, or health. "Be very choosy . . . upon what you set your heart. For if you want it strongly enough, you will get it!" (Emerson)

Your Subconscious Has No Limitations

Select as many goals as you can think of. Use a divider for every basic goal in your looseleaf notebook. Your subconscious cannot be overloaded; it is working for you 24 hours a day. Keeping your mind on what you want will start the subconscious mind power working, guiding you in thought and action, so that you will attain your objectives.

Make Up Your Mind on Your Goals

Have clearly in your mind what you really want to accomplish. Write your goals down specifically and precisely-in detail. This is very important. Define them; plan them; expect them. *As soon as they are written down, they start to work! Decide what you want—then go* ahead and get it. "YOU CAN'T LOSE FOR WINNING!" Winning is a habit. Nothing can stop you. Develop the Winning Attitude. BE A WINNER. You cannot lose for winning.

Ask Yourself: Is this what I really want? Do I need it?

Is the time right to start now?

Is this in the best interest of everyone concerned?

Be sure your goals are realistic in terms of your talents and the world you live in. To avoid frustration and defeat, goals should not be set at such high levels that they become overwhelming in the light of past performances. Lengthen your stride, they should be challenging.

If you can answer all these questions favorably, then it is full speed ahead, with *all your heart* and *energy.*

THE PROCEDURE FOR PROGRAMMING YOUR GOALS
INTO YOUR SUBCONSCIOUS MIND.
EXERCISE IN FIVE STEPS

STEP I

Read Goals. Sit down comfortably and read all the pages of

your goal book aloud, or mouth every word with great enthusiasm and belief and a burning desire for accomplishment. Expect the materialization in your life. There must be no doubt in your conscious that the goals will be realized in your life, although you can't visualize yet how they will be actualized. Give your subconscious a chance; assign this incredible force to bring to pass what you desire. Read your goals always with the attitude of the Mind Track Formulas, interwoven and in conjunction with your goals.

I want it, I expect it, I am going to have it, I know it is mine. Everything is possible. (Re-read Mind Chart 3, Part III)

Read your goals twice daily, morning and evenings.

It is especially beneficial to read them shortly before you fall asleep.

STEP II

Proceed With Standard Relaxation

(Part III, Chapter 3)

STEP III

Do Nothing

Breathe evenly and regularly, don't try to remember what you have read. Don't make it work—let it work. You may see yourself in real life situations, having the goals already achieved. If your mind tends to wander, focus your eyes, while closed, on the tip of your nose and you will experience the feeling of heightened concentration. Stay relaxed for the programming state of mind.

STEP IV

Arouse Yourself

At the end of that time, count up from zero to six as fully explained with Standard Relaxation (Part I, Chapter 3).

STEP V

Listen

to the promptings and act accordingly.

"THANK YOU" METHOD

Sign your goals, date them, and add "thank you." "Thank you" means that you believe that you have already received them. If they pop up in your mind, it is a good sign that they are on their way to you. They are working, moving and growing in your mind. Greet these thoughts with "Thank you, (believing that you have received and you will receive)."

Never think or say: "I will try; maybe it will work." The thoughts "try," and "maybe" are negative and will fill your mind with doubt and fear. Replace these thoughts with: *"I Can, I Will, I Do, I know it is Mine. All things good for me will materialize in my life."*

A MENTAL PICTURE OF YOUR GOALS THE END RESULT OR WHAT YOU WANT TO ACCOMPLISH CAN BEST BE DONE WITH THE COMPLETE "POSITIVE MIND TRACK" FORMULAS AND STANDARD RELAXATION

THE SECRET OF MENTAL PICTURING REVEALED

Some have difficulties with mental picturing at first. If you do, remember that you are not alone. The problem is usually caused by a misunderstanding of what you may have read on this subject.

You have read that the subconscious computer can't understand words alone. But it is through thoughts and words that your goal has to be expressed. It cannot be done by words alone. The word—the thought—has to be aroused by the vibration of such emotions as *enthusiasm, burning desire, mental picturing, imagination* and *expectation.*

Mind Track Formula I and II (Part II, Chapter 2—Chart 3)

It is enthusiasm which carries the meaning of the words on the positive programming MIND TRACK into the computer part of your subconscious. With the Positive Mind Track Formulas, and Standard Relaxation, *you will be able to hold your Mental Picture long enough in your subconscious for it to sink deep, deep into your subconscious.* "Imagination is more powerful than knowledge."—Albert Einstein

Dr. William James, the father of Psychology in America, stated:

"There is a law in psychology that if you form a picture in your mind of what you would like to be, and you keep and hold that picture there long enough, you will soon become exactly as you have been thinking."

Your subconscious will then work it over and incorporate it into your thinking and acting by way of the "Compelling Positive Feedback" into your daily life.

In my experience, I have found that no one is totally without imagination. Yes, many are negative because they applied this innate imagination and mental picturing ability in a negative way. But this can be changed.

You Must Have Visualization

It is the language of the subconscious. Before there can be realization, you must see yourself not as you are, but as you will become. Concerning other people, do as Goethe said: "Treat a man as he is and he will remain as he is. Treat a man as he can and should be, and he will become as he can and should be." (Johann Wolfgang von Goethe)

The power of visualization sufficiently developed will bring about the materialization. You can become what you can mentally see. You must use the magic power of imagination, the ability to see and feel things as they do not yet exist. One possessed with constructive imagination will see things as he wants them to be.

Identify yourself with larger and larger mental pictures of what you intend to achieve. Identify yourself so completely with success that failure will become impossible. For Review: re-read and practice Mental Picturing Exercises in Part I, Chapter 4.

Dr. William James said: "when there is a conflict between the will and the imagination, the imagination always wins." He also stated, "If you care enough for a result, you will most certainly achieve it."

MENTAL PICTURING IN VIETNAM PRISON

I heard about a pilot who was in solitary confinement in a Vietnam prison. To avoid insanity, he mentally pictured his release, his freedom, his flight home, and his reunion with his family, thousands of times. He saw himself building his home, drawing in his mind's eye the blueprint like an architect. Then he started to excavate over and over again, laying the foundation, erecting the structure, building the rooms. He said, "I actually had the sensation of sawing and driving the nails in!"

It became so real to him he said, he wouldn't have been surprised if he found the house already built and ready for occupancy.

This daily mental picturing saved his sanity and made it possible to endure his barbaric prison time. When he finally came home, he built his home exactly as he had mentally pictured it in prison.

YOU CAN'T FOOL YOUR SUBCONSCIOUS
Do not just wish you could change, or have this or that, but see and feel yourself as having already changed, being in possession of these things.

When you are programming your positive affirmations and goals, the words you mouth or think are only outward physical expressions of what you feel. What you feel with enthusiasm and a burning desire for achivement, you can be sure it will be achieved! If you expect it, your subconscious will bring it to pass.

Negative words, emotions, and thoughts create negative pictures and negative mental pictures create negative results. POSITIVE WORDS, EMOTIONS AND THOUGHTS LEAD TO POSITIVE MENTAL PICTURES. POSITIVE PICTURES CREATE POSITIVE, PLEASANT, RIGHT ACTIONS AND RESULTS.

DAY EXERCISE
You can emphasize your conviction, enthusiasm and burning desire more effectively by speaking out loud. This in turn will create the mental picture, which will automatically be flashed on the screen of your subconscious computer. YOUR PROGRAMMING EXERCISE WILL BE EFFECTIVELY REINFORCED WHEN YOU ADDITIONALLY SAY YOUR GOALS ALOUD TO YOURSELF DURING THE DAY, ESPECIALLY WHEN DRIVING YOUR CAR OR WHEN YOU ARE ENGAGED IN SOME OTHER AUTOMATIC ACTIVITY.

ZEPHYR

After I had been in America a short time, and not being able to pronounce some words correctly, I had to call Western Pacific to find out when relatives of ours would arrive on the Vista-Dome California Zephyr. I didn't know how to pronounce the word "Zephyr," and to the clerk it sounded as if I had asked: "Can you tell me when the Saviour will arrive?"

He replied with a chuckle: "brother, I would like to know that myself!" Then it dawned on me what I had said.

I cannot stress too often the fact that the subconscious cannot be impressed or informed by words only. This faculty of the mind can only be reached by emotions, imaginations, and mental pictures. You cannot joke with the Subconscious Mind. It will take your feelings as a command and act accordingly. A simple mis-pronounciation of one word in the question I put to the railroad clerk produced an entirely unexpected response.

We have to watch carefully what we think, speak, and feel as we create pictures upon the mental screens in our minds. How can we police these activities? By being constantly alert, watching ourselves and others, controlling our thinking, hearing and speaking with the highest awareness. Plant this self-suggestion for developing awareness in your mind, "My subconscious mind is assigned to watch over me and make me aware of my thoughts, speech, and whatever I see and hear, guiding me to a more positive way of life."

THE RADIO

I tried to listen to my radio program while visiting a doctor friend in his office, but I couldn't find it on the radio dial. This really disturbed me. Finally it dawned on me that the radio was set on FM instead of AM. The right waves were all around me, but I was not tuned in for their reception. The waves from many radio stations were all around, but I was unable to tune in and receive them.

This should bring home some understanding to us. I was on an entirely different frequency band. So it is with the conscious and subconscious mind, which are entirely different faculties. The subconscious cannot come through if you are set to accept only reason, will, and the judgment of the five senses of your conscious; the right switch has to be turned on.

The switch is Relaxation, Meditation and Prayer.

FIRST PLANTING—THEN HARVEST

Some try to reverse the process. They want to have the harvest before the planting of the seed, the reward before the service, the success and materialization before programming and expectation.

Do Everything You Are Prompted To Do

Let yourself be guided. The seed of the farmer needs water, sunshine, and cultivation. Don't try to make anything happen—let it happen. It is not your business to be concerned with it any more. Higher powers of your mind are working on it now. Just use positive affirmations to feed it. If *compelled* to do so, follow up with action. Listen to the promptings of your subconscious, and act accordingly. Obtain divine wisdom through your subconscious.

Make it Real to Yourself

The farmer looks forward to the harvest. He prepares everything for the harvest. In the same way you have to prepare yourself for the materialization of your goals. Think with great imagination what you will do after the goal is achieved—how you will apply it, spend it, enjoy it, live with it. Live in this state of mind ahead of time. Make it real to yourself—be excited about it—arouse enthusiasm.

WARNING
AVOID NEGATIVE MENTAL PICTURING

Unfortunately, it works the same way with fear and doubt.
A negative mental attitude will program your subconscious
negatively. Never lie awake in bed at night and brood
negatively over your problems. If you catch yourself doing
this, change your thoughts forcefully into a positive direction.

POSITIVE VS. NEGATIVE

REMEMBER, your subconscious is influenced by imagination and
mental pictures and emotions. The mind does not care what
you think; it will produce whatever you think and dwell on—
negative or positive. You are the editor.

POSITIVE MENTAL ATTITUDE

P.M.A.

IT IS ALL UP TO YOU

N.M.A.

NEGATIVE MENTAL ATTITUDE

A. The Negative Law of Doubt or Lack of Faith

1. I wonder when it will be realized?
2. I wonder from where it will come?
3. I wonder how it can be done?

You have to avoid these thoughts like you would a contagious illness. Replace negative thoughts with:

B. The Positive Law of Faith, Success, and Health

1. I want it.
2. I expect it.
3. I am going to have it.
4. I know it is mine.
5. I see it coming, and hear it humming.
6. I expect the best in every situation.
7. Everything is possible.

BE INVOLVED WITH PROGRAMMING YOUR SUBCONSCIOUS
Be a believer in this method, and your subconscious,
YOUR GENIE, will be your servant.

You can change your life by changing your mental attitude. Expect a positive result; expect the accomplishment; expect the materialization of your programmed goals and positive affirmations.

Expect the strong and compelling feedback, the extra booster, so that you can stay on the track of your goals and resolutions. Let it unfold and allow it to be released.

Expectation and faith in what you are doing will erase the doubt and fear of the past, and a positive attitude will always fill your mind.

DOES LIFE SEEM TO PASS YOU BY?
YOU TOO CAN BE A WINNER

STEP INTO THE
WINNERS' CIRCLE
YOU TOO CAN BE A WINNER

With the Magic Help of Your Subconscious
Your Subconscious will assist you to have a Positive Mental
Attitude, a New Positive Lifestyle.

Your Subconscious Feedback will compel you to stick to your Goals
with POSITIVE ACTIONS

Everybody Can Do It! Nothing Is Impossible! It Works! It Works! It
Works! You Can, You Will, You Do! It Depends All on You To Start
NOW

You too will Become more than you are now.
You will be Successful—when you want to be Successful.
You will be a Winner—when you want to be a Winner.
You will Become—what you want to Become.
You will Attain—what you want to Attain.
You will Achieve—what you want to Achieve.
You will Accomplish—what you want to Accomplish.

YOU HAVE NO LIMITATIONS ANYMORE.
YOU CANNOT LOSE FOR WINNING!!

TODAY STARTS THE REST
OF YOUR LIFE

THE ACCORDION SOLOIST

In "The Swiss Chalet Restaurant" at Lake Tahoe, we heard a young accordian virtuoso whose fingerwork was so exceptional that I felt I had to ask him a few questions. I inquired: "How can you think so fast about so many things at the same time—the melody, the notes, your left hand, your right hand, and every finger?" He replied, "I just hear the melody in my mind, and my fingers follow, fully coordinated." I retorted: "Are you doing this subconsciously?" "What is that," he questioned. Obviously he had never heard about the subconscious.

Three German couples sang old German folk songs to him, which he had never heard before. Before long he began to accompany them, then played them alone by ear. I asked: "How can you do this?" "Well," he answered, "I hear it, and play it. Afterward I just do it automatically. I can't permit my mind to wander. I have to concentrate on what I am playing. I hear the melody in my mind, section by section, chord by chord, and my fingers react accordingly. Sometimes the notes just dance in front of me; I read them and play them. It isn't easy to explain, and I have never thought much about it. But it works and that is all I am concerned about."

Isn't that another proof of the power of the subconscious mind? What he really did, without being aware of it, was to permit his conscious mind to program the music into his subconscious computer for later replay or automatic feedback.

What I want to emphasize is that the programming of the subconscious is extremely easy. The accordion soloist wanted to play the new melody. He expected that he could do it and had the self-confidence to do it. Through a lot of practicing he knew that he

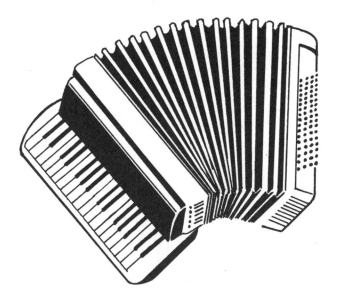

was capable of accomplishing it. He concentrated on the music and played it. It is a learning process.

When you first practice typing, you have to think of each individual letter and its position on the keyboard. After you acquire the skill through practice, you only think of the text you have to type.

We could do many things in our lives if we wanted them, expected them, and programmed them through exercises. We are limiting ourselves only by doubting our abilities and potential.

THE LION AND THE GAZELLE

Hunters in Africa have observed that a lion will always approach a herd of gazelles very cautiously. When he is close enough to attack he has selected from a distance the gazelle which will be his prey. Then he begins to circle in closer and closer, always watching his chosen victim. He will not take his eyes from it. The lion knows from experience that gazelles are fast, and that he will have to time his attack very precisely. He finally leaps from the tall grass. The gazelles run for their lives; some are faster than others.

Hunters have noticed a strange thing. The lion is blind to all gazelles except the chosen one. In his obsession he actually passes other gazelles, which he might have caught easily. But he just doesn't care. He leaves everything else behind him, and goes after his goal.

If a lion can be goal-directed and learn to stay on his target until he succeeds, then we human beings, blessed with such marvelous minds, can do likewise. People who are successful always have a primary goal. This goal must be chosen with a selective, open and reasoning mind. After the decision is made, one must be obsessed with a burning desire and be highly focused on the selected goal, so that nothing else can distract him from it. The primary goal, the life goal, should not be changed. All other goals—for the day, week, month, and year can and must be constantly replanned and redirected. The main goal, however, must always stand out as the target. Just like the lion we should stay on course. Our goal-striving Subconscious Mind, programmed for our life goal, will always bring us back on course and guide us toward the target. Use the following affirmation: "I wish success; I want success; I expect success; I work toward success; I will enjoy success."

PART III
CHAPTER 3
SUMMARY

1. Start Goal Book with Dividers for the following goals: Family— Spirituality — Profession — Finance — Health — Education — Recreation.
2. List all your basic goals; select as many as you can think of.
3. Write them down specifically and precisely.
4. Be sure your goals are realistic.
5. Date them; give them a deadline; add "Thank You," which means "It is accomplished already."
6. Read the goals twice a day.
7. Proceed with the Standard Relaxation Exercise creating a programming state of mind.
8. Remain in Standard Relaxation for five minutes and let the goals you read sink into your subconscious.
9. Arouse yourself by counting up from zero to six, and be fully awake.
10. Listen to the promptings and act accordingly.
11. Read the goals aloud to yourself from time to time to create enthusiasm.
12. You too can be a winner—step into the Winners' Circle. You cannot lose for winning.

How to Program Your Subconscious Mind with "Print Tapes"

Samples of "Print Tapes" Affirmations

Explanation: How to Program Your Subconscious Mind with "Print Tapes"

Phyllis Diller "It Is Psychic"

Sidney Portier "Success a By-Product"

SAMPLES OF PRINT TAPE AFFIRMATIONS

I encourage you to buy a Tape Printer for programming slogans. Print all kinds of positive affirmations, like:

TODAY I EXPECT THE BEST IN EVERY SITUATION
I EXPECT THE BEST, AND I WILL GET THE BEST
IF GOD IS WITH ME—WHO CAN BE AGAINST ME?
ALL THINGS GOOD FOR ME WILL BE REALIZED IN MY LIFE
I EXPECT MIRACLES TODAY
IT IS WONDERFUL THAT GOD CARES FOR ME
I CAN ENJOY DRIVING MY CAR ONLY WHEN I OBEY ALL TRAFFIC LAWS
I RECOGNIZE MY BLESSINGS
I AM THANKFUL FOR MY BLESSINGS

EXPLANATION
HOW TO PROGRAM YOUR SUBCONSCIOUS
WITH PRINT TAPES

First:

Place a tape on the dashboard of every car in the family, on doors, mirrors, drawers, the refrigerator, or the oven door, put them all about your home and office.

Second:

Change the tapes once a month. You will be surprised at how good this will be for your family. Soon they will look forward to the changes. These tapes must be so conspicuous, that none in the family can escape reading them. Be ready for a fast change to a positive mental attitude in yourself and your family. These tapes have a great programming effect. The positive affirmations will be absorbed unconsciously. The subconscious will take the affirmations as commands, and with its immense power will proceed to bring them to pass.

What are you waiting for? Get a Tape Printer!

PHYLLIS DILLER

The straggly-haired comedienne, Phyllis Diller, was interviewed and quoted as saying, "I don't accept negative thoughts or comments. It's psychic. I am a doer, self-motivated, inner-driven, vitally interested in everything, all life." She has done quite well with this philosophy, hasn't she? It is fascinating and most profitable to study the lives of people to find out what makes them tick, and to hear their success stories, and methods. Most of them are humble and eager to share their secret.

Really, it isn't a secret. They have all discovered the Fundamental Laws of Right Thinking for themselves, and are willing to apply these higher principles in their daily lives and professions. What's holding you back? Why must you remain only hearers of the word? Today can be the day that starts the rest of your life.

Let's summarize: *First*, as Phyllis Diller said, "it's psychic." You have to recognize the extrasensory perception of your mind and train yourself to use it. *Second*, self-motivation. It can be done with positive affirmations, the success method with which to program the subconscious. The affirmations have to be repeated over and over again. Third: Don't accept negative thoughts or comments. Neutralize and reword them instantly in your mind; change every negative, devastating, unethical, immoral and hateful statement to the opposite. These three steps will train your mind to succeed in all endeavors, to bring health and happiness, and to free yourself from mind bondage. Life has so much for you.

Take a short cut to success. Use positive affirmations like this: "I think abundance, health, acceptance, spirituality, a positive attitude, and a new self-image, and therefore these conditions will be realized in my life."

SIDNEY POITIER, "SUCCESS A BY-PRODUCT"

In an interview, the likeable actor, Sidney Poitier, said, "work is therapeutic for me. Work and love are the mainsprings of life. Success never was my goal; it was a by-product." His statement struck me, and I meditated on it, often.

Too often we put the carriage before the horse. We seek success as a goal, and forget about the price. Success should be the by-product of service, work well done, and unselfish love. Then it is the mainspring of life. Let's analyze it in the light of the Fundamental Laws of Right Thinking. It is not so much lack of knowledge or understanding of what we should do, as how to do what we know we should.

Daily we are showered with "thou shall's" and "thou shalt not's," but no one offers road signs, and explanations or provides the inner drive and conviction to carry out the directions. There is no doubt that we should follow the directions, and take the advice. Most have the necessary good will and good intentions. We make resolutions to improve our work, family, church, community, we plan education, and other projects, but we become side-tracked, or lose sight of the goals.

There should be a better way. There is a better way! The answer is Dynamic Mind-Training and programing the Subconscious Mind. Some people do it this way without having to be taught. Most of us have to be introduced to it and motivated for it. We all have the key for it, but we have to be shown its location. Studying the stories of many successful people, I found that just like Sidney Poitier, many found success to be a by-product of service.

We should learn that we have to program service to others into our subconscious and then assign the subconscious to find ways and means for us to follow our call. With this goal "in mind" we never have to worry about limitations. What we need, and much more, will abound in our lives. Success will come to us as a by-product.

PART III
CHAPTER 4
SUMMARY

1. Buy a printer and tapes in different colors.
2. Choose positive affirmations according to your needs
3. Change them from time to time.
4. Enjoy the great motivating effect.

PART III
CHAPTER 5

The Universal Law of Abundance

Fourth Principle: Expectation
Case Histories
Self Examination
Pay Your Debts Promptly
Case Histories
"But Seek Ye First the Kingdom of God."
The Law of Abundance Engraved on a Coin
as a Tangible Reminder.

The Apostle John wrote: *"Beloved, I wish above all things that thou mayest PROSPER and be in health."* (III John:2)

It is expected that we will PROSPER and enjoy the riches and the beauty of the earth.

"And God saw EVERYTHING that He had made, and behold, it was very good." (Genesis 1:31)

The Universal Law of Abundance and prosperity is not in conflict with the teachings in the Bible.

You have probably heard this statement before: "Money is the root of all evil." The quotation actually reads, *"For the LOVE of money is the root of all evil."* (1 Timothy 6:10)

"LOVE OF MONEY" was criticized by the Lord. *"Lay not up for yourselves treasures upon earth . . . for where your treasure is, there will your heart be also."* (Matt. 6:19-21)

Money is a symbol of compensation for service. It is a medium of exchange.

Service done in the right quality, quantity, and with integrity will be rewarded with well deserved money. Poverty or love of money can destroy peace of mind.

Constructive, honest work will bring money as compensation, as well as other benefits. *"For we hear that there are some which walk among you disorderly, working not at all, but who are busy bodies."* (II Thessalonians 3:11)

Sounds familiar for our time also.

Our country is endowed with riches and opportunities for everyone to make an honest living. There are many who are lazy. There are others who are merely getting by.

THE FOUR PRINCIPLES OF THE UNIVERSAL
LAW OF ABUNDANCE
A Method To End All Of Your Money Troubles

Failure to obey the Universal Law of Abundance is the reason why so many people are in debt, never obtain financial independence, never have enough, and never find success. The practice of the Universal Law of Abundance works for religious and non-religious alike. It has been taught by many of the great minds and prophets. It works on the basis of observance of mental laws, expectation and faith.

The "Universal Law of Abundance" is flawless and absolutely dependable. These are the basic elements of the law:

First: Give "one-tenth" back to the Universal Storehouse (Malachi 3:8-10)

Second: Give freely and not begrudgingly (II Corinthians 9:6-7)

Third: Multiplication (Matthew 13:3-30) (Luke 19:11-26)

Fourth: Expectation: If you expect nothing, you will usually get nothing. If you expect much, you will receive much (Matthew 7:7)

FIRST PRINCIPLE
GIVE BACK ONE-TENTH TO THE UNIVERSAL STOREHOUSE

Let me give you again personal experiences.

My Introduction To This Law

A swimming club chose me to represent my state in the pre-swimming meet for the Olympics at Cologne, Germany. I stayed with my uncle who was at that time Secretary of the Interior under Chancellor Hindenburg.

My uncle was a good man, but he had raised his daughter the way my father had raised my brother and me; without any religion. We did not go to church. We never prayed. We never talked about God. We had a marvelous home life, and fine educational programs, but we had no religion.

One day my uncle took me aside and said, "Kurt, Hitler is coming to power, and I want to live in freedom. I plan to emigrate to America. Before I go, I want to tell you something that has helped me tremendously. I practice the 'Universal Law of Abundance.' Remember, this has nothing to do with religion. Churches use this law, but it is really beyond any dogma or creed. I owe my success to observance of this law. I can name you many great industrial leaders, scientists and government officials, people of all walks of life, who are living the 'Universal Law of Abundance,' and as a result have great success."

I was sixteen and had no money when my uncle talked to me. I had no goal in life except I wanted to be a swimming champion. My uncle told me, "Kurt, always pay 'one-tenth' of whatever you earn, back into the 'Universal Storehouse of Plenty'." I had not heard this before. I had no reason to doubt, because my uncle was a great success. I put it to the test, and practiced it. The idea worked, and is still working for me today. I can now say just as my uncle did: "I owe my financial success and financial independence to the 'Universal Law of Abundance.' "

My uncle added: "Observe all four principles; first, pay one tenth back to the Universal Storehouse; second, give it freely, not begrudgingly; third and fourth, expect a multiplied return for yourself."

Whether you are rich or poor, I promise you it works. It is the Universal God-given law of Abundance. If you haven't tried it, test it for yourself. You will be surprised at how many opportunities will open for you. Blessing after blessing, success after success will be poured out and you will attract good luck!

It works. Start today! You will never regret it. You too will reach financial independence. You will get out of debt and never be in debt again.

The divine storehouse, the inexhaustible reservoir, is lavish in its rewards, bountiful, gracious and extravagant. Giving will bring you rewards beyond your needs. You can't lose for winning!

IMPORT BUSINESS

While I was writing a book a friend of ours told me the following story:

"Years ago, as immigrants from Germany, we had quite a struggle. My parents took over a part of our property and their regular monthly payments were a necessity for our existence. Without this money, we wouldn't have been able to make ends meet. When the time for the last intallment came, we looked forward to it with fear. What made the situation even worse was the fact that we hadn't met our last month's obligation to pay our tithing. We had lived the Law of the Universal Storehouse since we were married and did not want to neglect it. Therefore our decision was to use our money even if we couldn't afford it, to pay first our obligation to the Universal Storehouse of plenty. The money we owed would have provided us with food for the next 3 weeks. It took all our faith and expectations to pay this tithing.

Afterwards we felt at peace and we were sure that something good would be on the way for us. We had no idea where it would come from. We had never told you this, Kurt, but it was that evening we visited you. We didn't want to bother you with our financial troubles, but we needed the positive booster, which we always received from you. At the end of the evening you had said to us 'Are you interested in my import business? I have chosen insurance as my new career!' My husband was very reluctant, but I immediately saw the possibilities, the miraculous multiplication of our tithing. It took some big talk and persuasion to convince my husband of the value of this great opportunity. All of the time that we were standing in the open door to say goodbye, we came very close to missing this good fortune. Then we turned around and came back into the house, where we talked and planned for hours.

Well, you know the rest of the story. We decided to take over the business. We came together almost daily for years and discussed every phase of the business until we were thoroughly familiar with it. Now my husband and I cannot imagine ourselves being without this thriving and highly successful business.

What occurred involved a direct relationship between the law of Abundance, Faith and Expectation, and our financial independence. Now I can only say it works—it works! I give you permission to use our story so that others will benefit from our experience and act accordingly."

What is the basic principle behind this law of one-tenth? I don't know how it works. I know from experience as do many others, that this law is real, and that it works.

I once watched a dowser searching for water. His rod reacted suddenly with wild jerks and he proclaimed excitedly, "Here is water!" (It was proven—a well was dug.) I asked the man, "How could you know; how does the dowser work?" He said, "I don't know, but it works!"

So it is with the "Universal Law of Abundance." No one knows exactly on what basis and principle it works other than faith, expectation and obedience, and observance of mental laws, but it works! We all use many things without understanding how they work, the car, electric light, television, radio, X-Ray, or microwave ovens. We do not know how the answer comes to prayer, or healing of the body. Why not give this great Law of Abundance a chance? Unfortunately, many of us are negatively programmed and feel when we give, we lose. We have to obtain an understanding of the principles of the Law of Abundance. Understanding comes through obedience to mental law. Do it—and you will know it!

The crop is always greater than the seed planted. You will find that when you observe the Law of Abundance, you will prosper.

My writing will reach some who are in sad financial conditions, close to nervous breakdowns, with no hope in sight. People in such situations often feel tired, sick, tense, nervous and grumpy. They have contentious dispositions, and are unable to reason clearly.

There is a way out of every situation! It is easier than you think! I am thankful that I have known hopeless situations myself. I endured inflation, devaluations, and political persecution under Hitler. I was politically imprisoned during the Second World War. During the bombings I lost everything. I emigrated to the United States of America, and arrived there with very little. I have tasted the bitter and the sweet. I write from experience. No one is too old or too young to change. Anyone can do it IF they really want to.

I vividly remember many downtrodden people. They embraced the "Law of Abundance." They started small and worked themselves up the ladder to a new and better life. The "Law of Abundance" is one of the many Fundamental Laws of Right Thinking and Living. Get acquainted with all these laws.

The intangible elements of the "Law of Abundance" are Faith, and Expectation. Money is the tangible part. Your rewards multiply through the power of Faith and Expectation. You must give the money freely to receive the multiplied return. You need to give service freely to receive increased love in return. Spend time, and help others freely, and it will come back to you multiplied.

This giving has to be done without doubt. Fear of losing will invite lack and limitations into your life. The Universal Storehouse can never be exhausted. The Law of Abundance is a sound Investment. Try it. IT WORKS! IT WORKS! *IT WORKS!!*

Let me share with you some more of my life experiences.

HOTEL ADDRESSBOOK

Following the "Truce" at the end of the Second World War, business and industry in Germany lay dormant. The economy was paralyzed and money devaluated to 10% of its former worth. Everyone was in a state of panic, searching for ways to earn money, and to build up the economy again. My family and I were living in a resort town high up in the Black Forest in Germany.

One day I drove to Freiburg, 150 miles away, and with my last money paid my obligations; I contributed one tenth of my income to my church. In my mind I believed, I multiplied my contribution for the best of all concerned. With an empty pocketbook and backpayments due for rent and food, I stepped out into the street, and expected a miracle to happen—and it did!

Suddenly someone in a new Volkswagon called my name. He called: "Kurt, what are you doing here?" Then I recognized him. He had been president of a large coal company when I was president of the steel company in Strassburg, France. He stopped the car, and exclaimed, "Kurt, I have had a heart attack, and I have to take it easy. If you need a car, you can have this one." I inquired, "what in the world will I do with a car? I have no work." As we talked he said that he knew a company which was putting together a post-war hotel-motel, sanatorium and resort town addressbook. I went home with him, took over the car, and applied for the job.

They were happy to have a representative with a car and gave me an orderbook. I asked for more books. They thought one was plenty. On my way back to our home in Schoenwald, I filled thirty orders, and to my amazement, even collected cash. Upon reaching home, I called up the company officers, told them of my success, and asked for more order books. They were amazed. Now they were willing to send a dozen orderbooks to me. With my wife and two young sons in the car, I traveled from one resort town to the other, criss-crossing the Black Forest. We were fabulously success-ful. After a month, I was promoted to Sales Manager of the company for all Germany. I went from financial distress to success in a very short period.

A coincidence? No! It was a direct result of obeying the Law of Abundance. It works without fail. It will work for you, too.

Re-read the promises on tithing in your Bible:

"Prove me now herewith, saith the Lord of hosts,
if I will not open you the windows of heaven, and
pour you out a blessing, that there shall not be
room enough to receive it." (Malachi 3:8-10)

WHAT A PROMISE!
HOW CAN ANYONE MISS?

Many believe prosperity is a sin!
"If they obey and serve him, they shall spend their
days in prosperity, and their years in pleasures."
(Job 36:11)
Think about it!

THE CONCEPT :

MY COVENANT AND PARTNERSHIP WITH

THE UNIVERSAL STOREHOUSE

Picture yourself with a firm Handshake with the Universal Laws of Abundance—with the Universal Storehouse, with Infinite Intelligence.

You will be rich beyond your needs.

Isn't this the best way you ever heard of, to get out of debt, pay all your obligations, and live a prosperous life?

". . . MY CUP RUNNETH OVER." (Psalm 23:5)

HERE IS ANOTHER SECRET! AS SOON AS YOU MAKE UP
YOUR MIND TO PRACTICE THIS LAW OF ABUNDANCE,
IT STARTS TO WORK.

SECOND PRINCIPLE
GIVE FREELY AND NOT BEGRUDGINGLY

The Law of Abundance and multiplication is a universal, irrevocable law. It works in a chain reaction, for all of us. Whether we obey it and recognize it or not, it is as automatic as nature. If we give willingly, freely, and with full understanding, it will return multiplied to us.

Give freely and not begrudgingly, service, love, money and time. Take every opportunity for contributions, gifts, and paying your "ONE TENTH."

Do it with the right positive mental attitude, and a deeply rooted spirituality.

Here is another promise from the Bible.

Every man according as he purposeth in his heart, so let him give; not grudgingly, or of necessity: for God loveth a cheerful giver.
He which soweth sparingly, shall reap also sparingly; and he which soweth bountifully shall reap also bountifully. (II Corinthians 9:6-7)

A student of mine approached me saying, "I have lived the Law of Abundance for the past six months, and nothing has changed yet. I am beginning to doubt." I questioned him about the four principles and found that he paid his "one-tenth" grudgingly and with an attitude of resentment. He was always thinking of the many things he needed to buy with this money. When he accepted my explanation, he changed his frame of mind, and observed the second principle. His whole financial situation changed dramatically in a very short time.

Let me introduce you to the "frosting on the cake," a principle not much known and not practiced.

THIRD PRINCIPLE—MULTIPLICATION
NOT ONLY MONEY BUT ALSO LOVE, SERVICE AND TIME CAN BE MULTIPLIED IN ACTION

IT IS THE MISSING LINK:
THE GREAT SECRET REVEALED

Is it selfish to expect a multiplied return of your gifts?

First: You decide to give because you want to help; this takes an unselfish character, and motivation—Right?

Second: You must arouse Faith and Expectation for the multiplication of your gift. "Nothing comes from nothing—nothing ever will." *It stands to reason that if you can arouse faith for the multiplication of your gifts, then you will have faith for anything else you desire. It strengthens your Faith and Expectation.*

". . . If thou canst BELIEVE, all things are possible to him that believeth." (Mark 9:23)

In the Bible Jesus gave the parables, who has ears to hear let him hear!!!

"The Sower," (Matthew 13:3-9):

". . . And he spake many things unto them in parables, saying Behold a sower went forth to sow; And when he sowed, some seeds fell by the way side and the fowls came and devoured them up:

Some fell upon stony places, where they had not much earth; and forthwith they sprung up because they had no deepness of earth:

And when the sun was up, they were scorched and because they had no root, they withered away.

And some fell among the thorns; and the thorns sprang up, and choked them.

But others fell into good ground, and brought forth fruit, some an hundred-fold, some sixty-fold, some thirty-fold.

Who hath ears to hear, let him hear.

The seed is the word, the thought, the good deed, love, service, time or money freely given away. The ground is our mind, our attitude, our faith, our expectation, our feelings toward giving.

But the marvel of the Universal Law is the MULTIPLICATION from what you give: "thirty, sixty, or a hundred fold." No set percentage is given for multiplying. We only limit ourselves. The Universal Storehouse can give you anything in return. It is wide open to the receiver. Your mind must be able to conceive and expect it before you can receive.

The "Multiplication Pact" with Infinite Intelligence, the Universal Storehouse—works!

But remember, "NOTHING" can not be multiplied!

Even the Lord asked for some bread to multiply. Then he fed 5,000 people from five barley loaves and two small fishes, and still had baskets of fragments left over. (John 6:3-13)

What Can Be Multiplied?

It is all up to you. Your "one-tenth" contributions, gifts, service, love and time *for which you have not received a direct compensation, renumeration or reward will all be multiplied.* Examples are: Payments to churches, philanthropic organizations, associations, clubs, etc., drives, fund raising and donations to charitable, humanitarian causes. To be more detailed: even wedding presents, or collections. Gifts to widows and unfortunate people.

How Does This Principle of Multiplication Work?

How can we apply it in daily life? I will give you some real life experiences which will demonstrate this exciting universal principle.

My church asked me to pledge a large amount of money to help in the maintenance of a chapel. I was so surprised at the amount they asked that I checked the name and address on the envelope. It was beyond our family budget. I asked my wife what we should do. She said, "Be thankful for this amount. Don't you remember the Law of Multiplication?" So we paid, believed, then left everything open for the universal storehouse to supply us. We pictured a big return, expected much and we received much.

I had a real war of papers with the German Government for many years to establish eligibility for my German retirement benefits, without making any progress. I was informed that it was hopeless, because some of my records had been lost during the war. One day I received good news from Germany. They informed me that everything could be cleared and that I would receive my pension plus back checks for the months that had been missed. A fulfillment of the Law of Abundance? Yes. The multiplication did it. We received many times over.

The Law of Multiplication Works Whenever You Apply It

During my insurance career, I was approached by a college to sell philanthropic policies. I bought one myself and pledged an additional monthly cash amount to the institution. Then I mentally multiplied my contributions and let myself be guided to the right prospects. The return in commissions is still coming in from that.

Do you know what a philanthropic Life Insurance Policy is? You can buy a Life Insurance Policy and make a church, university, or any non-profit organization the beneficiary. Your contributions are tax deductible. The proceeds can be included in your gross estate and will give a favorable tax picture for the taxable estate. You are creating a living memorial that will outlive you.

BUT THE FROSTING ON THE CAKE IS THAT YOU CAN MENTALLY MULTIPLY THE PREMIUMS CONTRIBUTIONS AC-CORDING TO THE LAW OF ABUNDANCE. What a reward! In this day when charitable gifts are so needed, can you think of anything that would give you more satisfaction or be of greater benefit to your favorite foundation?

Charitable Bequests

I want to be thoroughly used up when I die for the harder I work the more I live . . . Life is no brief candle for me. It is a sort of splendid *torch* which I hold for but a moment, and I want to make it burn as brightly as possible before handing it on to future generations.

George Bernard Shaw

For Many Years I Was A One-Man Operation

Many times I have taught church groups free of charge, given free lectures, taught seminars too small to bring monetary gain, and helped people who could not afford the tuition. Sometimes I have been cheated out of complete or partial tuitions. I never became upset. I tried to collect, but if I could not, I would multiply it as a contribution on my part, and I was richly rewarded.

I programmed my subconscious for a secretary, supplemental teachers, Colleagues and business associates, with whom I could improve the Golden Keys Success Seminar. Two ladies fell in love with the teachings of the school for Dynamic Mind Training, and received a glimpse of what it would do for their own lives as well as for others.

See how it works? I received my multiplication a thousand fold. My friends have peace of mind for themselves, a harmonious and happy family life, an understanding of service to others, and a brand new professional career with a bright and exciting future. We are thrilled at how successfully it works. The Law of Abundance is flawless and absolutely dependable. All that is required from you is EXPECTATION, FAITH, and RIGHT ACTION WITH INTEGRITY. Then just let it work for you. Let me share with you another experience of mine:

A lady friend of ours, eighty years young, broke her leg and was alone and helpless in her apartment. She had no relatives to help her. For two months I went to her home two or three times a week to take care of her. Love, service, time and money were freely given, without hesitation. We multiplied the love, the service, the time and money and left it up to the Universal Storehouse of God to bless and multiply it to the best of all concerned.

A month later my son called from Japan and invited us to take an extensive study trip to the Orient, fares, hotels, and meals, all paid for. But this was not all! Our friend gave up her apartment shortly afterwards and moved into a fine old folks home. Many of her beautiful things were given to us. This was the return and the multiplication of our service and time. I can only say that it works!

This is the most fantastic financial law of abundance conceivable. Why don't you try it out for yourself? It works! It works! It works! It works!

". . . For whatsoever a man soweth, that shall he also reap." (*Galations 6:7*)

THE UNIVERSAL STOREHOUSE HAS TO BE REPLENISHED

"One-tenth" has to go back to the Universal Storehouse. This is the law of nature. It is logical, reasonable and fair. Include yourself. Step into the Winners' Circle. Be a Winner. You can't lose for winning. Nobody dare neglect this law of "One-tenth." It makes much more sense to return "One-Tenth" in a positive way, expecting the multiplication than to ignore this commandment and have it work against you, in a negative way. The Universal Storehouse has to be satisfied. (Luke 19:11-26)

After my lectures on this subject, there are always people who come to me and say, "Now I understand why I suffer: Why my car broke down; Why my heating system failed; Why I became sick; Why things were stolen from me, Why I lost goods and money; Why I was not lucky, Why I did not get the sale; and why I was not promoted." This law works in a chain reaction. Your loss may be the reward for someone else; your reward may be the loss for another person.

It operates in a positive or negative way, fully automatic and in multiplication. Nobody can win by stealing and lying. For a while he may think he has escaped the laws of nature until the universal storehouse has caught up and collected in its own way.

You may have thought that it was up to you to keep or neglect the Universal Law of Abundance. You probably took blessings and the good life for granted. You considered losses to be unfair to you and blamed God, the Devil, or the world around you, never yourself! Remember, the negative course of your life can easily be changed.

WORDING OF THE MULTIPLICATION
AND
HOW IT IS DONE

Lift your right hand up and say or mouth, "I am thankful for the knowledge of the Universal Law of Abundance and for the opportunity to give and serve. I expect the multiplication now, leaving it up to Infinite intelligences, the Universal Storehouse— God—to bless and multiply the return for the best of all concerned. Thank You. Thank You. Thank You." "Thank You" means: "*Believing* that you have received, and you will receive. It is on its way to me." Then just sit back, so to speak, and let the law work for you.

Keep records in your diary. Reinforce the multiplication from time to time. Impress the multiplication on your Subconscious Mind with Mental Pictures and a burning desire for the multiplication for the best of all concerned.

The following are examples of "Positive Affirmations" which you may use for the multiplication in Relaxation, Meditation and prayerful attitude or just say it aloud or silently to yourself often.

"I know a multiplication nominator is on the way for me, and I know it can only be good. I give thanks in advance for all good things in my life, whatever they may be, and from whatever direction they may come. I set no limits. I am not concerned with where, why, how or when good things will happen to me. I know everything will come to me in proper order. I give thanks for all these good things in advance. Today and every day I expect the best in every situation."

"I give thanks that this multiplication is already spiritually created. I completely identify myself with it. I await with confidence the rewards in my life."

"I want the multiplication."

"I expect the multiplication."

"I am going to have the multiplication."

"I know the multiplication is mine."

"For the best of all concerned."

WARNING:
DO NOT DWELL ON NEGATIVE
QUESTIONS SUCH AS: WHEN? WHERE? OR HOW IT
WILL BE DONE? THIS IS NOT YOUR CONCERN ANY MORE.
YOU TURNED IT OVER TO "HIGHER POWERS."

Change your thinking to:

"I Want it—I Expect it—I am Going to Have it—I Know it is mine. I see it coming with my mental eyes, and hear it humming in my mental ears."

"I Expect the best in every situation, for the best of everyone concerned."

"WITH MEN THINGS ARE IMPOSSIBLE: BUT WITH GOD ALL THINGS ARE POSSIBLE." (Matthew 19:26)

I made a covenant and partnership with God. I will REJOICE and be exceedingly glad!

". . . But my GOD shall supply all your (my) needs according to his riches . . ." (Philippians 4:19)

How To Change From A Negative To A Positive Mental Attitude

If you find yourself speaking or thinking negatively, and doubting the Law of Abundance, you should immediately say "NO" and push your left hand down forcefully. Say or think, "I have turned the Multiplication over to Higher Powers—and I expect the best for all concerned." Replace your negative, doubting thoughts with a positive form and lift your right hand up saying or thinking, "Thank You." "Thank You" means, "I know the multiplication is on its way to me in due time to the best of all concerned. Thank You."

Make + (Plus Signs) all over the house on the mirrors, refrigerator, doors, T.V. etc., as well as in your car and place of work. This will remind you to expect the multiplication with a positive thankful mental attitude.

BAHA ULLAH

While studying the philosophy of the East, I was struck by the saying of the Persian prophet, Baha Ullah: "Work done in the spirit of service to men is equal to worship of God." Christian literature is also full of this wisdom.

I want to motivate you with another Golden Key of the Fundamental Laws of Right Thinking. We think first of ourselves and of the advantage something may have for us. Many of my students had such a mental attitude.

The Fundamental Laws of Right Thinking teach that you never need to worry about limitations, promotions, sales or recognitions if you give service to man first. *The higher law will multiply and bring to you all you have done for others. What you send out comes back multiplied to you.*

If you are dissatisfied with your environment, position, business, or sales, all you have to do is to give more and better service. Does that sound too good to be true? Not at all. The Law really works that way. You must, in your own mind, in your own opinion, honestly deserve a reward for your service. If the reward is not enough, give more service. If you think your reward is too much, increase your service.

One more principle will close the circle of the Law of Abundance.

FOURTH PRINCIPLE—EXPECTATION
IF YOU EXPECT NOTHING, YOU WILL
USUALLY GET NOTHING.
IF YOU EXPECT MUCH, YOU WILL RECEIVE MUCH.
VERY SIMPLE, ISN'T IT? CAN YOU SEE WHY SO MANY FAIL?
THEY DON'T EXPECT ANYTHING!

". . . Give, and it shall be given unto you; good measure, pressed down, and shaken together, and running over, shall men give unto your bosom. For with the same measure that ye mete withal it shall be measured to you again." (Luke 6:38)

A missed chance to give is a lost opportunity to expect—and receive—multiplied.

Your attitude of mind of giving and expecting is very important.

". . . And as thou hast believed, so be it unto thee." (Matthew 8:13)

Merely thinking, wishing and dreaming about it is not enough.

"Therefore, I say unto you, what things soever ye desire, when ye pray, believe that ye receive them, and ye shall have them." (Mark 11:24)
"And all things, whatsoever ye shall ask in prayer, believing, ye shall receive." (Matthew 21:22)

Continuous giving brings continuous blessings.

Some of the many testimonies which have been expressed to me:
"The Law of Abundance increased my faith."
"I had my doubts first, but success breeds success. I am on my way up."
"We were so much in debt that we took any straw to hold on to. We have overcome. It feels good to be out of debt."
"We always thought tithing is for church goers only. We love the Law of Abundance. It is easy to live. We would rather have 90% of our money with the Universal blessings than 100% without."
"In our case, we recognized the multiplication to be better health and harmony in our marriage."
"I only wished I would have heard this down to earth explanation of the Universal Law of One-Tenth sooner."
"I had to work my way through college. I give credit to the 'Law of Abundance' which helped me to have sufficient all the time and to be able to receive my B.A. Degree."

After an ensuing lecture on the Law of Abundance, a group of young people stood in line to shake hands with me, expressing themselves in this manner: "I like it—it works! I couldn't be without it." "My savings account is growing." "I feel a closeness with God." "My prayers are more focused— I am getting along better with my family—I see a great future."

Many married couples said that their budgets are well balanced, and their many needs are well taken care of. Comparing their family lives with others, not living the Law of Abundance, they feel that they are far ahead and secure.

One man stated: "In my youth I was taught that I have to give to my church without expecting anything back. I quit this false concept. What a difference to believe in a loving God who will supply all my needs. My life has turned about 180 degrees through the Law of Abundance."

After a lecture a lady said to me: "I do not feel worthy to expect anything from God. How can I even expect to multiply?" I said, "Lady, aren't you a daughter of God? Yes, you are. So why do you feel insignificant and undeserving? The Lord himself said, ". . . Ask and it shall be given you; seek and ye shall find; knock and it shall be opened unto you, for everyone that asketh receiveth; and he that seeketh findeth; and to him that knocketh it shall be opened. (Matthew 7:7-8)"

If you feel unworthy because you have transgressed His commandments, then you should repent and sin no more and live a uplifting spiritual and positive life."

The poor and needy think limitations and therefore they are in need, and in want all the time. Those who succeed are thinking beyond their needs, without limitations.

After you have given and multiplied, the higher powers will work in your favor so that you can receive a magnified return.

You Probably Were Told Not To Expect Anything In Return When You Give.

You shouldn't expect it from the person or organization you give to. "Don't let your left hand know what the right hand is doing." Don't speak about your giving, keep it a secret and hold it sacred. That does not mean you cannot expect multiplied returns from the "Universal Storehouse."

From numerous case histories of students of mine, and my own experience I chose these few stories to start you on the road to a positive new life style—happiness, health and total success.

A Student of the Seminar, Fell in Love With This Great Law

He said, "If a kernel of corn can bring a hundred fold or more return through nature's law of multiplication, then the same law should work for me." With love, service, time and money freely given, he and his wife kept track of all their expectations and waited with thankful unselfish hearts for the multiplied returns. They really went all the way and seized every opportunity. Originally he owned two grocery stores. After one year of application of the law, he has four big, successful markets. Under his direction, his staff is positive, industrious and devoted; and full of integrity. They work harmoniously together. Customers love this kind of atmosphere.

To Whom Shall It Be Given?

If you have joined a church, give to the denomination of your choice, whether it teaches the Law of Abundance or not. If you do not belong to any organized church, give it according to your affiliation, to an organization you patronize, to a group or to some one in need.

Is it Your Responsibility to Determine
How Your "One-Tenth" is Used?

NO! Don't even think or talk about it! It is not your concern any more.

Who Has Ears to Hear—Let Him Hear!

Most of the people are brainwashed and negatively programmed with the idea—"When I give—I loose. I experience a lack and limitations afterwards. Any contribution is a loss, any loss is a loss, period!" This is negative thinking. The positive approach is to do it with the FOUR PRINCIPLES and enjoy the multiplied return.

SELF EXAMINATION
WERE YOU ABLE TO DETECT ALL OF THE FOUR PRINCIPLES?
WRITE THEM DOWN WITHOUT LOOKING THEM UP AGAIN.
FIRST:

SECOND:

THIRD;

FOURTH:

The crop, the harvest, is always greater than the seed planted. That is a law of creation, a law of nature, a law of abundance. It stands to reason then that we have to seed more to experience a greater harvest. Very simple—Right?

THE MORE YOU GIVE, THE MORE WILL COME BACK MULTIPLIED TO YOU.

THIS IS ANOTHER OPPORTUNITY TO LIVE AND APPLY THE UNIVERSAL LAW OF ABUNDANCE

I will never forget the good advice I received from a Jewish businessman I had smuggled in my car trunk to safety during the Hitler regime. He said, "Pay your indebtedness promptly. When you send your check away, express your thankfulness toward the Universal Storehouse, that you are able to take care of your liability. Then kiss your check and say "come back multiplied in assets to me for the best of all concerned. Thank You."

The return will not always be in currency. It may be in the form of: TIME, health, a new job, love, service, spirituality, faith, protection and harmony with God and the world around you. Leave it up to the Supreme Power. God knows best what you need the most.

A True Principle Discovered and Properly Applied Will Bring The Expected Success

With this knowledge of the Universal Law of Abundance, it stands to reason that NO ONE should neglect to pay his debts. Paid debts and obligations will then psychically release frozen assets and credits of yours—obligations others owe you. There is no shortage in the Universal Storehouse—only lack of demand, claim, expectation, want and desire from us. ONLY YOU—YOURSELF are limiting the return. Right action brings success and blessings. Wrong action, lack and limitations. Be honest with yourself.

A young girl and a boy, representing a group of teenagers of a youth organization said to me after a lecture:

We don't have money to pay tithing. We have not enough for dates, to buy all the clothes, and shoes we want, and take care of our cars and stereos. We are constantly in the hole. Our money is spent before we get it. How do you expect us to pay One-Tenth? That is only for adults.

They described it accurately! "We are constantly in the hole." It might sound strange but I replied, "*First* one needs FAITH, EXPECTATION and a full understanding of the "Law of Abundance" and secondly money." After a soul searching discussion and a down-to-earth explanation of the Law of Abundance, they understood it quite differently and said, "It sounds like an investment, and fun! How can we miss? In the past we considered it as another debt or a cold contribution to the church. Now we understand it is for our own benefit. We will give it the test."

Six Months Later

I had another speaking assignment to the same group. I couldn't believe it. Every personality and life had changed wonderfully. To look in their happy faces and sparkling eyes was a glimpse of heaven.

As one voice the group testified enthusiastically to me: "It was easy. * The Multiplication worked instantly. * I can't lose for winning. * I paid honestly my One-Tenth, enjoy all the good things as before, and have money left over. * You were right. We needed the power of faith which we now apply to everything we do in our life. * I do better in school. * I am getting along better with my peers, and my parents, and my family. * I am more successful in whatever I undertake. * My scores are much better playing basketball!" (Winning in competitive sports was mentioned just about from everyone.)

REMEMBER
"BUT SEEK YE FIRST THE KINGDOM OF GOD, AND HIS RIGHT-EOUSNESS: AND ALL THESE THINGS SHALL BE ADDED UNTO YOU." (MATTHEW 6:33)

To live the "Law of Abundance" will be a spiritual unfolding for you and will add new dimensions to your life.

The Best Way To Keep Success Steadily Flowing
Is To Be Thankful For It All The Time

"Our doubts are traitors and make us lose the good
we often might win by fearing to attempt."

—William Shakespeare

PART III
CHAPTER 5
SUMMARY

The Four Principles of the Universal Laws of Abundance:
First: Give One Tenth
Second: Give Freely
Third: Multiplication
Fourth: Expectation

WORDING OF THE MULTIPLICATION IN THREE STEPS

1. Express thanks for the knowledge and opportunity.
2. Leave the multiplication up to the Universal Storehouse—God.
3. To the best of all concerned.
   Case Histories to spark your imagination.
   Create your own positive affirmation for multiplication.
   Always carry the COIN of the Universal Law of Abundance with you.

PART III
CHAPTER 6

How Your Subconscious Mind Can Help You to Achieve A Congenial Marriage

HARMONIOUS MARRIAGE THROUGH THE POWER OF YOUR SUBCONSCIOUS

Love is the energy by which everything lives. Love is the basic element, the energy and vibration by which everything prospers. Humans, plants, and animals wither away without love. Love generates emotions.

Women are especially gifted with psychic phenomena. One of the gifts women possess is love. Every woman can be a "Love Generator" and "Love Transmitter." A woman's nature is to bring love into being, and build love into an unconquerable force. When the "Generator" is sparked and turned on, this Love Energy glows mightily. The source is inexhaustible.

Women are much more intuitive than men. A man can turn on the "Generator" and "Transformer" in a woman to release this natural, universal energy of love. The woman sparks the energy field in man for creativity and success. This mental energy field, transformed into love by a woman, will create in man endurance, ingenuity, inventiveness, resourcefulness, imagination, skillfulness, and an understanding of love and tenderness and romance. As long as the woman's love vibrations are appreciated and recognized with admiration and consideration, the flow of Love Energy is unfailing. This energy must be received and accepted in the same spirit of love. It has to be absorbed and used.

If not, it will return to the woman like a boomerang as unused energy. Rejected, unappreciated or ignored love, will transmute into dislike, hostility, animosity, resentment, and hate.

WHY MARRIAGES FAIL

Failure in marriage is easy to prevent when one has an understanding of the nature of woman. She functions the way she was created to function.

It is up to you to choose the right partner, and to be the right partner. It takes two to quarrel. If you strive to be a peacemaker, you can avoid serious disagreements. Every man must accept the challenge and create an aura of respect for his wife in the home. A wife generates overflowing Love Energy if her husband is courteous, considerate, understanding, helpful, appreciative, tender, attentive, thoughtful, and dedicated. Even a few of these qualities stimulate the exciting "Love Energy" and dedication of a wife. Devotion, faithfulness, and loyalty leads the wife to offer high esteem and admiration for the husband she loves.

All a husband has to do is to treat his wife as a queen, and she will see him as her king. It is like an echo. What you shout out will come back to you multiplied. A husband has only to honor and respect his wife and treat her with dignity; then all doors between the partners, parents and children will swing open.

A.B.C.'S FOR THE HUSBAND

A.   Speak to your wife; exchange ideas; fill her in, make her a part of your daily activities.
B.   Take advantage of her intuitive mind. Seek counsel from her, brainstorm with her. Follow her suggestions, precognitions, and inner feelings about people, things, and time. Trust her.
C.   As a bonus token of appreciation, do something together. Take her out. Make short and long trips. Choose exciting vacations. Be alone with her. Love her; be good to her. Be tender, understanding, caring, compassionate, warmhearted.

This will create a happy and harmonious marriage, filled with trust and fidelity. It will foster a loving atmosphere in your home, your castle, your sanctuary. This can all be yours by programming it directly into your subconscious.

In the middle ages, a great many women were burned at the stake because they were accused of "magic powers." Why women, and not men? Women have always been more gifted than men with psychic phenomena. Men would do well to be in harmony with their wives and the gifts and talents they possess.

MY WIFE CHARLOTTE SUGGESTS TO EVERY WIFE

On our various train rides throughout Japan, we experienced much frustration because of the language barrier. People we asked for directions could speak few words of English, and we knew no Japanese.

One day we were lost. We didn't know exactly where we were, or which way to go. We approached a business man, whom we thought might know some English. He was extremely friendly, but we had a hard time making him understand. We succeeded because both parties had a sincere desire to communicate.

The first pre-requisite for understanding is the desire, the determination to do so. This simple principle is essential in marriage. Each partner has the responsibility to achieve harmony, happiness and love. One person is not accountable for the success or failure of the marriage. Wife and husband must adjust to the mental, emotional and physiological needs of the partner. It is easy to blame the other partner and withdraw from responsibilities. Lively communication will assure success.

At first we were in love and we overlooked and forgave all kinds of negative character traits. When the first love fades, many a young woman is upset, frustrated, disappointed about the short-comings of her husband. Have you ever heard this passage in the Bible, "A man . . . cleaves to his wife; and they twain shall be one flesh." This means being one not only in the physical sense, but in mind also. The couple should be open to each other—no secrets. They should exchange inner feelings, expectations and goals.

Inasmuch as most women are especially gifted with E.S.P. let's use them and get them to work in our families.

A.B.C.'S FOR THE WIFE

A.   You can help and influence your husband and children with the Winners' Circle through mental telepathy. You must impart, share and understand. (PART 2, CHAPTER IV)

B.   You must make and keep yourself as attractive as possible. Get through with routine housework before he comes home, if at all possible, so that you may have time together.

C.   You are responsible for the beauty and harmonious Aura of the home. You have to strive to be a devoted and happy wife.

Is that too much? I tell you, it's worth it! It brings rich rewards. Women are often blamed for nagging and bickering. I know that all we are doing is applying positive criticism, but we are often misunderstood. Sometimes we can achieve better results by taking it easier.

It is time to put Father back into his place. He is supposed to be the head of the family. Encourage him to be that way. Father will then set the home in order. He will like the authority. He will be pleased to organize a home where love, affection, spirituality, counseling, study, brainstorming and fun can prevail.

Spiritual enlightment (positive) or spiritual darkness (Negative) influences our marriages and homes. Happiness is walking together in the light. "But if we walk in the light . . . we have fellowship one with another." (John 1:7) "I am the light of the world; he that followeth me shall not walk in darkness, but shall have the light of life." (John 8:12)

"Nothing can take the place of the home in rearing and teaching children, and no other success can compensate for failure in the home."—David O. McKay

"A home divided against itself cannot stand."—Abraham Lincoln

A great church leader, discussed this idea at one time and said, "Parents should love and respect each other and treat each other with decorum and kindly regard all the time. The husband should treat his wife with the utmost courtesy and respect. The husband should never insult her; he should never speak lightly of her, but should always hold her in the highest esteem in the home and in the presence of their children.

"The wife also should treat her husband with the greatest respect and courtesy. Her words to him should not be keen and cutting and sarcastic.

"She should not make slurs or insinuations at him. She should not nag him. She should not try to arouse his anger or make things unpleasant around the home.

"The wife should be a joy to her husband and she should live and conduct herself at home so the home will be the most joyous, the most blessed place on earth to her husband." (George Albert Smith)

THANK YOU, CHARLOTTE SCHNEIDER

HAPPY PEOPLE MAKE A HAPPY HOME

Once a business man, sad and depressed invited me to come home with him and explain the teachings of the Golden Keys Success Seminar. As we approached the front door I noticed a poster printed by a child's hand, "Happy people make a happy home. If you can't smile, walk around the block, and come back when you can smile."

Sherry, his little girl, opened the door. She examined her dad's face, and said, "Come on, daddy, let's walk around the block first." As we walked around the block, I found out that she had just brought this poster home from school. The walk gave me a good opportunity, and some Fundamental Laws of Right Thinking fell on fertile soil.

When Sherry finally admitted us into the home, I couldn't believe what I saw and heard. They were wealthy people, had all the comfort and security one could ask for, but for some time the family had lived in mental misery. They had a house, but not a home. They lived under one roof, but didn't have much love and companionship.

They accepted gratefully every Fundamental law, and were willing to apply it. Do you want to know what the first lesson was?

1. Speak to one another.
2. Look at one another.
3. Swing one another around. And, the last,
4. Praise one another and find good in each other.

We programmed this with mental exercises and affirmations into their subconscious and laid the ground for a new, positive self-image.

Be open-minded and start a new, happy, joyful and rewarding life. How many of us need a poster on the front door? "HAPPY PEOPLE MAKE A HAPPY HOME. IF YOU CAN'T SMILE, WALK AROUND THE BLOCK AND COME BACK WHEN YOU CAN SMILE." Maybe you ought to make one.

Let me share with you a few more stories from my radio program, "The Fundamental Laws of Right Thinking."

A POSITIVE ATTITUDE IS CONTAGIOUS

A student of mine, reported: The husband had left early for work. The mother with six children, stayed behind. Three of the children had to get ready to go to school. Three stayed at home. The weather was inclement. Their home was small, with little room to play inside. Quarreling and fighting started. The mail came with more bills. Disturbing news came from the radio and T.V. A neighbor arrived with bad news about her family. Another neighbor came in tears to say that she had filed for divorce.

In the late afternoon, when all six children were together again, more problems and disturbances came up. The mother was trying to settle them down and prepare dinner. Who could blame her for being nervous and depressed, or that she had a splitting headache?

At last the husband came home. He sensed the situation. He

went over to his wife, embraced her, kissed her, and expressed his love and appreciation. The kids calmed down, feeling his strength. Love, harmony, affection, and willingness to help one another was reestablished in minutes. Mother sang as she finished her dishes. Neighbors passing by heard her singing, and it changed their depressed attitudes. The happy mood travelled along the street from home to home. Why? Because one husband showed understanding and appreciation to his wife by looking at her, embracing her, speaking encouraging words, expressing his love, affection, and gratitude.

DIVORCE

Statistics on divorce reveal that 52 percent of all divorcees have not finished high school; 66 percent married between the ages of 15 and 21, and 51 percent eloped without a family or church ceremony. What can be done to avoid these tragedies? Over and over again, adults tell me, "I wish I had been introduced to the Fundamental Laws of Right Thinking in my teen-age years."

The subconscious mind can be programmed with right ideas and goals, but only through the method of affirmation. The affirmations have to be worked out in positive language and incorporated into our daily lives. Such positive suggestions should be used at least three times daily with burning desire and mental picturing to achieve the end result. Soon you will be able to work out your own suggestions according to your needs, and develop the ability to picture mentally the desired goal. Say, for instance, "by applying the Fundamental Laws of Right Thinking, I will draw to me a partner who is thinking in the same direction. I expect my Subconscious Mind to guide me to the right decisions. I am willing to prepare myself in every way for an everlasting, joyful marriage, and I expect the same of my partner. When we are both mature enough for marriage, I expect that we shall meet under the most favorable circumstances."

This attitude will certainly bring you the best results.

THE WEDDING

My wife and I have had the honor of being invited to many weddings. We like to see newlyweds. Somehow it brings a renewing of our own vows. Oh, how much in love they seem, how considerate the bridegroom, how lovely the bride! It is easy to see that the parents have only one wish—that love, happiness, consideration, the wonderful feelings the newlyweds have for one another may endure forever.

It would be the natural thing. But, regrettably, this does not always happen. Why? Divorce often starts at the altar. For too many couples, courtship and consideration for one another end with the honeymoon. To those who have learned self-control, consideration and unselfishness, happiness lasts forever.

With the application of the Fundamental Laws of Right Thinking, you will have an advantage, a special tool to use, if your marriage should shake from time to time. By controlling your thinking, by good feelings for one another programmed in your subconscious mind, right actions will come even in the most trying situations. The lifetime-guaranteed bond is daily prayer while self-suggestions with positive affirmations should fill your mind daily.

Here is an example on which you can dwell: "We have mutual love, consideration, respect, faith, inner peace, happiness, and joy. The highest ideals are woven between us. We are constantly attracted to each other through the law of loyalty and faithfulness. We prosper spiritually, mentally and physically in everything we undertake."

THE BREAKFAST

I knew one couple who had not had a happy family life for some long time. They let it go far too long before trying to change. One day the wife began to study the Fundamental Laws of Right Thinking, and was ready to make a move for the better.

One morning she got up earlier than usual and asked her husband what he wanted for breakfast. He said, "two pieces of toast, 2 strips of bacon, 2 eggs, one fried and one scrambled, and a glass of orange juice." She fixed everything nicely and called him. He looked at the set table, and said, 'You fried the wrong egg." What do you think she should have done? You are right! But she didn't.

She remembered the saying, "A quitter never wins and a winner never quits." She had made up her mind to have a happy family life. Although her husband did not deserve it to begin with, she used mental conditioning to herself and Positive Mental

Telepathy in the Winners' Circle, with faith and trust in him. She expected a result, but not as quickly as it came. Her Positive Mental Attitude worked like magic. Day by day he became more and more understanding and considerate. She almost fainted when he came home one day with flowers for her. He hugged her. They embraced and kissed each other, tears were running down their cheeks. With that kiss they put behind them the miserable times of the past, and started a happy life.

I hope your marriage is better than this but all have room for improvement. Life is too short to ruin it. Try this affirmation: "I want to have a happy family life. I love him/her and he/she loves me. I am willing to forgive and forget the past. We will attract and be attracted to one another again with love, appreciation, and consideration." I assure you it is really easier to be happy. It works!

One of my students told me:

At one time my wife and I were deeply concerned about our youngest son. He was attracted to a girl, a most unhappy and disturbed girl, who alternately encouraged or repulsed him and made him most unhappy. We began to seek, and believe and expect a better girl to come along for him. We told him continually that this girl would come if he would be patient and believe. Every chance we could we told him. She will come to you. Expect it. Believe it. Tell yourself each time you feel sad: "I know there is a right girl for me. I know she wants me as I want her. I know she will come to me." Privately my wife often said: "If only a girl could come along like Naomi—a young and lovely lady we had both known.

One day my son was introduced to a pretty girl, and later dated her. Both my wife and I were encouraged, and as their friendship deepened we met this young lady, and liked her. We really *knew* that she was the one for whom he had mentally sought when we learned her name . . . Naomi.

They were engaged to be married, and we believe and expect they will be happy.

FATHER, THE HEAD OF THE FAMILY

A very happy man mentioned to a friend of his that he had never had a quarrel with his wife. "You want to bet?" said the other?

"Tomorrow when you leave the house, say to your wife, just as you are walking to your car, 'tonight I want to have fish,' and then drive right away. If your wife has fried fish you say you wanted it broiled. Try to create an argument over it." Shortly afterwards, the men met again. The happy husband reported he couldn't fight with his wife, because half of the fish was broiled and the other half fried. She gave him a choice!

"All right, let me give you another test for your wife," said the friend. "The next time it rains, come home and say, 'it is raining so hard that the water is running uphill.' You will see, she will demur and you can make an argument out of it.' " But not as it turned out. His little boy was there and he corrected his father, saying, "Oh, dad! Water can never run uphill." Mother reprimanded him, and said, "Boy, remember if your *Dad* says water is running uphill, then it is running uphill!"

It is only a story. But an important one! Husbands should earn their places as head of the family and households with consideration and love. Fathers have to earn respect in the home. After you have changed your image and programmed the right attitude toward the family with the Fundamental Laws of Right Thinking, you become the heads of the family, pillars of strength and sources of happiness.

PART III
CHAPTER 6
SUMMARY

A.B.C. for Husband to Wife: Speak with her—look at her, Swing her around—praise her.

A.B.C. for Wife to Husband: Be the psychic center in the home, Be as attractive as possible, Be the source of beauty and harmony and the center of love.

"NO OTHER SUCCESS CAN COMPENSATE FOR
FAILURE IN THE HOME.
David O. McKay

In search and pursuit of LOVE—HAPPINESS—HARMONY in our homes, let's romanticize and glamorize our marriages.

Things to Do
Constructive Use of Your
Time With the Help of
Your Subconscious Mind

Story of Mr. Ivy Lee and Mr. Charles W. Schwab
"Things to Do"—My New Concept in Six Steps
With the Help of the Subconscious
Sample Card "THINGS TO DO"
What is Your TIME Worth?

Make yourself a list of "Things to Do" for every day of the week. Put them in order of importance. Work on one item at a time until it is finished without concern over the next thing on the agenda.

This idea was presented by Ivy Lee to Charles W. Schwab, the business manager and trust for Andrew Carnegie. He paid Mr. Lee $25000 for this practical idea.

MY NEW CONCEPT
DO IT WITH THE HELP OF YOUR SUBCONSCIOUS

First: Write down on the "THINGS TO DO" card all your appointments and obligations for the next day.

Second: Number the items in order of importance, the most urgent first.

Third: Read the card five to six times in connection with the "Mind Track Formula"—"I Want It; I Expect It; I am going to have It; I Know it is Mine. Everything is Possible. I can; I will do it." Create a vivid mental picture of having the goal already achieved. Sign the card with "Thank You." "Thank You" means it is on the way to you; it is done.

Fourth: Go into "Standard Relaxation," and let it mull around and sink into your subconscious. Expect promptings, new facts, and additional help beyond your own planning. Stay in this programming state for five minutes and then arouse yourself. (For more details see card method, Part III, Chapter 3.)

Fifth: Let your subconscious start overnight to work on it, to prepare the way, the situation and the timing. You will be amazed at how much more you will get done. Everything will fall into the right place.

Sixth: Next morning start with item No. 1. Don't be concerned about the others. Complete them one by one and express thanks for every item accomplished by scratching it out on your card. Transfer the remaining items to the next day's card.

During my time of selling, I passed out this "Things To Do" card with my name on it. Many businessmen told me, "You are the first one to bring me an idea. Everybody else just wants my order." As a reward they bought from me.

If something comes up during the day, write it on the card. Scratch it out when you have taken care of it. It will increase your sense of performance and efficiency.

On the following page is a sample card.

There are 244 working days in a year. If you make $20,000 a year, every working hour is worth $10.25. Find your salary in the table below and ponder the value of your every working hour.

If you Earn Per Year	Value of Every Hour
$ 5,000	$ 2.56
7,500	3.84
10,000	5.12
12,000	6.15
16,000	8.20
20,000	10.25
25,000	12.81
30,000	15.37
40,000	20.49
50,000	25.61
75,000	38.42
100,000	51.23

Pick out your own income and interpolate the hourly value and decide for yourself how many hours per day you can afford to waste. I believe if you are sincere you will try to stop wasting time. Learn to say "NO" to unimportant and insignificant things.

HERE ARE THE COSTS OF ONLY ONE WASTED HOUR PER DAY OVER THE COURSE OF A YEAR:

If you Earn Per Year	Cost of Lost Hour
$ 5,000	$ 625
10,000	937
12,000	1,500
16,000	2,000
20,000	2,500
25,000	3,125
30,000	3,750
40,000	5,000
50,000	6,250
100,000	12,500

THINGS TO DO

DATE _____

1	
2	
3	
4	
5	
6	
7	
8	
9	
10	
11	
12	
13	
14	

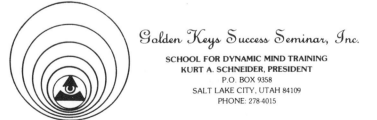

Golden Keys Success Seminar, Inc.

SCHOOL FOR DYNAMIC MIND TRAINING
KURT A. SCHNEIDER, PRESIDENT
P.O. BOX 9358
SALT LAKE CITY, UTAH 84109
PHONE: 278-4015

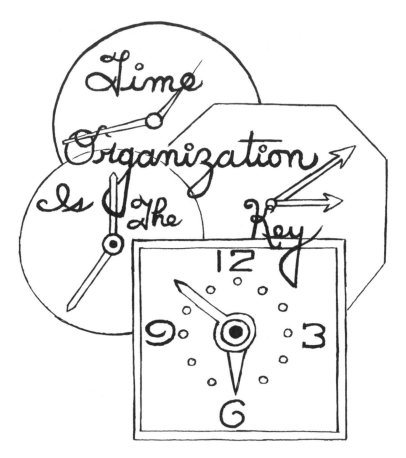

PART III
CHAPTER 7
SUMMARY

1. Plan your time—Do not let Time Plan You.
2. Have a card printed "THINGS TO DO"—with your name or your company name for advertising.
3. Use the six steps to program daily "Constructive Use of Time" with the help of your Subconscious.
4. Be an Organizer. Keep the value of your time in mind.
5. Act—Don't Be Acted Upon.

PART IV

How to Forgive and Forget With the Help of Your Subconscious Mind

The Reckless Driver
Avoid Living in the Past
Explanation of the Subconscious Mind
Live Up to Your Full Potentials
Cast Off Your Negative Emotional Chains
The Universal Law of Forgive and Forget
Case History: To Forgive a Loss of $3500
Case History: Two Letters of Appreciation
Technique and Wording of the Exercise in Four Steps
Hand Movements During the Exercise
Pictures of the Hand Movements
Make Allowances for Thoughtless Cruelties of Others
Forgiveness Turned Into Friendship
You Can Expect the Best in Every Situation
Cassette Tape With Exercise Available

The purpose of this chapter is to give understanding, how to "FORGIVE AND FORGET" with the help of your Subconscious Mind Faculty.

NOTICE: The following chapter is not designed to take the place of the service of a physician, psychiatrist, psychologist or psychotherapist. This chapter is to help each individual become what he or she desires to become. I wish to motivate and stimulate you to right thinking and right action.

THE RECKLESS DRIVER

My daughter and I visited some friends into whose life tragedy had come hoping to express our sympathy and to bring peace of mind and faith in the hearts of these fine grandparents. This is what happened:

A car driven by a reckless intoxicated man in the company of a woman, went through a red light, skidded onto the sidewalk, killed a father of four, and injured his pregnant wife for life. The driver had no job and no insurance. The husband was buried while the widow was in surgery. Two thousand people attended the funeral to pay their respects to him as an educator and church leader.

Susi and I were so overcome with sadness that we could hardly speak a word. As long as I live I shall not forget the look in the eyes of our friends, the parents of this ill-fated couple. It almost tore me to pieces. I came to bring them peace, understanding and help, but the grandmother gave me more than I could give her. She had a moral right to be angry, and filled with hate toward the reckless driver, who had brought such misery into their lives. But she had really and honestly forgiven him, so that the Lord could forgive her and her husband and bless them. This grandmother said, "Why should I be grief-stricken about yesterday? I cannot change it. I cannot say, 'turn back this day for me.' I have to live every day, and take care of the things which every day brings. I have forgiven him so that the good Lord can forgive us."

Just a year ago she was introduced to the Fundamental Laws of Right Thinking. Through the benefit of Subconscious Mind Training she was able to continue to carry on during her time of trial and tribulation.

FORGIVE AND FORGET

I heard this story about missionaries in the jungle preaching the law of forgiveness of your enemies. They quoted from the Bible, "For thou shalt heap coals of fire upon his head, and the Lord shall reward thee." The natives took it literally. This is the way to deal with enemies! It was a breakdown in communication and in understanding. Some would like to handle enemies the same way.

Let's see how the law of "Forgive and Forget" has to be understood in order for you to make it work for your benefit.

Stop Living in the Negative Past

There is a mythical bird that flies backwards. That bird doesn't care where it is going; it only wants to see where it has been.

Sometimes we dwell on past glory and achievements, re-live losses and failure and miss present opportunities and responsibilities.

Someone said: Fifty percent of us live in the past. The past is like a cancelled check. Thirty percent live in the future. The future is like a "Promissory Note." Twenty percent live in the present. The present is ready cash.

EXPLANATION OF THE SUBCONSCIOUS

The following is a brief explanation of the conscious and subconscious faculties of the mind, their functions, potentials, and how they can be put into service for you.

Each of us has only one mind. However, the mind manifests itself in two phases of mental activity, the conscious and the subconscious. Each of these faculties is capable of independent action or synchronized interaction. It is in your greatest interest to explore the working of your subconscious mind faculty.

For this exercise "Forgive and Forget" we need to work with both faculties of the mind; our head representing the Conscious Mind—our heart representing the Subconscious Mind.

LIVE UP TO YOUR FULL POTENTIALS

We all fall short of our potentials. Every one of us is capable and able to increase his mental powers. Most of us use a fraction of our mind power. If we had access to all the money in the world and took only a penny, it would indicate the use of our mind power. We use only a tiny part of that which could be ours if we used our subconscious. We must learn the way to release the energy within us. We must throw off inhibiting complexes and other factors. It does not matter how long you may have used your mind in a negative and destructive manner, the day you begin to think positively, positive results will follow.

"WHAT YOU CONSCIOUSLY CONCENTRATE ON, DESIRE, AND EXPECT, YOUR SUBCONSCIOUS WILL ACHIEVE FOR YOU"

Your subconscious receives your emotionalized wishes, goals, and thoughts through the conscious faculty and bring them to pass. It never sleeps. (Your dreams are the proof.) It is your willing servant. All the automatic functions of your body are controlled by the subconscious.

The glandular system, the digestion of your food, the sympathetic nervous system, the reflex movements of your muscles, the operation of your organs, the circulation of the blood, the healing of the body, all this is done by the subconscious. Remember, the subconscious can not determine whether your wishes, goals and thoughts are good or bad, right or wrong, positive or negative. It accepts them, and moves to bring them about. You can't overwork your subconscious. It is tireless. The more you assign to it, the better it will serve you. It is your willing partner.

All your talents, emotions, and characteristics, everything you have seen, heard, and experienced is lodged in your subconscious mind. Teachings and beliefs related to your faith, religion, ethics, morals and patriotism are there. From your subconscious come inspirations, hunches, precognitions and all the phenomena of E.S.P., wisdom, creativity and the answers to your problems.

Deeply Lodged There Are Also:

Mental blocks, complexes, grudges, hatred, positive and negative patterns, habits, character traits, feelings of love, positive and negative emotions, and your total life experiences.

The following technique has helped so many during the Golden Keys Success Seminars that I have decided to put it on tape and into this workshop book to make it available to all.

You Have Been Taught, All Your Life, That You Should "Forgive and Forget"

You know that you should, but the concept was never

explained to you in the right way so that you can do it. Many of you are suffering because you have not forgiven yourselves. If you wronged someone, made restitution, and received forgiveness from the other person, then you can and must forgive yourself.

You may have tried in vain to forgive in the past. Why? Because you used conscious will-power instead of subconscious power. You used the power of a mouse compared to that of an elephant. A mouse might as well command an elephant to move as you try to overcome a negatively programmed and accepted hostility toward a another person by conscious will power.

Cast Off Your Negative Chains!

The world calls on you to reach your potential and to solve problems. You cast off the emotional chains that disturb your free thinking. It is most important that you overcome negative patterns of poverty, limitations, anger, hate and grudges, which have stopped you from living up to your potential.

Now you can remove the dark clouds from your mind. What you think and concentrate on, decide, desire, expect and accept consciously, whether it is positive or negative, becomes imbedded in your subconscious and is materialized in your daily life. You are the end result of your past thinking. If you are not satisfied with your life, change your thinking. Dr. William James, the father of psychology in America, said, "Human beings can alter their lives by altering their attitudes of mind."

It does not matter how often you have failed in the past. Nor does it make any difference how unhappy and hopeless your present life is. Success and peace of mind can be yours. Believe in these principles and your subconscious will start to work. You will get positive results. *This is the success and freedom you are longing for!*

Why Live the Hard Way?

There is an easier and better way for you. Stop torturing yourself with the past. There is a better way and I invite you to walk with me, find it and practice it.

"FORGIVE AND FORGET"
YOU ARE DOING THIS EXERCISE "FORGIVE AND FORGET"
NOT FOR OTHERS—ONLY FOR YOURSELF

The purpose of the following exercise is to dissolve long-lodged negative emotions, complexes, and limitations from the past and free the imprisoned energy for today's positive living.

Many of you have been able to forgive others but not yourselves. This is another great psychic danger. You must forgive yourself and free yourself from self-condemnation.

Forgiving others is the way that you can be free, healthy, and happy. You may have neglected this law of "Forgive and Forget" because you believed you had to *like* the person you should forgive.

You are old enough to see the faults in others, but sometimes not mature enough to forgive.

I Can't Say it Too Often!

You do not forgive for the benefit of the other person. You do it for yourself. The benefit is for you.

You only have to "Forgive and Forget." That is the Universal Law. All kinds of symptoms and sicknesses, unhappiness, misfortunes, obstacles and delays come from not forgiving and forgetting.

When you hold resentments or grudges toward someone, you bind yourself to that person by a negative emotional link, whether they live or are dead.

Perhaps you were cheated out of some happiness, but through forgiveness you avoid further bondage. To forgive means simply to give up.

TO FORGIVE A LOSS OF $3500

Let me tell you a story. I had a friend. He was the official Santa Claus in the Christmas Parade in my city, a well-known radio personality, and a popular man. One day he came to me and said, "Kurt, I need a new panel truck but I need a co-signer to purchase one. Will you help me out?"

My wife and my lawyer counseled me not to co-sign. I had known and respected this man and so I told him that I would be glad to do it. (I also remembered how a businessman, after only a short acquaintance with me, had co-signed for me to establish my first business.)

I did it without my wife's or my lawyer's approval, and even worse, without programming my subconscious for the answer! I was convinced of this man's integrity.

For three and one-half years I paid $100.00 a month, every

month, because this man and his truck disappeared. I haven't heard from him since. I had reason to be bitter, but who would I have been hurting? The man who disappeared? No, only myself. Hate, anger and resentment could have hurt my health, my working ability, and my peace of mind.

So I practiced what I write and teach. I completely forgave him for my own peace of mind. I used multiplication on the $3500 that I paid over the years and expected a many-fold return. I used my understanding of the Universal Law of Abundance, the law of "Forgive and Forget" the working method of the subconscious, and a simple mental exercise. Anyone can do it.

As a result, today I am in the best of health. I have peace of mind, and have experienced miraculous return of money from many sources. In every disadvantage there is the seed of advantage. Right thinking—right action. Wrong thinking—wrong action. All you have to do is let it work.

Maybe you have had a similar experience. You may be in a situation like that right now. All of us make mistakes. It takes courage to admit to error and choose right action to change it for the best of all concerned.

I have great hopes for you. I promise you peace of mind and great monetary reward. It is a universal law: "All that you send out will come back multiplied to you, good or bad, positive or negative." The principle fits many situations. It can change your life!

A DIVORCEE EXPRESSES HER GRATITUDE

During the writing of this chapter, I received the following letters of appreciation.

"I would like to thank you and tell you how much you have helped me. For years after I left my husband, I was bitter and resentful. All I could remember were the years of tension, unhappiness, the constant suspicions, yelling and fighting and never knowing what to expect next. The children and I suffered beyond description.

Still I felt that if I forgave and forgot, it would somehow benefit my ex-husband, and I was too bitter to do that.

Then I heard of you and listened to your tape of "Forgive and Forget With the Help of Your Subconscious," and I finally realized that in so doing, I would help only myself.

With wonder and joy, I listened to the tape the second time, and then I did the exercise. It's hard to believe the change in me. Even my family and friends are amazed. I'm happy! I set myself free from all the psychic burdens by shaking off the emotional chains. I can laugh again, and enjoy going out socially. My health has improved and my friends tell me I look years younger. I only wish I could have heard of you and listened to your tape years ago. My life would have been so much easier. I can't stop talking about your marvelous program and what it has done for me. Words cannot express my gratitude to you.

May your wonderful tapes and book reach out to touch many thousands of lives as you have touched mine. Again, I will be eternally grateful to you."

A BUSINESSMAN IS OVERWHELMED

"The road to success has been long and hard for me. There have been many individuals without scruples who have caused me to lose large sums of money, my beautiful home, and the respect of my close associates and friends.

"Several years ago, I had a truly marketable idea but I lacked capital. However, I had a good friend of long standing who had the necessary funds. We formed a partnership, and, to make a long story short, we were highly successful. Then one day, I woke up to find that my trusted friend had put the patent of my idea in his name, had taken over the company, and I had nothing. I lost my home; I lost my business; I lost everything!

"Quite naturally, I was bitter. My feelings began to affect my health, and my family relationships, to color my whole life negatively. My friends soon grew tired of listening to me. Then one day, I learned about you and purchased your tape on "Forgive and Forget." It was then that I learned that by forgiving and forgetting, I could free myself from this heavy burden of hate and anger, helping myself only, and doing nothing to help or hurt my ex-partner. I learned that hate hurts only the hater.

Today I am again a successful businessman with a beautiful home and the love of a close-knit family and my friends; I truly feel that I owe it all to you. If you had not shown me the way to rid myself of all my hurt and disappointment, I would not have what I have today.

I wish you constant success."

THE TECHNIQUE OF EXERCISE
FORGIVE and FORGET
IN FOUR STEPS

You may use the following mental exercise for any person (including yourself) whom you have to "Forgive and Forget," or for any incident from which you want to be freed. However, use this simple exercise for one subject at a time. Each time choose another episode or another person.

Step One:

Choose your subject or the person you want to "Forgive and Forget."

Step Two:

Proceed with the "Standard Relaxation Exercise" to reach your subconscious for erasing the life episode in question from your subconscious. (Part I, Chapter 3)

With the highly effective, simple "Standard Relaxation Exercise" you can enter into a programming state of mind where body, mind, and emotions are pleasantly relaxed. This is a breathing exercise by which your mind, body, and emotions are relaxed. You should always create this receptive state of mind for meditation, prayer, or programming your subconscious.

Step Three:

Use the following suggested wording to "Forgive and Forget" to free yourself:

SUGGESTED WORDING OF THE EXERCISE

"I am convinced that this is and will be good for me. Of my own free will and choice, I forgive and forget the following incident." (Think of the person or incident you have chosen.)

"Herewith I set free (think of the name) so that I can be free and will have peace of mind again, so that God can forgive me also. I release you. May God be with you and forgive you also."

Meditate for a few seconds to get yourself into the right frame of mind . . . you want to be free from and relieved of this person and from this episode. Dwell once more on the experience. (Now you can easily stand the negative emotion which has upset you for so long because you know that you will be free from it now.)

HAND MOVEMENT OF THE EXERCISE

Then lift up your arms and bring your hands to your forehead, the fingertips of both hands touching each other in the middle of your forehead. Take a deep breath. Then exhale slowly, and stroke your fingertips slowly toward the temples left and right and at the same time express your thankfulness for this newly obtained freedom. *MOUTH:* "Thank You. Thank You. Thank You." "Thank You" means it is accomplished. "I have forgiven and forgotten of my own free will. It will never bother me again. Never again will I suffer from this life experience. It is gone. I will never bring it up again. It can never return to me. It is gone forever, out of my heart, my subconscious."

Then Let Your Hands Fall Down Again.

1   2

YOU WILL FEEL THAT HUNDREDS OF POUNDS OF PSYCHIC WEIGHT HAVE BEEN LIFTED FROM YOUR HEART—YOUR SUBCONSCIOUS.

Originally it was taught to me to "wash the hands." I never liked this procedure. So, I have developed the "Hand Movement" which can be done anytime and anywhere. Even among other people without being noticed.

AFTER THE EXERCISE:

If conflicting thoughts try to sneak into your mind again, say or mouth to yourself: "Yes, I will keep my promise. I have forgiven _____, and I will never bring it up again. I have forgiven so that I can and will be free, healthy, successful, and well-adjusted in life again. I have forgiven so that God, Infinite Intelligence, can forgive me, too." A wonderful feeling of freedom and peace of mind will then envelope you.

Step Four:

Arouse yourself by counting up from zero to six.

SUGGESTED WORDING:

Counting up from zero to six will end the programming and meditating state of mind and at the same time multiply your energy.

Zero: I am free; I have forgiven. I am free of this specific mental complex. Day-by-day in every way I will feel better and better.

One: I have made contact with my inner core, my subconscious.

Two: Today starts the rest of my life; a life of expectation that all things good for me will now be realized in my life. I feel buoyantly well.

Three: I will never let this come up again or let myself become discouraged again. I will now expect the best in my life. A feeling of comfort and security is with me now and forever.

Four: I will blink my eyes and be wide awake.

Five: I am awakening. I open my eyes. I am wide awake and alert and ready for action. I am feeling fine. The relaxed programming state of mine is completely erased.

Six: I am happy, goal-directed, greatly assured and full of self-confidence. I can expect the best in every situation.

Say Aloud: "TODAY AND EVERY DAY, I EXPECT THE BEST IN EVERY SITUATION."

Be creative and develop your own positive wording.

The Positive Always Overshadows the Negative

After completion of the exercise, this injury will not arouse any negative emotions and feelings in you anymore. It does not concern you anymore. It is as though you have read it in a book, or seen it in a movie.

IT IS ABSOLUTELY NORMAL FOR CONFLICTING THOUGHTS TO TRY TO ENTER OR SNEAK INTO YOUR MIND AGAIN

If this should happen, just say "NO" and push your left arm and hand downward. Lift your right arm and hand up and say, "Thank You." "Thank You" means: "I am free, I have forgiven and was willing to forget it. It cannot bother me anymore."

You see, the positive always will replace the negative. Fill your mind with a positive affirmation such as, "All good things will come to me now," or "I expect the best in every situation in my life," or "I expect the best and I will get the best," or "I can, I will, I do," or "With the help of God I can and will do my best." You replace the negative with a positive mental attitude. You chase out negative thoughts or emotions by reciting positive affirmations.

Mental Blocks Will Be Eliminated From Your Subconscious

Your subconscious will create the new mental image in reality, bringing the realization into your life. You actually feel then that this episode with this person has been eliminated, just as if it had never existed. Just as if you had done it for somebody else. It is not with you any more, in any way, shape or form. This conviction is growing stronger and stronger in you, by the second. You are absolutely assured that this exercise has brought you the help you wanted for so long. With this exercise you have wiped out the emotions from this episode with this person, wiped it from your subconscious where it was lodged for so long.

BELIEVE and *EXPECT* THAT YOU ARE FREE
AND YOU WILL BE FREE

You may use this method for other complexes in the same manner. Do Not DOUBT: let it work, undisturbed. Believe and expect that you have received and you will receive. Believe and expect that you are free, and you will be free.

MAKE ALLOWANCES FOR THOUGHTLESS ACTS OF OTHERS

From now on, take the faults of others in your stride. Make allowances for thoughtless cruelties and negative statements and actions from others. Don't let them again inflame your negative emotions. Anybody who tries to upset you from now on, is really doing you a favor! Practice on this person how to remain cool and calm. Ignore his inconsiderate actions. Stay on your own positive ground—don't react emotionally. Act instead of being acted on. Don't come down to the other persons level. Be patient and understanding. With mental telepathy put yourself in his place and ask yourself: "Why is this person acting this way?" This is the way you solve the problem. Evaluate the situation without emotions and influence this person afterwards with the "Winners' Circle." (See Part II, Chapter 4)

Expect the Best in Every Situation

Today starts the rest of your life. Day by day, in every way, you will be positively affected and compelled and blessed by your decision. Your subconscious will guide and impel you to right action all the time.

Your subconscious has accepted your new freedom and your willingness to forgive. You will feel free. You made your choice to forgive. You can start in the right direction now with the help of your subconscous. Your subconscious is and will be your faithful partner in all life situations from now on.

Do not depend alone on your own genius and natural strength, knowledge and wisdom. Don't ever think they are sufficient to guarantee your day-to-day success.

Remember, you can receive—*through your subconscious*—help above and beyond all that your conscious efforts can produce for all your problems. Remember that your subconscious is in direct communication with Infinite Intelligence. You will add a new dimension to your life, a spiritual dimension that will become your "NEW POSITIVE LIFESTYLE."

I hope you have received a glimpse of what the super power of your subconscious can do for you now.

THIS EXERCISE WAS FORMULATED AFTER THESE BIBLE VERSES:

"And Forgive us our debts, as we forgive our debtors." (Matt. 6:12)

"And when ye stand praying, forgive, if ye have ought against any: that your Father also which is in heaven may forgive you your trespasses. But if ye do not forgive, neither will your Father which is in heaven forgive your trespasses." (Mark 11:25-26)

"I can forgive, but I cannot forget, is only another way of saying, 'I will not forgive.' Forgiveness ought to be like a cancelled note torn in two, and burned up, so that it never can be shown against one."—H.W. Beecher
"Little, vicious minds abound with anger and revenge, and are incapable of feeling the pleasure of forgiving their enemies."—Chesterfield
"A wise man will make haste to forgive, because he knows the full value of time and will not suffer it to pass away in unnecessary pain."—Rambler

One of my students reported:

"I was transferred to an office of the British Government in Lowestoft, and there met my superior officer, a man who immediately disliked me. Although I worked earnestly, and with all my heart, nothing I did satisfied him. My work was always done quickly and well, but he found fault every day with something I had done.

In a very short time I disliked him as much as he did me. Many of the short stories I wrote at this time had this man as villain, and in imagination I killed him in hundreds of ways. I longed, hoped and yearned for a transfer out of his jurisdiction.

One day I made up my mind to change my attitude, and my thoughts about this man for every time I read "love your enemies, do good to them that hate you, pray for those who despitefully use you," in my Bible I knew I was doing wrong.

I began late one evening to wish this man well. I thought about him. I considered his family situation—how unhappy he was. I began earnestly to think, and hope for good things for him. I blessed him in my heart and in my thoughts. I determined never to dislike him again. I programmed myself never to be troubled or hurt by him, but to pour out feeling and thoughts of good toward him. I fell asleep after some hours, and forgot about it.

The next day I went in early to work as usual, and started work before many of my fellow employees were at their desks. This man came into my office, and to my desk. He called me by name. He said, "I know that in the past I have not been your friend, but I want to change. I like you. I appreciate the great job of work you always do. If you will accept it, I will be your friend from now on? And he was my friend from that day forward. All this came from one intense mental programming to change my feelings toward this man, and to wish him well.

I have used this programming of my thoughts and feelings many times since then. It always works. Without them being consciously aware, it changes people antagonistic to you to friends. I believe that the thoughts and feelings of love, friendship and good that I send out, are heard, received and accepted by the subconscious minds of these people, and from their subconscious minds come feelings and thoughts that change enemies to friends.

NEW CASSETTE TAPE

From the Golden Keys Success Seminar (School for Dynamic Mind Training) "How to Forgive and Forget With the Help of Your Subconscious"

Contents: Side A

1. Short life story and achievements of the author: Kurt A. Schneider, President of the Golden Keys Success Seminar.

2. Explanation of the working method of the subconscious.

3. Explanation of the Universal Law of "Forgive and Forget."

4. Case histories from people of all walks of life, who have successfully applied this method.

Side B

1. "Standard Relaxation" (worded by Mr. Schneider so that everybody can learn, practice, and experience it).

2. In detail a described flight to Switzerland and a trip to a resort hotel in the Alps to educate the listener in how to create an effective mental picture. (The language of the subconscious). The ability of mental picturing, imagining and visualizing developed sufficiently will help bring about the actual materialization in daily life.

3. When you are very dramatically and emotionally involved with imagination you will be mentally guided by select wording to shape and knead the abuse, hate, anger and pain into a snowball. Then you throw this imaginary formed ball from the balcony of your hotel suite into the deep mountain lake. It sinks and melts, sinks and melts away forever, together with the complex which you rolled into it. Then it is lifted out of your subconscious, where it was lodged for so long.

THE EXERCISE WAS FORMULATED AFTER THIS BIBLE VERSE:

"Whosoever shall say unto this mountain, be thou removed, and be thou cast into the sea, and shall not doubt in his heart, but shall believe that those things which he saith shall come to pass, he shall have whatsoever he saith." (Mark 11:23)

How to Order the Tape:

"How To Forgive and Forget With the Help of Your Subconscious"

Please send your check for $10.00 plus 75¢ for postage and handling to:

Golden Keys Success Seminar, Inc.

P.O. Box 9358

Salt Lake City, Utah 84109

PART IV
CHAPTER 1
SUMMARY
EXERCISE FOR "FORGIVE AND FORGET" IN A NUTSHELL

1. Identify the person or life incident you have a problem with.
2. Proceed with Standard Relaxation creating the meditating state of mind.
3. Word the suggested formula in relaxation.
4. Hand and arm movement.
5. Awaken yourself by counting up from one to six with the suggested wording.

PART IV
CHAPTER 2

The Mensa-Bio-Rythmic Cycle

THE MENSA-BIO-RYTHMIC CYCLE

Have you heard people say: "Don't blame me—it's my bio-rythmic cycle. I am suffering and it is not my fault. I can't help myself. It is not my day."

Some will say, "I also suffer from these cycles." We are all going through these cycles physically and psychically.

A booming business has arisen to work out such cycles for people. Some observers regard it as an astrology—related system rather than a scientific tool. They claim these cycles start at birth and affect your chances of failure or success.

Whatever the cause, we do live under positive and negative cosmic and environmental influences. But we can control these influences very well by a very simple mental exercise.

THE MENSA BIO-RHYTHMIC CYCLE
NORMAL WELL-ADJUSTED, SUCCESSFUL, HAPPY AND
HEALTHY LIFE.

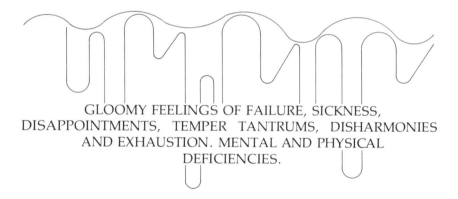

GLOOMY FEELINGS OF FAILURE, SICKNESS,
DISAPPOINTMENTS, TEMPER TANTRUMS, DISHARMONIES
AND EXHAUSTION. MENTAL AND PHYSICAL
DEFICIENCIES.

DEPRESSED, ON THE BORDERLINE OF A NERVOUS
BREAKDOWN, SUICIDE CANDIDATE.

HOW ARE YOU?

I had lunch with a student, a manufacturer and inventor, who lives in a big condominium. He said, "Kurt, you will enjoy hearing what happened to me this morning. We have a new, very grumpy manager. I wanted to be nice to her and to help her adopt a more pleasant attitude toward her tenants. I thought I had an opportunity this morning to apply what you have taught us in class, so I said to her, 'good morning, Mrs. _____. How are you this beautiful morning?" She answered, "Why do you ask me a stupid question like that?" My friend was dumbfounded!

If you are suffering from similar psychic bombardments and low cycles, there is a simple way to protect yourself. A mental exercise to program and condition yourself for a harmonious and positive lifestyle. Just keep on reading and you will be shown how to do it.

It pays to keep a record in your diary to discover your peak in alertness, your own personal energy cycles, and the rhythms in which they come. Through this log you will find out when your "high energy periods" are, and when the "run down feelings" set in.

EXERCISE

First Step:

State your problem.

Second Step:

Standard Relaxation (Part I, Chapter 3).

Third Step:

Attach the mental exercise counting down from sixty to zero with the conditioning word "DEEPER" and LISTEN (Part II, Chapter 2).

During this span of meditation, you will overcome and neutralize the gloomy feelings. You can expect all of the benefits of this exercise. With the help and power of your subconscious, new light will be shed on the situation.

LISTEN to the promptings and intuitions.

Fourth Step:

Arouse yourself by counting up from zero to six.

Fifth Step:

Act according to the new insight, new understanding and promptings of your subconscious. Peace of mind, assurance, hope and a positive mental attitude will envelop you. Act accordingly.

SUICIDE

A psychiatrist asked a person who had tried suicide: "What part of yourself did you want to kill, your loneliness or your depression, your frustrations, or your failure? Killing wouldn't solve anything. The problems have to be overcome."

This person hadn't failed in everything. Everything was not lost. Other solutions could be tried.

Thank heavens the rocking, shaking, and heavy blows don't go on forever. The downdraft in the Mensa-bio-rythmic circle can be stopped by adjusting your thinking.

"Anguish of mind has driven thousands to suicide; anguish of body—none! Health of the mind is of far more consequence to our happiness than the health of the body, although both are deserving of much more attention than either of them receives."—Colton

SELF-DESTRUCTION

More than 20,000 Americans commit suicide each year, and there is an ever greater number of attempted suicides. In the richest land in the world, in the land of opportunities, why do people commit suicide? What kind of thinking makes a person contemplate suicide? Do things suddenly become so unbearable that suicide is the only way out? If this were the case, anyone who suffered trying circumstances would commit suicide.

The fact is that people program their minds for suicide. They leave themselves no other way out. It comes from highly-focused negative thinking over a long period of time. Do we know where our uncontrolled negative thinking will lead us? Day by day, week after week and year after year, thoughts focused on lack, limitations, sickness, hate, anger, resentment, quarrels, revenge and bitterness program the subconscious for self-destruction.

There is a better way. The Fundamental Laws of Right Thinking bring us the answer. Mind Control will give us the inner discipline and free us from false concepts, thus re-programming a new self-image, a new reality-acceptance in our subconscious. Our lives are shaped by our thinking. What we thought and let our minds dwell on in the past shaped our lives for today. What we program into our subconscious from today on will form and create our future. It is never too late to change.

Affirmation: "Although I cannot see a way out, I know my subconscious will find a solution for me. I say 'Thanks' in advance."

BE PREPARED TO TAKE LOSSES

During the stockmarket crash in October of 1929, many financiers jumped from high buildings or killed themselves some other way. They had suddenly lost that which mattered most to them—their wealth.

People who are active in sports or who prepare themselves for competition develop self-discipline beyond the levels achieved by the average person. Their minds are schooled and trained through many trials and errors. They find they lose many times before they enjoy victory. Defeat becomes only a stepping stone to greater efforts, success and development. They learn how to take a loss.

Can we learn something from the athletic experience? Yes—to be prepared. We need well-adjusted leaders. We need people who can stand pressure, take losses, roll with the punches, and be willing to try again. An athlete must train day after day and he must endure that training for a long time before he can enter a meet. Championship is 90% discipline over mind and body. If we want to be a success, to be recognized as leaders by our country, community, church or family, we must start now. Subconscious Mind Training and adventuring in the Fundamental Laws of Right Thinking is the answer. I challenge you to try it! An appropriate affirmation will be: "I know that every loss and disadvantage has the seed of advantage imbedded in it. I will always be on top."

PART IV
CHAPTER 3
SUMMARY

1. Watch your Mensa-bio-rythmic cycles and keep a record.
2. Avoid or stop the sinking depressed negative feelings and moods by undertaking the exercise. Don't Postpone—Do It Now.
3. Work with positive affirmations and re-inforce your goals. Read motivating books, listen to harmonious music, visit with positive people. See uplifting movies.
4. Don't dwell on misery—Dwell on Success.

PART IV
CHAPTER 3

Psychic Protection

THE LOSS OF $7000.00

After I explained this mental exercise in the fourth session of a Seminar a lady said, "Why didn't you teach me this in the first session—I just totalled a $7,000.00 car!"

Another student spoke up and said, "Yes, and my house was burglarized last week."

Let me share with you some of my experiences.

FLIGHT FROM MIAMI TO THE BAHAMAS

On a beautiful sun-filled day, we boarded the airplane at Miami for our destination, the Bahamas. The airplane wouldn't take off. My wife leaned over and asked, "What have you done now?" She knew that I always protect our transportation.

Many service vehicles surrounded the plane and mechanics began to work on the boarding door at the center of the plane. Our seats were in front of the door. I inquired, "What seems to be the trouble?" I was told that the door couldn't be closed tightly enough. The stewardess said, "We have been flying six times a day for months. Everything has been fine until today, when the Aeronautical Commission stopped us."

The pilot explained to me that they were afraid that the air pressure could break the door open: "Then the cabin pressure would catapult us out of the plane and down to the sharks below." My wife and I were sitting by the door. Fortunately it wasn't our time to be shark bait!

A psychic protection? Yes.

DEEP SEA URCHIN

The day before we arrived at the Grand Bahamas Island, a great storm had roared over it. Natives serving on the beach suggested that this would be a good time to go shell hunting in the shallow waters. I did. The water was clear and warm; the sand soft and white. Everything seemed perfect. Suddenly some force beyond me stopped my right leg in mid-air. I stood there like a flamingo, one foot up, and one foot down. Looking down, I saw a round object that looked like a six-inch porcupine. I lowered my leg, careful not to step on it. Then I reached down and lifted it from deep under the sand with both my hands, and carried it out on to the beach. The natives, seeing what I had, yelled something I couldn't understand and ran away as fast as they could. I dropped the little monster and ran away also.

Later I was told that it was a deep sea urchin which secretes a poisonous substance in its many needle-like spines. This makes stepping on it extremely painful and dangerous. The highly toxic substance could have killed me, had one of the many spines entered my blood stream. A miracle? Yes! A Protection? Yes! A higher psychic power at work? Yes! I certainly believe in it. A higher power decreed my protection.

I expressed my thanks to God; I know that a thankful heart is like a magnet, that draws more good things to me.

Some of you may think: "How in the world can it be done?" Let me reveal to you the very simple, limitless mental exercise.

MENTAL EXERCISE

TO PROTECT YOURSELF, YOUR FAMILY, YOUR PROPERTY, YOUR BUSINESS, ETC. IN FIVE STEPS

Step One:

Start with Standard Relaxation (Part I, Chapter 3).

Step Two:

Lift up both arms and form circles, three dimensionally as if you want to describe a ball. At the same time, name the person or object you want to protect through your subconscious. Think or mouth with the "Mind Track Formula" for instance:

"I want to protect my car. I expect my car to be protected in every way. I am going to have this full protection for my car. I know that my car is fully protected against any harm, no matter who drives it. Thank You."

OR

"I want to protect my wife."
"I expect that . . . . . . is fully protected in every situation."
"I am going to have this full protection for . . . . . . day and night."
"I know that . . . . will be fully protected from any harm. Thank You."

OR

"I want to protect our home with all our belongings."

"I expect full protection for our home and everything in it."
"If anyone ever plans to burgalarize or vandalize our home and adjacent buildings and yards, it can't be done."
"I am going to have this protection."
"I know that this entire protection is ours. Thank You."

OR

"I want to protect our trip to . . . ."
"I expect our trip, our belongings, the transportation, including the roads, restaurants, hotels, etc., to be fully protected."
"I am going to have this marvelous protection in every situation so that we can fully enjoy our trip—our vacation."
"I know that this protection for us and our belongings, transportation, roads, restaurants, hotels, is ours. Thank You."

ALWAYS REPEAT THE ARM MOVEMENTS WITH GREAT EXPECTATION DURING THE WORDING. *WHY THE ARM MOVEMENT?*

IT WILL HELP YOU TO AROUSE FAITH, EXPECTATION AND ENTHUSIASM. IT WILL CREATE THE NECESSARY MENTAL PICTURES FOR PROTECTION.

If you are used to praying, do it in the same way as you start and end your prayers and as you address Diety. Many of our students have told me it helped them to understand how prayer or psychic protection works and arouses the positive emotions and faith and expectation with the help of the arm movements.

Repeat from time to time this protection for you, your family, and all your possessions, and personal belongings.

Repeat this protection exercise whenever there is an additional special need for it.

Step Three:

Express: "I now seal the protection for the best of all concerned."

Step Four:

Proceed with the countdown from sixty to zero. WHY THE COUNT DOWN? It will bring you many of the benefits specified for the mental exercise, counting down from sixty to zero (Part II, Chapter 2). You can expect: Promptings, intuitions, new facts, or a strong warning.

Step Five:

Arouse yourself by counting up from zero to six. Say or mouth "Thank You." "Thank You" means the protection is accomplished.

SUSI'S TRIP TO CANADA

My daughter Susi was invited to vacation in Canada by her aunt and uncle. At the time she went, her uncle was so busy as president of an insurance company, that he would not seem to have time to travel around with her and to show her the country.

Susi and I practiced the Winners' Circle exercise and unforeseen opportunities opened up so that her uncle had more time than expected for them. My sixteen-year-old daughter, witnessing the chain reaction of the Winners' Circle exercise and receiving a testimony of the working method of the mind exclaimed, "It works, it works, it works!"

You can be sure that we put Susi under protection before she started on her trip. Close calls in the air, on the ground and in the water were turned to positive experiences.

The most exciting demonstration of psychic protection came on the last day of her trip. A canoe run on a famous white-water stretch involved my brother-in-law, his 12 year old son, and Susi. A huge log appeared in the middle of the white-water and caused an accident which could have been fatal. Seven people had died in this area in the past few months. The boat capsized, my brother-in-law was pinned under a floating tree, and Susi was caught beneath the big log.

She said later:

> "I was sure I would lose my life. I saw you getting the telephone call, and how terribly sad and upset everyone was that I had died. In those few seconds, my whole life passed by. I had a recollection of everything, just like in a movie. I swallowed water and was unable to breathe for a while. It was a horrible, horrible feeling. Then all of a sudden, a peaceful sensation came over me. Later, I couldn't believe that I was still alive. I really experienced the power of the unseen world. I know you were instrumental in my protection and that my guardian angel, my psychic helper, saved me under the direction of the Lord. I know that psychic protection is real and that it works. They were rescued in time with only bruises and cuts.

FIRE IN THE BOY'S ROOM

One night, Carl M., age 10, came sleepwalking down to his parents in the living room. "My room is on fire," he said. The parents were sure he was dreaming and took him back up to his room. To their horror, they found his room filled with thick, black smoke. A fire had started in his electric blanket and had burned the mattress, which started smoldering. Had he remained in bed a few minutes longer, he could have been suffocated and burned.

You may say that this is nothing extraordinary. His parents assured me that the boy had never slept so deeply before and that he never sleepwalks. The mother, a student of the Golden Keys Success Seminar, reported this experience as a proof of psychic protection. Was it just coincidental or was it something more? This was definitely Higher Sensory Powers at work. There is no difference between a "psychic protection exercise" and PRAYER.

God is working through our subconscious whether we acknowledge HIM through prayer or through a meditating mental exercise. This family for instance, didn't accept any church, but they have faith in God as Ruler of the Universe.

WARNING THROUGH E.S.P.

During the second world war in my executive office in Strassbourg, France, I had a built-in radio, hidden and undetectable behind the wall paneling. Several times daily I heard the news from the U.S.A. and then informed my friends as to how the war was proceeding.

One day, when I was at lunch, I had an urge (E.S.P. clairvoyance warning) to rush back to the office and change the radio station from the "Voice of America" to a German station.

About the time I was ready to leave my office again, two tall Nazi SS men in black uniforms with the swastika on their sleeves and guns in their belts entered my office. One leaned against the wall and touched the exact spot in the paneling which opened the secret compartment holding the radio. They acted surprised, but I could tell that they had been tipped off. One of them reached over and turned on the radio, which began playing music from the German station in Stuttgart.

Had the "Voice of America" still been on, they would have taken me away to be executed without further delay.

My wife said to me that evening, "It is well that you have trained yourself in E.S.P., living the kind of life you do. You'll need it if you plan to be around much longer." It is very evident that this was not a coincidence. A psychic warning? Yes! An answer to our prayers and exercises for protection? Yes!

LISTEN TO THE PROMPTINGS

A student of mine, T.I., shared a memorable, moving story with me about a prompting of the spirit. He said:

"We have a very close-knit family and a splendid relationship with one another. During dinner my daughter asked for permission to go with friends to a dance in a neighboring city. An unusual feeling suddenly came over me. It's hard to describe in words how strong this sensation was. Fear descended on me. I trembled all over. I said emphatically, "NO." My daughter and even my wife couldn't believe me. Many times before my daughter had gone with the same friends to the same dance. I re-emphasized my position. 'I'm sorry, but I have a strange feeling that tells me that you should not go this time.'

My wife and daughter must have doubted my sanity. I was on the verge of changing my mind. My daughter began to cry and ran out of the room. I couldn't blame her; I was upset myself, but I had the courage to stick to my decision and to follow the psychic guidance I had received. The prompting was too urgent to doubt or disobey.

After midnight, we received a telephone call inquiring about our daughter. I said, 'Why? she is sound asleep! The other party hesitated for a moment, then reported a horrible accident involving the car my daughter would have used. Three people were dead, three other badly injured.

I woke up the family and told them about it. With tears in our eyes, we kissed and hugged each other and expressed our thanks to God in a family prayer.

Whatever you want to call it—revelation—a miracle—a prompting of the spirit—precognition—guidance of the Lord—God is the source.

TRAIN ACCIDENT

After a long day filled with speaking assignments, I had to rush to catch a train for an appointment in a nearby city. At the ticket gate I was informed, "It is too late. Impossible. The train will be leaving right now. Stay back." I have never accepted the word "impossible" and ran through the tunnel and up the stairs to the train. The conductor yelled at me, "Stay back; you will get hurt!" I ran and ran, handicapped by a suitcase, and briefcase, to catch up with the train. He wasn't kidding, the train had left. I ran with all my heart. I had to catch that train. I expected it, and through the superhuman power of my subconscious aroused sufficient strength and succeeded. It was one of those local trains where each car had six separate compartments and doors to the outside with a runningboard in front.

I reached the last compartment of the last car of the train, jumped on the runningboard, suitcase, briefcase, and all, and opened the door. Instantly I slammed it shut again. What I had seen frightened the wits out of me! A horrible face like that of a huge devil had stared out at me. I jumped down and ran again. Two conductors tried to hold me back.

Meanwhile people looked out the windows and cheered me on. They encouraged me and I ran, faster and faster until I reached the third car. A passenger opened the door, and helped me into the fifth compartment. After everyone congratulated me, I settled down and fell asleep, exhausted.

Thirty minutes later, an express train ran into the back of our train. There was a terrific jolt. Everybody screamed and the luggage fell from the racks. It was one of the worst train accidents in Germany. All of the passengers in the last car were killed. Most of them in the second car and in the first three compartments of the third car were badly injured. In my compartment, the fifth, people were just thrown around. If I hadn't been warned by the projection of the horrible face in the last car, I would have been killed too. The picture of this tragedy, dismembered bodies strewn around, the wounded crying in pain and agony, haunted me for years. Even the sound of the squealing brakes of a train would terrify me.

A coincidence? No! I believe in and expect psychic protection and assistance from spiritual helpers. I believe in the power of prayer and the Almighty.

THE OVERCOAT

At lunch with some other businessmen in an exclusive restaurant, my head suddenly turned toward the entrance without my conscious awareness. To my surprise, I saw a man take my overcoat and start to walk out with it. I excused myself from the table, ran to the door, and said: "Excuse me Sir, you have taken the wrong overcoat." He was quite startled and acted insulted. I said: "Sir, I may be wrong, but reach into the right pocket; my car keys must be there." He did and this was the proof I needed. He apologized. He gave me my coat back, and walked out without any overcoat at all.

My business friends were very anxious to hear all about the incident and wondered how I sensed what I did. I explained the psychic protection exercise, and how it works. One said, "I do this all the time by prayer." "Yes, prayer for protection is just the theological name for psychic protection," I said. The other business friend joined the debate with the explanation: "That is right, I pray too, but now I understand how effectively prayer works. In my prayers, I have left too much room for 'maybe.' I can see now the value of expectation without fail."

FIRE IN THE ROOM

During my bachelor years, I had an apartment in the home of a fine family. One evening I was playing an absorbing game of chess with my landlord when I suddenly heard a clairaudient command: a voice said, "Go back to your room." I didn't like this advice in the middle of a game, but I went anyway. I had received too many proofs in the past of the power of E.S.P.

As I opened the door, I discovered that my room was filled with smoke. Wood stacked behind the ornamental tile stove was on fire. I ran to the window and opened it; then grabbed towels, to protect my hands and tossed the burning wood from the third floor window into the street below. The pedestrians probably thought that fire was falling from heaven!

This psychic warning not only saved my room, but very likely the apartment and the entire house.

All my life I have had such marvelous protection and promptings. I am not special; anybody can have them. You must live in harmony with the universal laws, and expect that all good things will be realized in your life in order to be protected.

DROWNING EXPERIENCE
(My First E.S.P. Experience)

My friend and I were playing on a pier. We couldn't swim. My friend fell into the deep water and sank. I forgot all about the fact that I couldn't swim and jumped in to save him. We both sank, clinging to one another. Just then a private boat came in and a man from the boat jumped in to save us both.

The people in the boat told us, "We had no reason to come in yet. Some force urged us to do so." A higher intervention? Yes! Many times my parents talked about this incident. From my earliest youth, I enjoyed this wonderful protection.

In my diary many more such experiences are recorded. When you expect such phenomena, you attract them to you.

PART IV
CHAPTER 3
SUMMARY
PSYCHIC PROTECTION

1. Get comfortable.
2. Proceed with Standard Relaxation.
3. Lift up your arms and form a three dimensional circle as if you want to describe a ball (See picture).
4. Word your protection in a prayer-like attitude. Go into details, mentally picture the person or object.
5. Express: "Thanks"—"Thank You" means it is done. It is accomplished.
6. Seal it to the "best of all concerned."
7. Proceed counting down from sixty to zero with the conditioning word DEEPER. Expect: Promptings, intuitions, warnings and special instructions.
8. Arouse yourself by counting up from zero to six.

PART IV
CHAPTER 4

Psychic Protection for Escape Door Method

DOOR METHOD
PSYCHIC HELP—PSYCHIC PROTECTION
WITH THE HELP OF YOUR SUBCONSCIOUS MIND

Early in my youth I was taught by one of the great mind teachers of Europe how to escape. During the Hitler regime and World War II, I had many opportunities to practice it.

THE EXERCISE:

Whenever you are cornered physically or mentally, draw in your minds-eye a closed door, open it, escape, and then close it again. No one is able to follow you. Lift up your right hand and say "Thank You." "Thank You" means, it is done, everything is possible.

Why a door? It will help you to create a mental picture—the language of your subconscious. This mental picture in turn will arouse faith and bring a way out of every situation. You will be able to arouse faith, expectation, and creativity. You will be led to act courageously sparked by higher powers through your ever willing subconscious.

It might sound too simple to you. Please swallow it, practice it and you will experience for yourself, it works. Let me share with you some personal experiences.

ARE PSYCHIC HELPERS REAL?

On the last stretch home from a beautiful trip, our left front tire blew out. The car swerved to the left into the oncoming lane. We had a heavy load, and despite all my strength it was impossible for me to gain control of the vehicle.

My wife saw an oncoming car before I did and cried out: "We are going to crash!" I exclaimed in my mind: "Good-bye, my love; thanks for everything. See you in heaven!" I was about to close my eyes, expecting the collision, when suddenly the car swerved back into the right lane. We all felt that a higher power had taken control.

I finally brought the car to a stop. For quite a while we couldn't believe that we were alive. We were still shaking when the other car turned around and a man came to our window and asked: "Are you all right?" He told us that he, too, recognized the helplessness of the situation and witnessed the sudden turn. He also believed it was a miracle—an intervention of higher powers.

In Part IV Chapter 3, I acquainted you with the mental exercise on how to protect yourself, your family and all your possessions.

Let me share with you some more of my experiences:

THE COMMANDER ON THE ARABIAN HORSE

Near the end of the second world war, we lived in the Black Forest. The truce was signed and the French occupation began. One evening a regiment of Moroccans on Arabian horses came to our resort town to make quarters. When the long line of horses came to a halt in our street, the commander rode into my driveway to find quarters for his men. Suddenly his horse neighed, pranced as if startled by a strange vision. It must have been an angel or a psychic helper who had frightened the horse. There was absolutely no one around because of the curfew.

Observing this through the window, my wife turned around and said, "Could that mean we will be spared—we can escape?" The commander remained seated on the horse, but he looked very frightened. Then he turned around and gave the command to ride on, all the way to the next village, as we later learned.

The soldiers' departure was a marvelous blessing for us and our town. The next village was not as fortunate. The people were ravaged by these soldiers, in the most horrible way. Every female from the very young to the very old, was abused and disgraced. Husbands who protested were shot down.

I asked and programmed for protection. I expected protection and we received protection from higher powers. *It is wonderful to live under such protection.*

CHARLOTTE AND THE MOROCCAN

Shortly before the end of the second world war, we lived in the Black Forest, high up in a resort town in the French occupied section of Germany. An overworked heart, among other factors, had prevented me from being drafted into the German Army. My doctor placed me in the hospital for a few months of treatment.

One day my wife, Charlotte, walked about eight miles down into the valley to visit me. There was no transportation of any kind. On her way back up the mountains, she had to walk through a forest. As she climbed up a steep trail alongside a waterfall, she saw in the distance a Moroccan soldier of the French occupation. Since she was half-way up the waterfall, at the point of no return, there was no use running down again. She wondered what to do. No other human soul was near. When she saw the Moroccan approaching her, she quickly slipped her raincoat over her light summer dress and buttoned it up all the way. As she tried to pass him, he stepped in her way, stretching out his arms and said: "una bussa, una bussa." Instead of showing that she was frightened, she spoke up in French and commanded him to get out of her way and leave her alone. With his arms almost around her, Charlotte declared that she knew his commander down in the city. She would report him; he would be shot for mistreating her. (Charlotte told me later that she had no idea that she still remembered French so well not having used it for fifteen years.) She struggled out of his embrace, and passed him, as he stood there open-mouthed. He probably had never seen such great courage before.

The very next day, we heard that close by the scene of this incident a girl had been attacked and left dead, with her right hand cut off as if by a surgeon. The blood had been drained from her body. We learned that on this day there was a special celebration for the Moroccans in which they drank human blood.

A miracle for Charlotte? Yes. Was she protected? Yes. "All things are possible to him that believeth." "With man things are impossible, but with God, all things are possible." It is all a matter of faith and expectation. You too can arouse this mental attitude. Today starts the rest of your life.

THE BRIDGE OF REMAGEN

The following story was told to me. A young man was drafted into the army in World War II, and fought on German soil. When the U.S. troops reached the Rhine River, it was essential for them to take the bridge at Remagen. During the fight the young man was wounded and left to die. Then the Germans came back. An officer saw him lying there, dying and in great pain. He drew his pistol, cocked it, intending to put him out of his agony. He was not moved by hate, but by pity and the human compassion of one man for another.

The American opened his eyes and the expression in his face stopped the officer from shooting. He just could not do it. Higher powers had stopped him and prevented the mercy slaying. The war ended. The American was rescued and recovered from his wounds.

Years later he was called by his church to fulfill a mission in Germany. During his mission he met an industrialist, who had been approached on several prior occasions by ministers without success. But the American missionary was able to influence the industrialist and his family and he was instrumental in converting them.

One evening when they were sitting together, they spoke of the war. The German said: "I am glad I didn't have to kill anybody. Once, however, I came very close. During the fight on the Remagen Bridge, I found an American lying in agony, mortally wounded. I wanted to shoot him to end his misery because there was no help or hope for him. I cocked my pistol, ready to shoot, but he opened his eyes—a sight I will never forget. His expression pleaded with me not to shoot. I could not fire the pistol. I left him with a silent prayer, and went on with my group. Now I see—it was an intervention of God. I am sure it would have haunted me for the rest of my life. How thankful I am for it."

Tears were trickling down the American's cheeks. He asked one more question, then he stood up and embraced his German friend. He revealed to him that he was the American soldier on the Bridge at Remagen whose life had been spared. In return he was able to give his German friend and family a new spiritual life with added understanding and happiness.

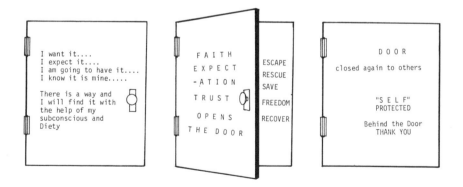

SUMMARY

DOOR METHOD
PSYCHIC HELP—PSYCHIC PROTECTION
WITH THE HELP OF YOUR SUBCONSCIOUS MIND

THE EXERCISE:

Whenever you are cornered physically or mentally, draw in your minds-eye a closed door, open it, escape, and close it again. No one is able to follow you. Lift up your right hand and say "Thank You." "Thank you" means it is done, everything is possible.

How to Solve Your Problems, Make Decisions, Be Creative, and Obtain the Right Answers With the Help of Your Subconscious

THE SUPER SUBCONSCIOUS

Research in the past few years has led some leaders in mind-power to suggest the existence of a supra, or super conscious. They see the mind as:

1. Conscious Mind—the center of thought.
2. Subconscious Mind—the control center for all involuntary body functions.
3. The Super Conscious—or perhaps better The Super Subconscious—since it is not under conscious control—but has to be approached and handled in the same way as the subconscious.

This SUPER SUBCONSCIOUS seems to be in continual contact with Infinite Intelligence and appears to be able at will to communicate with others, and exercise all the vast range of mind power known as the E.S.P. faculties.

When you program your subconscious for problem solving, or the Winners' Circle, it is this SUPER SUBCONSCIOUS that comes into play, and reaches out to change the world about you for your good.

Actually, it makes little difference whether you envisage this separation into subconscious and *super* subconscious or treat your subconscious as one magic, wonderworking, all powerful entity.

The programming of the subconscious is unchanged by these discoveries. After all I have repeatedly told you not to be concerned *how* it brings about these wonders in your life, just be sure that what you consistently imagine and believe, your subconscious, or your super subconscious will bring about in your life.

SPIRITUAL SELF RELIANCE

So many of us seek counsel and help but do not follow through with it. We seem to have contracted an epidemic of "counselitis" in family counseling, welfare and church, which is a drain of spiritual as well as monetary strength.

It is important that we understand that we are innately gifted to know right from wrong and to make right decisions.

We seek after wisdom. Never say or think: "I can't. He or she can do it, but I can't. The pressure is overwhelming me. I can't solve my problems by myself."

Do you realize WHAT you are doing? You are a son or daughter of the Almighty God! Powerful resources from the Universal Storehouse are waiting to be called upon to give you needed help, steadfastness, courage and self-confidence.

When you have a problem, work it out in your own mind first. Ponder it; analyze it; meditate and pray about it. Then practice the following exercise: "How to solve your problems with the help of your subconscious."

THE INDIAN WISDOM

An Indian story tells us: "If white man takes advantage of Indian, white man is smart. If white man takes advantage of Indian second time, Indian is dumb." That is a wise statement. It is insight and ability which distinguishes successful people from the unsuccessful ones. How can people be persuaded to do something which they should not do? Why can they be talked into buying something which they don't need? And sometimes don't have the money to pay for? Why do young people allow themselves to be stampeded into marriage?

The Fundamental Laws of Right Thinking recommend that we start young to make right decisions. Parents are advised not to overshelter their children. Youth should talk with their parents and then make their own decisions with full respect for the consequences. Decisions should never be made when you are depressed, emotionally upset, or sick. They should be delayed until you are calm, rational and well. Your thinking must be realistic and impartial. You must consider all the information available to you. Past experiences of your own or of other people will help. Future consequences for you, your loved ones, your community and your country must be considered. When all facts are in your possession as far as possible you should free yourself from the problem in question. Assign the subconscious faculty of your mind to scan through everything and bring forth the answer. If it is not right, you will have a feeling of emptiness and restlessness and your mind will be uneasy. If your decision is right, you will experience a feeling of assurance, self-confidence and harmony that everything will be all right. Your subconscious is your partner. Affirm: "Consciously based upon what I know I would do this . . . but in all humility I now turn the question over to Higher Powers and expect the guiding answer."

THE HOURGLASS

In an hourglass, fine crystals drop one by one through the

narrow neck from the upper part to the lower half. If two or more crystals tried to pass at the same time, the flow would stop and *nothing* could pass through any more.

You may have admired people who are able to manage many projects, who are active in several enterprises and give counsel in a number of board meetings effectively. This is the secret of their success; their method.

The conscious has to be focused on one problem at a time. Under no circumstances allow your mind to wander away and think of other things at the same time. Set aside everything else during the time you work on a specific project. If you are involved in different projects and enterprises apply the following method: Your subconscious has an entirely different working method than your conscious. After you have consciously spent the time allotted for the selected job, using reason, will power and judgment, turn the task over to your subconscious. The subconscious has the ability to work out your unsolved problems without you having to think about them consciously. You can assign this computer as many problems as you have, you can never overload it. It will never break down; and when you have prepared yourself with expectation, awareness and receptivity, it will pop the answer into your mind. A frustrated nervous feeling comes when you overload the conscious and struggle from one problem to another. If you want to avoid this

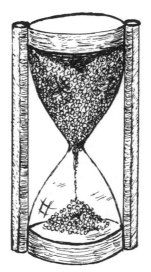

difficulty start today to turn your problems over to your subconscious. Let it work for you. Use the following affirmation:

"I am calling on my subconscious to use its powers to seek the answer to my problem."

PREPARATION FOR THE EXERCISE: HOW TO SOLVE YOUR PROBLEMS, MAKE DECISIONS, BE CREATIVE, AND OBTAIN THE RIGHT ANSWERS WITH THE HELP OF YOUR SUBCONSCIOUS

(See Appendix #5)

"Study it out in your mind."

Collect all facts. Write them down, weigh them. Compare them over and over again.

Consult experts in the field of your problem. Discuss it with friends and with your partner. Let the light of knowledge shine on your problem from every angle.

Take two sheets of paper—one marked Right,—the other with—Not Right—and write down the accumulated opinions and facts.

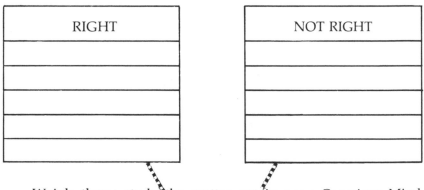

Weigh them; study the matter out in your Conscious Mind Faculty, and then make your decision.

RIGHT

In this case you decided, based upon al the available data, for Right. You are ready now to turn your decision over to your subconscious mind faculty.

Humbly, prayerfully, but with a positive mental attitude and expectancy that you will receive the right answer, you can then proceed with the following mental exercise:

MENTAL EXERCISE FOR SOLVING YOUR PROBLEMS WITH THE HELP OF YOUR SUBCONSCIOUS

1. State your decision.
2. Proceed with Standard Relaxation (Part I, Chapter 3).
3. Continue with counting down from sixty to zero with the conditioning word "DEEPER" (Part II, Chapter 2). The purpose of counting down is to bypass your critical and analytical thinking and to forget about the problem in question. During this time your conscious will be occupied with counting so that your subconscious can then freely without distraction, work on the problem. The counting will also help you to stay partially awake and keep you from falling asleep. You turned your question over to your subconscious. It is not your concern anymore. "LET IT WORK INSTEAD OF MAKE IT WORK." TRUST IN THE RIGHT OUTCOME, AND START TO *LISTEN* WITH UNDIVIDED ATTENTION.

YOU CAN EXPECT ONE OF FOUR DIFFERENT ANSWERS DURING THE TIME YOU ARE COUNTING DOWN.
1. RIGHT
2. NOT RIGHT
3. INFORMATION AND NEW FACTS
4. WAIT FOR FURTHER INSTRUCTIONS

1. Right:

A clear and strong feeling that you are on the right way. A confident feeling that your decision is right. No doubts in your mind. You will feel an assurance beyond your five senses. You will feel that it is right.

2. Not Right:

You may feel a real life situation with strong emotions or see and hear in pre-cognition or clair-audience, or clairvoyance, definitely a strong NO. It will be absolutely clear to you that your decision was wrong, that you are on the wrong track. This means, "take your hands off; STOP, WRONG WAY!" Put an end to it.

3. Information and New Facts:

Suddenly during your relaxation exercise, new facts may pop up in your mind, and creative, untried, original ideas develop. You may be guided to think in a different direction. You may have the experience that your mind will be focused in a completely different direction. You might feel that you are sitting in the center of a web with an inflow of new facts which will change your decision to the right evaluation. This can be manifested to you by an answer to your prayers; through intuitions, promptings, clairaudience, clairvoyance or any of the phenomena classified as extra sensory perceptions. (E.S.P.)

4. Wait for Further Instructions:

This is one of the "problem solving Golden Keys" very often overlooked. We are living in a time of the "hurry-scurry" attitude and we often lose the knack of relaxation.

The time may not be right. New connections and facts which are not now available will be revealed in the near future when you are ready to comprehend the real situation. The subconscious moves in a mysterious way not comprehensible to your conscious thinking. You must learn to trust. You must learn to expect the right answer.

When you get the strong feeling "Wait" although your own conscious decision was different—don't doubt. Do what higher powers counsel you to do. The time will come when your subconscious will compel you to make another exercise. When you are not thinking of the problem at all, the right answer may flash up into your conscious automatically.

You may be moved to collect new facts.

Again you break it down. Think it over; talk it over with friends, and your partner. If you have come to what appears to be a wise decision, consciously state your verdict again for a new exercise. There might just be a better way. Find it!

As soon as you think that you have the right answer, whatever it may be, stop counting down immediately, interrupt your relaxation exercise, blink your eyes and simply arouse yourself by counting up from zero to six. This will awaken you, clear-headed, full of energy and happy. Say aloud or think, "Thank You." Act accordingly without delay. This is the way to make right decisions without having to change them over and over again.

Forgive me when I am personal again. Let me give you some of my own experiences.

THE BOOKS

An Example of "WAIT"

One evening when I came home from work, later than usual, I found a book salesman waiting in the living room with my family. Books, illustrations and maps were scattered all over the floor. The family had decided to order the books and they were waiting for me to sign the order!

Pretty soon, I had also made up my mind to buy. We were all excited about the books. As the salesman gave his closing pitch, I sat leisurely on the couch, engaged in a problem solving exercise to inquire about the final decision. To my surprise, I heard in my mind, a strong "WAIT, Don't buy YET."

It was hard for me to understand. We needed the books. We were able to afford them. I talked back to my subconscious, "How can I tell this to my family? Again there came the same answer, "WAIT."

Finally I aroused enough courage and said, "Sorry, I am not buying tonight!" The family was speechless. The salesman who had waited for hours was furious. Angrily he collected his samples and stormed out of the house. My wife asked, "Why did you do that? We need the books and can afford them!" I explained that I did the exercise and was told to wait. That ended the discussion.

A few days later a friend of mine called and asked for an appointment to show us his new line of books.

He had the same books; he needed insurance from me, and I was able to pay for the books with my commission. Was it worth doing a three-minute problem solving exercise?

TERMITES

An Example of "NEW FACTS"

After a year in America we began planning to buy a home. In looking around we received what appeared to be an unusually good offer. The house we were looking at seemed to be built especially for our needs. Consequently, I was anxious to close the transaction. Then my wife said, "wait a moment. Have you done your mental exercises? Have you inquired of your subconscious about the purchase?" I replied: "No, I don't have time. I am sure it is the right house for us." But my wife insisted that I do the "subconscious problem solving exercise," and I did.

During my five-minute exercise the word "termites" flashed in to my mind. I didn't know what the word meant. I looked in the encyclopedia and discovered that these little insects were eating up the forests in South America. I asked: What has this to do with the house we want to buy? I read further and found that these tiny creatures were eating up the houses in North America. I talked to the realtor. "We are certainly not buying a house with termites. How can you have the audacity to offer it to us?" The man stood there speechless. He didn't understand how we had come to such a conclusion. When he had recovered, he said: "This house has no termites." After some discussion, he admitted that the house had had termites. It had been professionaly treated and shielded inside and out and the affected wood removed and replaced. He showed us the proof in the basement. I didn't give up, because I had been informed that there were termites.

We insisted that a professional inspector of our choice check the house over once more. The inspector found that the house had had termites, but was now well protected. I still could not find peace of mind, and had a definite impression that all was not right. Another examiner was employed. He found one wooden support pillar in the basement coming through the cement floor from the ground. He split the wood open and I saw, under his powerful magnifying glass, termites going up one side and coming down the other.

When this man was through he assured us that the house was now 100% protected. He told us that we had nothing to worry about anymore.

The best part of the story came when we again discussed the house with the realtor. We were able to get the house for $3000.00 less in price because of the termites. Not bad for a five minute "Problem Solving Exercise" with the omnipotent subconscious! Why do I call the subconscious omnipotent? With the help of the subconscious we can reach out to God. If we had had any doubt about the down-to-earth reality and effectiveness of this mental exercise, it would have vanished then and there.

What if there is very little time to do the problem solving exercise? Assigning and working with Your Subconscious Mind regularly will condition and speed the interaction and you will soon be able to make accurate, dependable, "on-the-spot" decisions, guided by the inner wisdom of your subconscious.

THE IRON CURTAIN

It is heart-breaking to look behind the "Iron Curtain." People there are deprived of their freedom and cannot come and go as they please. Families, friends and business relations are torn apart and progress is impeded. Almost all of the people would like these restrictions removed.

Isn't it the same with the mental, cultural, race and religious barriers we set in front of us from time to time, depriving ourselves of a wonderful life, rich in experiences, blessings, and successes?

We all suffer from this? The barriers are prejudice. We judge before we know all the facts. Pre-Judice means pre-Judged!

Students of mind have had great success in removing prejudice from their lives by using self-suggestions for self-adjustment. For instance they say, "I will keep my mind open for every truth and will be slow in condemning others. Before I judge, I will always ask myself the question, 'Why did he do it? He must have had a reason and there may be facts I am not aware of.' My subconscious mind will now bring forth the answer." If you are willing to use this guidance system and saturate your subconscious mind with affirmations according to your needs in a relaxed state of mind, you will enjoy a new, happy and well-adjusted life.

LEARN TO TAP THE HIDDEN POWER OF YOUR MIND.

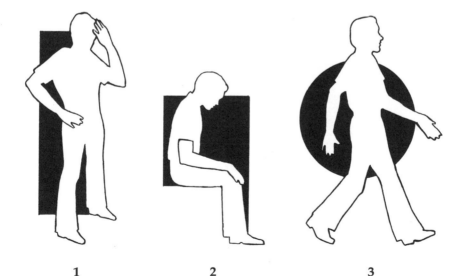

1   2   3

PART IV
CHAPTER 5
SUMMARY

1. Study it out in your mind.
2. Collect facts.
3. Consult experts.
4. Take two sheets of paper RIGHT and NOT RIGHT and make your conscious decision.
5. EXERCISE.
6. State your decision.
7. Proceed with Standard Relaxation (Part I Chapter 3).
8. Follow up with counting down from sixty to zero with the conditioning word "DEEPER" (Part II, Chapter 2).
9. Let it work—trust—LISTEN to the prompting coming through your super subconscious mind.
10. As soon as you feel the answer, stop counting—count up from zero to six and act accordingly.

PART IV
CHAPTER 6

Self Evaluation
Be Honest With Yourself

You Can't Eat the Cake and Keep it Too
Self Examination for Self Graduation
Workout in the Health Studio
Summary of TIME SCHEDULE of all
the Mental Exercises
Marcus Tullius Cicero
Winston Churchill
There's No Way to Go—But Ahead
There is Only One—Yourself
FAITH
Gyro Compass
Life With God
ETERNITY
GOD—MARRIAGE—U.S.A.

SELF EXAMINATION FOR SELF GRADUATION

YOU CAN'T EAT THE CAKE
AND KEEP IT TOO.
YOU CAN'T NEGLECT THESE EXERCISES
AND EXPECT TO DERIVE THE
BENEFITS WHICH THE FAITHFUL
FOLLOWERS GAIN!

	YES	NO
PART I CHAPTERS 1 to 4		
I memorized and used the "Positive Mental Attitude" Formula		
I memorized and used "My I Am" Formula		
I practice them faithfully every night and during the day as explained.		
I kept a record with the 31-day sheet.		
I am practicing the daily Standard Relaxation		
I practice with the Pendulum for mental picturing and heightened concentration.		
I practice Mental Picturing through magnetizing fingers.		
I have memorized Formula I and II of the Mind Track and incorporated them in all my daily activities.		
I practice hand movements "NO" and "THANK YOU," to resist intruding negative thoughts.		
I read and reread all pages, Session I, Chapters I to IV.		
I studied Mind Chart No. 1, the negative vicious cycle.		
I read and signed the pages in Chapter 1.		
PART II CHAPTERS 1 to 7		
I studied Mind Chart No. 2.		
I practice twice daily and more the exercise: Counting down from 60 to 0 for all the 14 benefits.		
Daily between 12 and 2 P.M. and as often as needed I practice the Winners' Circle.		
I practice Hand Levitation.		
I am aware of my Aura.		

	YES	NO
PART III CHAPTER 1 to 7		
I read and reread Mind Chart No. 3		
Twice daily I use the Positive Affirmation Card.		
I decided on my goals and wrote them down. I will evaluate them once per month. I program them daily.		
I practice the Law of Abundance.		
I practice constructive use of time with the "Things To Do" card.		
I practice "Silent Speaking, Silent Closing."		
I use "Print Tapes."		
I practice "Multiplication."		
I do all my programming with Mental Picturing.		
PART IV CHAPTER 1 to 6		
I studied Mind Chart No. 4.		
I try to solve all my problems with the help of my super subconscious mind.		
I psychically protect myself, my family and all my possessions.		
I live the law of "Forgive and Forget."		
With the understanding of the Mensa-bio-rythmic cycle I avoid depression and can neutralize the negative psychic bombardments.		
I started a diary to keep a record of my improvements and my experiences.		
I read at least one book in the field of mind improvement every month.		
I expect E.S.P. phenomenon every day.		

	YES	NO
I will do something good for someone every day.		
I keep myself mentally, physically and morally fit and strive to be well-adjusted.		
I keep smiling, being positive and in harmony with my loved ones and God.		
Time will pass anyway—whether you do the exercises or not. Use Your Time Constructively.		

WORKOUT IN THE HEALTH STUDIO

During a workout in the Health Studio I overheard the following conversation between a participant and the instructor. "I bought a package deal from you for a six month workout and I have been here three times a week. You also gave me a chart to use at home. After six months I look in the mirror, and I don't like what I see; I am still paunchy and overweight. I am not husky and athletic looking." The instructor said: "Why did you stop coming in to exercise? Did you exercise at home according to the chart I gave you?" The man said: "No. I thought six months should be plenty of time." The instructor said: "Nothing comes from nothing—nothing ever will."

Don't be like this chubby man at the health studio. Practice the mental exercises daily for the rest of your life (not just for a few months) and you will be the person you want to be.

Practice—Practice—Practice

I asked my Yoga teacher in Bangkok, Thailand, "How can I achieve real tranquillity of mind and body?" He replied, "By relaxation and meditation." How can I be sure that what I experience and feel is the desirable and right state of mind?" I wanted to know. The master answered: "Don't worry about it. Just do it. Accept the explanation and start practicing!" Through practice you will gain the assurance and the mastery.

Later that year I was in a situation with my ski instructor. He told me, "Kurt, you have to re-program your subconscious and get the old German technique out." I said: "I have done that. What else can I do?" He advised me: "Go ahead and ski; practice, work at it; ski often, it will come to you through practice."

Standard Relaxation and all the other mental exercises can create for the beginner the kind of problems I had with Yoga and skiing. It is difficult to express in words exactly the feelings these relaxing exercises create. Everyone reacts differently. Some people feel as if they are floating, others as if they are sliding down an escalator, or just taking a break from daily tasks. Other thoughts, even noises, will drift and fade away. They will escape your attention.

You will feel an ability to cope with your environment. Suddenly circumstances appear in a new light—you are able to master your problems with a fresh perspective. Self-confidence will be yours. Abrupt promptings from your subconscious may break through. Answers to questions you could not previously solve will be revealed to you. You can have E.S.P. experiences and meaningful dreams.

So I tell you what my Yoga teacher and my ski instructor told me: "Practice; practice; practice!" I can assure you that if you do, you shall gain the mastery. Be ready for an exciting, new, positive lifestyle.

Our students practicing these exercises say: "They are the Best."

SUMMARY OF TIME SCHEDULE OF ALL MENTAL EXERCISES TO BE PERFORMED DAILY

You must not allow yourself to skip any part of the time schedule. It is like the observance of the Ten Commandments. You don't keep them occasionally you keep all the Commandments all the time. Work with the 31-day self-improvement and psychic recharge. After 31-days of rigid daily discipline, this time schedule will become a positive, desirable habit, guiding you to total success with a positive mental attitude and physical and mental energy.

You have the choice of being an idle spectator or an active participant.

Marcus Tullius Cicero 106-43 B.C. Roman Orator, Author and Politician taught the Roman Senate with his polished and styled method of repeating communique's in different ways at least *three times*. Later, this became known as the "CICERO METHOD" "REPETITO EST MATER STUDIOSUM ET ARTIFICIUM." (Repetition is the mother of learning of all arts.)

THIS WILL DISCIPLINE YOU FOR ABSOLUTE DEVOTION—TO SPEND 45 TO 60 MINUTES DAILY TO PRACTICE THESE EXERCISES.

	MINUTES
AWAKEN—IN THE MORNING—COUNT UP FROM 0 to 6 AND EXPRESS YOUR THANKS FOR ANOTHER DAY. PRAYER	3
READ GOALS WITH STANDARD RELAXATION PROGRAMMING	5
MIDMORNING: CARD METHOD	3
BETWEEN NOON AND 2 P.M. WINNERS' CIRCLE, PROBLEM SOLVING. PRAYER	10
MIDAFTERNOON: CARD METHOD	3
EARLY EVENING BEFORE YOU GO OUT FOR WORK OR PLEASURE: EXERCISE, COUNTING DOWN FROM 60 TO 0. ENERGY BOOSTER.	5
BEFORE RETIRING: READ GOALS WITH STANDARD RELAXATION PLAN NEXT DAY WITH "THINGS TO DO" CARD AND STANDARD RELAXATION	10
WINNERS' CIRCLE—POSITIVE MENTAL ATTITUDE FORMULA. PRAYER BEFORE FALLING ASLEEP.	10

THIS TIME SCHEDULE HAS TO BE OBSERVED AS ACCURATELY AS POSSIBLE FOR THE NEXT FOUR WEEKS FOR THE PURPOSE OF HABIT—FORMING PROGRAMMING. THERE IS SOME PSYCHIC POWER IN CHOOSING THE SAME UNDISTURBED PLACE AND TIME FOR THE EXERCISES.

IF YOU ARE AWAKE 16 TO 18 HOURS THEN YOUR DAILY TIME SCHEDULE FOR MEDITATION, PRAYER, PROGRAMMING YOUR SUBCONSCIOUS AND BUILDING UP YOUR PHYSICAL AND PSYCHIC ENERGY AMOUNTS TO ONLY 5 TO 8% OF YOUR WAKING HOURS. THERE IS NO EXCUSE FOR OMITTING THEM.

Many Are Drifting Through Life Without Any Destination or Strong Resolution

They are the ones who are bitter against others, who are not successful, not spiritual, unhealthy and lack energy. They don't want to pay the price. They would not set aside 60 minutes each day for meditation, prayer, and the programming of their subconscious. Instead they waste their time sitting around day-dreaming and watching successful people.

WINSTON CHURCHILL

Shortly before his death, Sir Winston Churchill was honored in a special parliamentary session. Many paid tribute to his service and accomplishments for England, Europe, and the world.

But one speaker claimed that Winston was an alcoholic and was a bad example in that respect. He pointed out a line on the wall and said: "If we poured all of the whiskey he has consumed into this room, it would fill it up to here."

Later when the Prime Minister was asked to speak, he stood contemplating the mark on the wall, then looked up to the ceiling; then down to the mark and up to the ceiling several times. "there is still so much to do and so little time," he exclaimed!

That's how I feel about the subject of the subconscious. There is so much to say and so few pages!

What can we do to make faster progress? Re-read all of the exercises, explanations, stories and affirmations. Incorporate them into your daily life *right* away. I hope I have sparked your interest sufficiently so that you will follow through.

THERE'S NO WAY TO GO—BUT AHEAD!

"If you live these mental laws
    for the rest of your days
You don't have to tell it;
    it shows in your life and in your face."

Don't claim each accomplishment and improvement as a personal success. Give credit to God. Also, God didn't put any limitations on you; therefore, allow yourself no limits.

Think Huge! Don't let yourself fall into a trap or discontinue this exercise because you already feel so much better, buoyant and successful. There has to be a constant growth. The mental exercises will lead you to a happy, healthy, harmonious and positive lifestyle. If for some reason you interrupt the practice of mental exercises, you may fall back into the old way of life.

Never Allow Yourself to Think or Say:

"It is too good to be true. It is too simple. Will it last?" Negative statements like that, would erase the good you have done.

The results will create a successful life only when practiced daily. Those who use these mental exercises daily experience a great difference in their lives. They are happier, calmer, better-adjusted, better protected against the many psychic blows we all receive daily. They are healthier and more successful in all undertakings. They are morally and spiritually elevated.

Many things will be experienced by the person who is willing to follow through with this self-help book.

Don't be impatient with your development. Do your exercises regularly and "let it work." By practicing these exercises you can reduce mental and physical anxiety and tension, and improve your relationship with your family. In your business, and with others; you will calm down, eliminate temper tantrums, and achieve a sense of peace and security.

Keep in mind that I am teaching you only "How To Do It." What You want to program and what you want to do with your life is up to you.

THERE IS ONLY ONE YOURSELF
BE YOURSELF
LIKE YOURSELF
BELIEVE IN YOURSELF

FAITH

Throughout my stories I have mentioned "faith" as the essential element in subconscious mind training. As I have interviewed many people in Europe, the Orient, and the United States, I have asked the question: "What do you think 'faith' is?" Most people have expressed the opinion that faith is a technique used to understand church dogmas and creeds and to pray to God. Unfortunately, that is a widely-accepted concept. Critical and analytical thinking has ruled out faith in daily life. But faith is a state of mind. Faith is Focused Mind Power. Faith works in and through the subconscious mind. To have faith, or apply faith, means to overrule the faculties of reason in the conscious mind. Faith removes limitations of all kinds. If you have faith, you don't need to have a perfect knowledge of things or of the way they work. Faith is an undivided positive attitude, a hope of things which can't be seen or experienced yet, but which are nevertheless true.

Your desire will arouse your conscious and subconscious faculties to the extent that the growth of faith will be accelerated, and in a chain reaction more and more faith will develop.

Faith enlightens our understanding. The mind expands and we

start to think in new dimensions where the impossible is eliminated. To assume that faith is only involved in religion would be as incorrect as to assume that electricity is light. Electricity is used to produce light, but there are numerous other ways to use the power of electricity. The average person doesn't need to know what electricity is and how it works; just how to use it. So it is with faith. Add particle on particle of faith with repetition of affirmations, and soon your mind will be programmed and ready to use it. You can apply the magnetic power of faith in every endeavor of your life.

THE GYRO COMPASS

During a stop-over on a flight we were taking, the pilot invited us up to see the cockpit. He described the workings of the gyroscope, a navigational instrument which indicates any change in the direction of the aircraft. This sensitive instrument enables the pilot to read the altitude of the plane.

This brought home to me the understanding that we have a kind of psychic gyroscope in our minds. If it is plugged in and not misdirected by negative thinking, we will have a sensitive feeling radiating from our inner minds. It is the reflector of our thinking. This "psychic gyro-compass" reminds us when we are not balanced, or not goal-directed. We then have the opportunity to change our attitudes, and our direction according to the principles programmed into our minds. Dr. William James said, "Human beings can alter their lives by altering their attitudes of mind."

It wouldn't hurt to re-program our Subconscious Minds from time to time with the following affirmation: "I want to be aware of my inner guidance. All my decisions are influenced by Infinite Intelligence. I hold myself clean physically, spiritually, and mentally. I keep myself morally straight." I challenge you to acknowledge your "psychic gyroscope." Be aware of it; believe in it. It will work for you, if you can have FAITH in it.

LIFE WITH GOD

Let's face it—we cannot live without God, even though some of us have a hard time accepting that fact. For many of us, God is dead. We blame Him for the miseries we have brought upon ourselves. If we develop individual virtues, many social, political, economic and family problems would not exist. It always makes me feel grateful to hear great men and women testify that they believe in God.

I realize that I have to build up my own way or I would not be able to enjoy direct communication with God. How we conduct ourselves is an hourly matter. Just as every man has to shave and every woman has to put on her makeup every day, we have to renew daily our convictions about God. We shouldn't be surprised if our concept of God becomes diluted, if we are not constantly, *and I mean hourly*, nourishing our souls.

The purpose of this book is to show you a success system which will work in every endeavor. Doing it right means success; doing it wrong means failure. How can it be done? By prayer? Yes—that is very important. But I have additional help for you. Through many years of studying, teaching and interviewing, I have found that a thankful heart is always close to God. To make you aware of the power in and around you, practice the surprisingly simple "Thank You" method. "Prayer is and always remains a native and the deepest impulse of the soul of man."—Thomas Carlyle

Here it is. When you are protected, or feel fine, or have a good idea, or when some wonderful thing happens to you, always say, "Thank You." "Thank You" means you recognize and are aware of the almighty Godpower and the Fundamentals of Right Thinking. Remember, what you are seeking is searching for you. My students have had great success with this system. Try it out.

ETERNITY

It is my conviction that our spirit, our personality, our identity, will never die. Neither will the spirit of any of our loved ones, departed from this dimension, die.

"So-called 'death' is not the end, as 'birth' was not the beginning." Our spirits will always exist to function in an assigned and deserved dimension. "Death is only an incident in life."— William De Morgan. There is little in *this* life that proves to be permanent; this makes it hard to comprehend ETERNITY.

It is said: "Whatever principle of intelligence we attain to in this life, it will rise with us in the resurrection. And if a person gains more knowledge and intelligence in this life through his diligence, and obedience than another, he will have so much the advantage in the world to come."

GOD—MARRIAGE—AMERICA

I wish to share with you the three most sacred, important, influential, and dominant factors in my life.

1. My Communication With God:

I am thankful that I have been chosen, gifted and created to have faith and expectation in a Universal Power, a higher power beyond my wisdom and control. I call this power, "GOD," my Creator, and Father of my spirit.

2. My Wife—My Children—My Family:

I am thankful for my eternal marriage which continues beyond death. I share the same interests with a brilliant, warmhearted wife and three fine children. We experience love and affection for one another. Family togetherness for us is the most profound and rewarding experience in our lives.

3. Our Citizenship in America:

I am thankful for the naturalization and citizenship papers that we have been accepted as citizens of this great country AMERICA. We are proud to be Americans. Do you know the meaning of the last four letters of the name, American? Amer"I CAN."

I don't like to hear people saying, even politicians, "This country." This is OUR COUNTRY, YOUR COUNTRY, MY COUNTRY. Let us preserve our constitutional principles. May God bless us that we will cherish all three: GOD, OUR MARRIAGE AND FAMILY, AND OUR GREAT COUNTRY.

This is the last page, but not the end. Re-read this book many times and practice all the exercises faithfully and daily. The ungrateful have done so little for so long, and have received nothing. We, the willing, led by the Higher Powers are qualified to do everything—even the "impossible."

"It is better to wear out than to rust out!"—Richard Cumberland

One can not play a piece of music with one key on the piano. The whole KEYBOARD is necessary. So with the mental exercises. The practice of all of them will bring total success—a new positive lifestyle.

PRAYER FROM PRESIDENT GEORGE WASHINGTON

Almighty God, who has given us this good land for our

*heritage, we humbly beseech Thee that we may always
prove ourselves a people mindful of Thy favor and glad
to do Thy will.*

*Bless our land with honorable industry, sound learning
and pure manners.*

*Save us from violence, discord and confusion: from pride
and arrogancy, and from every evil way.*

*Defend our liberties, and fashion into one united people
the multitudes brought out of many kindreds and tongues.*

*Endue with the spirit of wisdom those whom in Thy name
we entrust the authority of government, that there may be
peace and justice at home, and that through obedience to
Thy law, we may show forth Thy praise among the nations
of the earth.*

*In the time of prosperity, fill our hearts with thankfulness,
and in the day of trouble, suffer not our trust in Thee to
fail.*

All of which we ask through Jesus Christ, our Lord. Amen.

**PART IV
CHAPTER 6
SUMMARY**

Summary of all exercises—Self Graduation—Daily Time
Schedule for all Mental Exercises.

Without programming your Subconscious—something terrible will
happen to you—

N O T H I N G

APPENDIX

1. The Pendulum Exercise was designed by M. Chevreu, a Frenchman, primarily for the purpose of testing a person's suggestability. Mr. Harry Arons, an American, also uses it for testing suggestibility. The exercise has also been used by Leslie M. Lecron, Aaron A. Moss, D.D.S., Mevlin Powers, Dr. Perry S. Lim from Manila, and probably many others in America and in other parts of the world this author is not aware of. The author uses the Pendulum Exercise as well as the Hand Levitation, Magnetized Fingers and Heavy and Light arm exercises to illustrate the reality of the Subconscious Mental Faculty as well as to increase the efficiency of the individual's mental programming exercise for any goal of his or her choice.

2. The exercise "I PLEDGE TO MYSELF" has been written of and taught by: William E. Edwards, and Earl Nightingale in a similar method as taught by this author. Most probably many other writers not known to this author have recommended a similar method.

3. This counting exercise has been taught and used in a similar way and for like purposes and principles by: Harry Arons, A. E. Van Vogt, Frank S. Capvio, M.D., Lewis R. Wolberg, M.C., Dr. Perry S. Lim from Manila, Phillipines, Oscar Schellbach, Germany, and most probably many others this author is not aware of.

4. This card exercise, with or without an accompanying relaxing exercise, is also taught by many teachers of the Subconscious. For instance: Harry Arons, Earl Nightingale, the late Oscar Schellbach, Germany, and probably many others have used and taught a similar card method in some form.

5. This problem solving exercise, with or without an accompanying relaxation exercise, is taught and used also in a similar way by Harry Arons and other Mind Teachers.

"THINK THIN"

There is a unique cassette tape album on the market that will help people to reduce, become well-adjusted and successful. "THINK THIN" cassette tapes program a person's subconscious and bring about amazing results. People testify:

● *I am happier, healthier, and more successful than I ever dreamed possible.*

● *I succeeded, after years of struggling, with this easy method of programming my Subconscious. Sure way to reduce and stay slim.*

- *Slim, happy, successful at last, thanks to the magic power of my Subconscious.*
- *After every conceivable method for reducing failed, I learned programming my Subconscious, which automatically compelled me to stick to my diet and goals.*
- *I simply listen to these cassette tapes in my own home, and reduce!*
- *I have lost 90 pounds in 9 months! I have never felt so good.*

As was evidenced by a recent *"60 MINUTES"* program on television, America is obsessed with being thin. People are willing to do almost anything to lose weight. They starve themselves, go through spartanic exercise programs and take pills (some of which are dangerous, addicting amphetamines). Looking good is important to America and that means being thin.

Kurt A. Schneider, successful businessman and resident of Salt Lake City since 1951, when he immigrated from West Germany, has come upon a revolutionary concept of weight reduction. Since his youth, Mr. Schneider has been a student of mind training. Over years of gathering information from numerous mind teachers the world over, he has accumulated a wealth of knowledge regarding the subconscious mind.

Since 1961, Mr. Schneider has successfully taught the GOLDEN KEYS SUCCESS SEMINAR, a school for dynamic mind training. This course has helped salesmen, actors, students, homemakers and people from all occupations and walks of life achieve their personal goals.

From his seminar, Mr. Schneider has now revealed an entirely new concept in weight reduction. "THINK THIN." These two words summarize the concept. With three tapes, Mr. Schneider explains how every action in life is first preceeded by thought. Thus, overeating can be rooted out by not thinking about eating. Sounds simple, doesn't it?

Many people have failed in weight reduction because they didn't know or understand how to program their subconscious minds, contends Mr. Schneider. With this three cassette tape album, Mr. Schneider explains the subconscious mind, how it is influenced, and how it can be programmed toward weight reduction or any other goal.

Why are we overweight?—because of negative programming. As children we were comforted with food when we cried. Every four hours we were taught to eat. That's alright for a child. As an adult we need to re-open our minds and develop a new attitude toward eating. Boredom, frustration, anxiety are no excuses to eat.

The first step to re-programming is relaxation, to release the tension, anxiety, frustrations, and fears that have been treated with food. Then while relaxed, the mind is programmed with vivid, enthusiastic words and mental picturing of the new, thin, happy YOU by means of positive affirmations.

It is never as easy to take off weight as it is to put it on, but with the help of your subconscious it is made easy, and anyone can do it. The magic works in a state of relaxation. It is for this reason that Mr. Schneider has perfected his programming on cassette tapes—first to induce a condition of deep relaxation and then, in direct mind-to-mind contact, the subconscious is programmed.

Mr. Schneider's three cassette tapes "THINK THIN" are indeed a new concept in weight reduction and are available through mail order.

EXPLANATION OF THE TAPES: "THINK THIN"

Tape 1, Side A:

An explanation of the working method of the Subconscious for reducing and a positive, new lifestyle.

Tape 1, Side B:

Additional explanations of how your Subconscious can help you to reduce, and be successful in all your undertakings.

Tape II, Side A:

Mental Training for Mental Picturing and Mental Command with the Pendulum Exercise. "Standard Relaxation," a new, exciting way to deep relaxation. You will learn to program your life the way you want it to be.

This tape will assist you to form a mental picture in your mind long enough until it will be fully accepted by your subconscious. It is a workshop for dynamic mind training with positive affirmations and programming the subconscious in a state of relaxation.

Tape II, Side B:

Two formulas to create a Positive Mental Attitude and a consistent positive SELF-IMAGE. Testimonies from the Achievers. Explanation and Application of Tape 3.

Before you begin Tape 3, use the enclosed list:
(1) list the foods and beverages you are going to restrict;
(2) list the foods and beverages permitted;

(3) your present weight and your goal weight;

(4) your three basic measurements as they are now (bust, waist and hips) followed by the goal for these measurements.

A set time limit for reaching these goals is essential. Be realistic in setting these goals.

Tape III, Side A: Night Exercise

Direct programming of your Subconscious in a new way of Relaxation, for reducing. Your Subconscious will be programmed to keep you on the food plan of your choice. You will also learn "SPOT REDUCING." This side of Tape III should be used before you go to sleep. A surprise exercise which will give you the absolute proof that you are able to achieve anything you desire by programming your Subconscious. It is your personal Genie. Get acquainted. You will be glad you did!

Tape III, Side B: Day Exercise

Direct programming of your Subconscious in relaxation for reducing. This will reinforce the NIGHT programming. You will learn to erase undesirable eating habits. It will help you to be aware

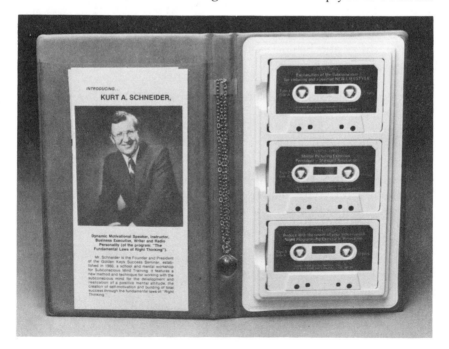

of what you eat, how much you eat, and when you eat. You will find yourself developing NEW and BETTER eating patterns.

As the days go by, you will find that your friends will remark, *"You are not just losing weight—you've changed! It's wonderful! What are you doing?"* It will be the most exciting experience of your life. Your SELF CONFIDENCE will soar.

HEALTH, HAPPINESS, SUCCESS, PROSPERITY, PEACE
OF MIND AND HARMONY WITH FRIENDS, AND
LOVED ONES WILL BE YOURS. IT WORKS.
IT WORKS. *IT WORKS!*

HERE ARE TESTIMONIALS FROM SOME OF THE ACHIEVERS

"I had lost and regained weight for years on every kind of diet. I had finally given up on myself, thinking that I would always be fat! A friend persuaded me to buy the 'THINK THIN' tapes and they really opened my eyes to a whole NEW WAY of living. Today I am slim and happy."

"How grateful I am for the great change brought about in my life by the wonderful 'THINK THIN' tapes!! Now I am happier, healthier, and more successful than I ever dreamed possible."

"I was more than sixty pounds overweight, and nothing in the way of diet ever seemed to work. It was not until I learned to use the magic power of my subconscious from the 'THINK THIN' tapes, that I was able to lose weight. I'll still use these tapes to keep this new, Positive Lifestyle I now enjoy."

"I had a miserable marriage, and I hated my job. I was way overweight. My wife heard of the 'THINK THIN' tapes and insisted that we get them. Today we are happy together and I have been promoted 3 times in my job. Along with my misery I lost about 30 pounds."

"I learned how to relax and fall asleep easily at night from the 'THINK THIN' tapes, in addition to losing weight. I had been able to lose weight before, but it always came right back. But with these wonderful tapes available in my home, all I do is listen to the tapes I need a few times. All three tapes have helped me."

"My husband was very heavy, and his doctor had warned him of the risk of a heart attack. He could not seem to control his appetite. I bought the 'THINK THIN' tapes for him, and after he had used the one for daytime, and the one for nights a few times, my husband changed. He quit overeating, and steadily lost weight. He is well and happy now."

"I never had any trouble with my weight, but I was irritable, nervous, and lived on a steady diet of tranquilizers. The wonderful 'THINK THIN' tape which taught me the Standard Relaxation Method brought me the *very help* I needed."

"Over the years, I must have lost five hundred pounds, but the weight always came back. My wife was constantly taking in or letting out the waistband of my pants! Since I used the 'THINK THIN' tapes, my subconscious watches my weight for me. My wife is surely grateful, and so am I!"

"If you want to lose weight, if you want to be successful and happy, believe me, there's nothing like the marvelous 'THINK THIN' tapes. I can't tell you how great they are, nor how much good they have brought into my life. *It was the best* money I ever spent."

- IT'S EASY!   • NO DRUGS!   • NO WILL POWER!
- IT'S SIMPLE!   • NO PILLS!

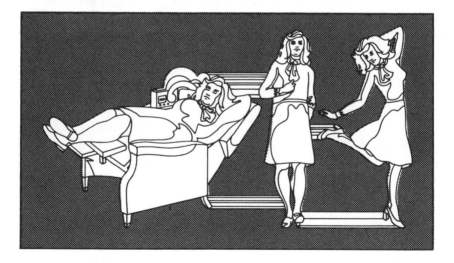

You may order the chapter "The Laws of Abundance" Part III, Chapter 5 in booklet form with an engraved gold colored coin representing the "Universal Law of Abundance."

Always carry the coin with you separately from other coins. Touch it often. It will remind you to keep and live the "FOUR PRINCIPLES of the LAW OF ABUNDANCE."

The Universal Storehouse can never be exhausted. The Universal Law of Abundance is awaiting you. Start today and enjoy the fulness of life. Send $4.95 plus 50¢ for postage and handling to:
GOLDEN KEYS SUCCESS SEMINAR, INC.
P.O. BOX 9358
SALT LAKE CITY, UTAH 84109

For your next seminar or convention, be ready for a great surprise—how the computer part of your subconscious mind works.

Mr. Kurt A. Schneider
Dynamic Motivation Speaker

Leadership and Sales Training for companies and groups to develop:
Self-confidence
Personal Magnetism
Positive Mental Attitude
Self-Discipline
Constructive use of time
Laws of Prosperity
Creative Thinking
Self-Starting Ability
Congeniality
Temper Control
Compatibility
Ethical Silent Selling
Strong Effective Closing
Dynamic Sales Presentation
Persistence

COMMENTS OF SOME COMPANIES FROM OUR FILE:

Our sales ladies and leaders want to express their deepest appreciation and gratitude for attending your seminar. They all agreed on these results:

Gained a Positive Mental Attitude—are now at ease during demonstrations and are able to close effectively, have remarkable enthusiasm to go out and sell with constructive use of time. With no more exertion they have already doubled their sales (Direct Sales).

Your personal effort has added immeasurably to the spirit and success of our agents. I have no question but that they will refer to you throughout their entire careers as the person who did most to instill within them confidence and a new self-image. Whenever they meet and discuss their problems, your name is constantly brought up as a source of inspiration and guidance. (Insurance and Investment Group)

We were very pleased with the report given to our Key Leaders' group regarding the Seminar we had with you. The group seemed to be most enthusiastic about the response of their instructors and leaders to the seminar. (D. B. Direct Sales)

If I had learned nothing more than how to relax instantly and thus make two days out of one, and how to solve problems through the wisdom of my subconscious, the lessons would be priceless. (J.C. Company)

I consider the time and money spent to be one of the very best investments I have ever made. I would not return the experience and information about the subconscious for money. (A. B. Company)

It would be impossible for me to relate the many different ways your seminar has helped me, but a total change has come over my way of thinking and my way of life. (C.B.)

A Ladies Apparel company wrote,
"To Whom It May Concern:

Mr. Kurt Schneider delivered a two hour lecture on motivation at our National Sales Convention in February of 1976. Our sales girls were very much motivated by the lecture and are still referring to the information received. We have received such comments as "My sales are increasing," and "Tell Kurt that I am still improving," or "I am going to make my goal this year; he helped me to believe that I could do it."

As a Company, we have been pleased with the results and are inviting Kurt back for our 1977 Convention.

If you would like to motivate your sales personnel or employees, we would highly recommend Kurt Schneider to you."

Brochure on request: For reservation call or write:
GOLDEN KEYS SUCCESS SEMINAR
P.O. BOX 9358, SALT LAKE CITY, UTAH 84109
TELEPHONE: (801) 278-4015 or 278-6735